BLESSED AMONG WOMEN

Also by G. Scott Sparrow, Ed.D.

Lucid Dreaming—Dawning of the Clear Light
I Am with You Always: True Stories of Encounters with Jesus

BLESSED

AMONG WOMEN

Encounters with Mary and Her Message

G. Scott Sparrow, Ed.D.

Harmony Books /New York

Published by Harmony Books, a division of Crown Publishers, Inc., 201 East 50th Street, New York, NY 10022. Member of the Crown Publishing Group.

Random House, Inc. New York, Toronto, London, Sydney, Auckland.

http://www.randomhouse.com/

HARMONY and colophon are trademarks of Crown Publishers, Inc.

Printed in the United States of America

Library of Congress Cataloging in Publication Data
Sparrow, Gregory Scott.
    Blessed among women : encounters with Mary and her message / G. Scott Sparrow.
        1. Mary, Blessed Virgin, Saint—Apparitions and miracles.
    I. Title.
    BT650.S62   1996
    232.91'7—dc20   96-25591
                                                                                CIP

ISBN 0-517-70443-9

10 9 8 7 6 5 4 3 2 1

First Edition

To Hsieh Ching "Mickey" Lin,
who introduced me
to our Holy Mother

Acknowledgments

I wish to thank each person who contributed their experiences for inclusion in this book. Obviously, this book could not have been done without their willingness to share their sacred encounters with the world. Many of the contributors also took a special, ongoing interest in the project, and supported me with warm letters and phone calls throughout the writing process.

The members of our monthly rosary group deserve special thanks for their prayerful support and for sharing their experiences with the Holy Mother throughout the unfolding of this project.

I also wish to acknowledge Mary Berke, Flo D'Ambrosio, Adelphia Galanopoulos and—of course—Mickey Lin, for their specific contributions to the project; Rob Grant for his invaluable assistance in soliciting accounts for the book and for publicizing the project; Ron Roth for his beautiful Foreword and for the friendship that he and Paul have extended to Mickey Lin and me; and my editor, Leslie Meredith, for encouraging me to explore personally uncharted territory to discover the essence of Mary.

Contents

Foreword

When one considers the violence and racial animosity that prevail in many areas of the world today, it is easy to become discouraged. And yet a ray of light continues to shine and expand throughout the world. In India, Mother Teresa ministers to the poorest of the poor with unlimited energy. At the age of eighty-five, and after several heart attacks, she works tirelessly while the world looks on in wonder. Not far away, the Hindu guru Sai Baba performs miracles reminiscent of Jesus' own miraculous gestures of love. And in my own work as a spiritual healer and teacher, I have witnessed the spirit working through prayer to heal people of crippling disabilities, terminal illnesses, and mental disorders. All of this points to an obvious conclusion: that God manifests his great love and mercy even in the most troubled times.

If all of these wondrous events were not enough to convince us of God's presence among us, the widespread apparitions of the Blessed Virgin Mary should dispel our remaining doubts. Even so, there was a time when I looked upon Mary's manifestations with skepticism. After making a series of pilgrimages to the site of the most famous current apparitions of the Blessed Virgin, my skepticism dissolved and my life began anew.

It all began in 1985. By then, I had already been involved with spiritual healing work for ten years, yet I was quite aware that something was missing from my life. While I had witnessed many people being healed or cured instantly from various maladies, it seemed my life was falling more and more into a slump—a dark night of the soul, if you will.

Around this time, my associate in the healing work, Paul Funfsinn, traveled to the tiny village of Medjugorje, which is located in Bosnia, a part of the former Yugoslavia. Upon his return, he shared with me his incredible experiences of supernatural phenomena surrounding the apparitions of the Blessed Virgin Mary that were reportedly taking place there.

At that time, I was still a Roman Catholic priest pastoring a small country parish. Even so, I found it hard to believe in such things as apparitions, although the spiritual healing in which I was involved could be considered a similar spiritual phenomenon. Paul decided he wanted to return to Medjugorje, and he wanted me to go, too. After much persuasion, I decided to go along, but for only one purpose: *I wanted to know and fulfill God's will for me.* In other words, it was not my purpose to go and be caught up in what I termed a "spiritual high." Without knowing it, however, I was in for a profound and unsettling awakening. Indeed, going to Medjugorje had traumatic and dramatic effects on my life. It was traumatic because I discovered through Mary's intervention that I lacked sufficient love to be serving Jesus adequately. The experience was dramatic because it ushered me into a transitional stage in my spiritual journey, through which I was eventually empowered to serve others more completely than ever before. Looking back, I now realize that my visits to Medjugorje prepared me to make a deeper commitment to the God I already claimed to serve.

We arrived in Medjugorje on a weekday, and immediately I could sense that indeed this was an extraordinary place in the spiritual sense of the word. On the surface, however, it was your typical poor Eastern European village.

As I was roaming around near the Church of St. James, a Catholic nun who worked with the visionaries—those who were said to be seeing Mary—approached me and invited me to be a part of a small group that would be with the visionaries at the time of one of Mary's apparitions. "Indeed, yes!" I responded.

My awakening was about to begin. Entering the room, we each found a spot where we could be comfortable. The room was a tiny cell in the home of the Franciscan priests who were serving the parish. The visionaries, along with one of the priests and the nun, entered the room. I did not know then that a bright light typically precedes the apparition, nor that the visionaries would literally fall to the floor on their knees when Mary appeared. Quite honestly, I really did not know what to expect. When the light appeared like a bolt of lightning, however, it knocked me off my knees and threw me against the wall!

I was afraid to open my eyes because I believed people were staring at me. When I was able to muster the courage to open my eyes, no one was paying any attention to me. In fact, their focus was upon God, to whom they were praying. At the end of the session, I left the room bewildered, unaware as yet that what had just occurred was about to transform me and my work forever.

Over the next few days, I had several deeply moving, extraordinary experiences. The chain of my new crystal rosary, purchased prior to my departure, turned gold—a "normal" phenomenon among the many visitors to Medjugorje, I was later informed. In the room where priests were allowed to celebrate Mass for the people coming to Medjugorje, the image of Christ suddenly appeared on a statue of Mary. My associate was able to capture the phenomenon on film. After he snapped the picture, the image disappeared.

We were able to stare at the sun without hurting our eyes. It danced and pulsated and was overlaid with what appeared to be a large whole-wheat wafer—like a Communion host. On the left of this image was the kneeling figure of the Blessed Virgin.

This was only my first trip to Medjugorje, and I had been given so much to digest. My second trip occurred only six months later. Between 1985 and 1988, I was prompted to make four trips to this remarkable sacred site. I guess I am a slow learner!

During the course of the other three trips, astounding things continued to happen. The chain of another rosary, which I had owned for a long time, turned gold. I witnessed more light phenomena in Medjugorje; and, upon returning home, I saw the sun spinning over my own parish in Illinois one evening prior to a healing service. Some fifty attendees witnessed this supernatural event with me.

I could go on and on, but these experiences in themselves do not change or transform one's life unless they are pondered prayerfully. In so doing, we allow the Holy Spirit to reveal the underlying truth of these events. My main purpose for going to Medjugorje was to seek God's will for my life. After much meditating on the events that occurred during my journeys to this isolated village, some deeply disturbing revelations were given to me; they would enhance the course of my life thereafter.

For instance, I was informed by an inner voice that I had been too hard in dealing with people who were sick and in need of help. Although the power and the healing were manifestations of

God's spirit, my lack of compassion was closing the channel for me to experience the same joy people were feeling through their communion with God.

I was also told that I lacked the quality of the feminine energy of God—that is, tenderness and mercy—which Mary, the mother of Jesus, symbolized. In other words, Mary could be viewed as the feminine aspect of God, or the feminine archetype of God.

This tenderness and mercy were evidently missing from my healing work. There was no doubt in my mind that these revelations were a true characterization of what I had become. I had been so busy with the work of the Lord that I had forgotten the Lord of the work.

I eventually realized that as I meditated more on Jesus, Mary, the Holy Spirit, and the Christ consciousness, God could mold me into an embodiment of love, mercy, tenderness, strength, and power. Recognizing God as a God of love enabled me to rise above the seeming tragedies of life and to see into the very heart of the mother- and father-God that Jesus himself knew.

I came to see that Mary and Jesus, taken together, express the completeness of both the masculine and the feminine energy found in the "personality" of God. These events and revelations have empowered my personal life and healing work in a profoundly moving way. I am now able, through the Holy Spirit, to be a clearer channel for God's presence and power and to introduce others to their God—a being not only of power but of tenderness, care, and mercy.

In the Gospel of St. Luke, a legalist approaches Jesus, seeking the answer to life itself. Jesus then asks the man to interpret the greatest commandment. The legalist quotes the words: " 'You shall love the Lord your God and your neighbor as yourself.' " Jesus then says, "Do this and you will *live.*" Similarly, God's message through Mary remains: Love God in one another and his peace will radiate from humanity's heart.

This is what it is all about. All other phenomena, including encounters with Mary and Jesus, serve only one purpose: to call us to return to our true natures, and to love and to experience life fully. In all of her manifestations, Mary tells how this can be accomplished—*through authentic prayer from the heart.*

Mary, the tender mother of Jesus, is also *our* mother. She is the mother of mercy and the companion of all, regardless of one's religion or the lack thereof. No religion can claim to have a monopoly on Mary's motherly love; Mary is for all of us. To embrace her is to become a humble servant of the Master. To be in communion with her is to experience the unparalleled empowerment that comes from saying yes to God.

This book is a marvelous read, and it is clearly a gift to her and from her. It is my prayer that as you encounter Mary in the life-changing experiences included herein, you, too, will experience the spirit of Mary—her humility, her strength, her courage, and her call to each of us to put love above everything else.

—RON ROTH
Celebrating Life Institutes for Spiritual Healing
Peru, Illinois

Introduction

Of all possible religious experiences, encounters with Mary, the mother of Jesus, seem to be increasing even more markedly today than when, more than 150 years ago, she began appearing to unlikely visionaries on hillsides and in other rural areas of Europe. This shift in Marian experiences away from the church and its saints and into the lives of unsophisticated children marked the beginning of an era in which the feminine face of the divine has been seen more widely by individuals of all faiths.

Some say that Mary brings an awareness to the world that we desperately need at this time—a nourishing spirit of self-sacrificing love that might, if embraced more widely, help to reverse the tide of hatred and bloodshed that prevails in many regions of the world today. In support of this idea, one can point to the timing of the major apparitions. They almost always precede, or coincide with, regional or worldwide upheavals and unprecedented opportunities. As Janice Connell says, "When the Blessed Mother appears, great things happen on earth and in heaven."[1]

The divine feminine spirit that Mary embodies assumes many forms, depending on the culture and the spiritual tradition in which she appears. One can feel her spirit everywhere, operating within religious and secular contexts alike, wherever love and forgiveness reign above age-old prejudices and grievances. In whatever form she appears, she calls upon us to make a difference by *sacrificing* for the greater good—not out of fear but *out of love*. She calls upon us, as well, *to foster love and growth*, and to leave something behind that can sustain life. Her spirit compels us to put transitory happiness aside and instead to undertake the more difficult path of *becoming "mothers" of all creation* by awakening to a timeless, moment-to-moment appreciation for one another and all creatures. In words attributed to Buddha, we are called upon to make this our sacred undertaking: "Like a mother, who protects her child, her only child, with her own life, thus one should cultivate a heart of unlimited love and compassion towards all living beings."[2]

An old friend of mine, C.N.,[3] who was a member of a women's group devoted to the Holy Mother, had a vision of this compassionate spirit in meditation. She saw the Holy Mother as a nurturing, protective presence enveloping the earth.

In October 1988, I opened my meditation with a prayer to Mother Mary to bless the children of the earth. I then had a vision of the Divine Mother. I saw her as a deep blue mass moving over the face of the earth. I saw her reaching out with silvery blue cords of energy, and I knew that these were touching children—the innocent and vulnerable ones of the world whose lives were being sacrificed at the expense of the self-centered consciousness and destructive activities of mankind. Then I heard her say, "Children seven years 'fore and seven years hence." I understood that the arms of the Mother were protecting

the children of the world who are at the mercy of abusive
situations—politically or environmentally or parentally.
I also saw that her protection extended to aspects of the
world's threatened ecology. I experienced her presence for
the rest of the day, and I felt an immense sadness and
compassion. (C.N.#1)[4]

C.N.'s vision effectively captures the spirit of love—as well as the sense of urgency and warning—that has come to represent the Holy Mother's influence on people today. Her vision also portrays the Holy Mother as a world-encompassing energy or consciousness that reaches into the lives of innumerable people at this very moment as she blends with and expresses herself through the diverse religious and mythical forms by which the world has come to know her.

Some of Mary's most recent messages, via the various visionaries who have disseminated them, contain warnings that may seem incongruent with the popular conception of Mary as a messenger of divine love. Mary does not typically appear to people who live in relative comfort, safely removed from the carnage of regional wars and political reprisals. Although she currently appears in many places around the world, including the United States, her messages universally convey an urgency meant to draw our attention to tragedies and injustices unfolding this very moment, and to the remedies that we can provide, especially through devotional practice. She reminds us of the grief that she carries for children who have no one else to care for them, and for those who are bereft of all hope and faith. We cannot turn to her without waking up to much of what we'd rather forget is going on in this world. Mary calls upon us to deal now with the ways things are, not merely to dream about the way we'd like them to be; and she points the way through these troubled times to the glorious promise of new beginnings.

Mary's consistently stated intent is to prepare us for the Second Coming—or the internal spiritual equivalent thereof. She tells us that unless we engage in more diligent spiritual practice, we may succumb to the trials and turmoil that might precede Christ's reappearance, or his spirit's heightened influence within us. Along these lines, some say that Mary models for us the ideal human response to the divine: Through emulating her, we can enter into a dynamic cocreative relationship with Christ, carrying his purpose to fruition in our lives much in the way that she graciously consented to her role in the conception and birth of Jesus. Three hundred years ago, Louis de Montfort prophesied that Mary's manifestations not only would be important but would necessarily precede the Second Coming: "In the second coming of Jesus Christ, Mary has to be made known and revealed by the Holy Spirit in order that, through her, Jesus Christ may be known, loved and served."[5]

Many orthodox Christians accept on faith that Jesus will manifest again as a person walking among us. Others, however—both Christians and non-Christians alike—regard the *Second Coming* as a metaphor for a vast spiritual awakening in which the spirit that Jesus and the other great masters embodied will infuse, for the first time, countless individuals who make themselves ready for this epochal transformation. Regardless of whether one accepts any version of the return of Christ, the idea still resonates with something within us that arguably transcends any particular religious view—an as-yet-nascent spiritual capacity that may eventually flower into a dominant state of awareness. If so, as this potential unfolds, Mary's qualities of love, forgiveness, self-sacrifice, and responsiveness will surely serve to midwife the divine spirit's fuller emergence in this world.

While one might accept the validity of Mary's contemporary manifestations—and the truth of messages that she has disseminated via those who have seen her—it is another thing altogether to *experience* the profound presence that the visionaries report. Most believers remain on the periphery of such events, deriving some faith and hope from a vicarious participation in the visionaries' experience of Mary's presence. While the apparitions appear to only a few, many who have visited the apparition sites can feel her presence, even years later. In making pilgrimages to these places, believers and nonbelievers alike may undergo healings or experience other inexplicable events that exert a lasting effect on their lives. Although most of us remain blind to what they have seen and removed from the ecstasy they have felt, the moving stories of their encounters convey faith-awakening messages of love that Mary clearly intends for us to receive, as well.

In the following pages, you will read many accounts of those who have *directly experienced* a presence whom they believe to have been Mary, the mother of Jesus. As has been true of the witnesses of the historic apparitions, the recipients of these heretofore-unreported encounters are mostly women. Further, as one might expect, the majority of the recipients were raised as Roman Catholics, although many of them had ceased to worship as Catholics when Mary manifested to them. Others, such as myself, are non-Catholics who became open to the Holy Mother through their own spiritual journeys. Regardless of their current church affiliations, many of the recipients have expressed a broad appreciation for other Western and Eastern spiritual traditions.

Just as the historic apparitions have brought Mary out of the church and into the lives of ordinary people, the accounts in this book will demonstrate compellingly that the phenomenon of

Mary's presence is becoming increasingly widespread and more personal—extending far beyond the doctrinal boundaries of the established churches and into the dreams and visions of individuals everywhere. Consequently, the reader—regardless of prior religious persuasion—may find himself or herself more ready and open to have an experience that once seemed beyond the reach of most seekers.

The Importance of Having a Relationship with Mary

In the case of virtually every modern apparition, the visionaries typically receive and disseminate a brief message from Mary after her appearance. More recently, lengthy "channeled" messages from Mary, which sometimes deviate considerably from the traditional Catholic view of her, have been made available through such intermediaries as Annie Kirkwood.[6] In contrast, most of the encounters that we will consider in this book reveal a Mary who remains silent or utters only a few memorable words. Indeed, some readers may puzzle at the contrast between the relatively quiet encounters in this book and the lengthy messages that have been reported elsewhere.

Mary's messages give us something that we can immediately understand and use to direct our lives. However, well-respected authorities have noted that even the most widely accepted messages from Mary—those derived from the major historic apparitions—"merely" reiterate the enduring spiritual truths espoused by Jesus and other scriptural sources.[7] If the message is familiar, then why does it inspire so many people? I believe that *we respond to her messages not because the information is new but because they draw us into a relationship with her.* By focusing on the content of the messages, we can overlook the fact that Mary initiates and sustains a relationship with ordinary people. Certainly, Mary's messages clarify the intent of the being who manifests to the visionaries; but the *relationship* that gives rise to these messages is, perhaps, a far greater treasure for us to contemplate and to seek for ourselves. For in knowing and relating to Mary ourselves, we can come to feel her promptings. We can move into a personal, intimate exchange with our own spiritual natures by communing with Mary's spiritual essence and wisdom.

Since I am a psychotherapist, I am naturally interested in the relationship dimension of the Marian encounter because, in my own field, researchers have found that psychotherapy's success depends primarily on the quality of the therapist-patient relationship. The *information* or guidance imparted by the counselor serves only a secondary role in the healing process. Likewise, I believe a case can be made that a mature spirituality is based on being in relationship with the divine, and serving its purpose, rather than any blessing or communication in particular. And yet to date, most books on the historic apparitions have focused on the *messages* conveyed to the masses from Mary, and the *miracles* that typically surround the visionaries and the apparition sites. By treating the apparition primarily as an *oracle* of information and blessings, it is easy to overlook the dynamic relationship that unfolds between the seer and the seen.

Mary's messages provide one avenue into a mystical relationship that we might have with her, but we might find a more direct route to knowing her by exploring the relationship with her that her visionaries describe. By examining this dimension of the Marian encounter, we may awaken to our *own* relationship with Mary. As we examine the experience of others, we might ask, What is the life context in which such visions occur? What are the feelings that accompany Mary's presence? What are the benefits and drawbacks of a relationship with her? What obstacles arise to prevent a closer, ongoing relationship with her? How does the experience affect the seer's relationship with friends, family, and colleagues when she keeps it to herself and when she shares with others? And, finally, what does the recipient feel called to do as a result of having experienced Mary's presence?

By taking such questions to heart, I believe we can gain a better understanding of the mystical relationship that develops between the visionary and Mary. We can learn what Mary might require of *us*, and how a relationship with her might transform *our* lives. Through this inquiry, we might ourselves enjoy an enhanced capacity to commune directly with Mary, or other manifestations of the divine.

The Importance of Focusing on Mary

For the purposes of this book, I have defined a Marian encounter as any experience in which a person encounters directly the presence of a being whom they identify as Mary, the mother of Jesus. Of course, such a definition rules out important experiences with the divine feminine that reflect a different cultural and religious orientation. However, given the importance of Mary in our Western, Christian tradition, we can perhaps justify limiting the scope of our inquiry to experiences with her. While we run the risk of being exclusive, a wider cross-cultural focus might overlook the meaning inherent in the encounter with the presence identified as Mary herself. Such a broad orientation might also overlook the additional responsibility that a personal relationship with Mary carries with it—that is, to have a relationship with Jesus, as well, and to act as if our spirits are informed by their spirits, ideals, and compassion.

Mary's qualities of love and self-sacrifice parallel those attributes associated with other female embodiments of the divine, such as the Egyptian goddess Isis, the Buddhist spiritual being Quan Yin, and the Tibetan Buddhist figure White Tara. In words attributed to Isis, we hear the essence of the divine feminine speaking: "At my will the planets of the sky, the wholesome winds of the sea, and the lamentable silences of hell are disposed; my name, my divinity is adored throughout the world, in divers manners, in variable customs and by many names."[8]

While one might consider the various expressions of the divine feminine as one and the same, except for cultural conditionings, one must remember that Mary differs from the goddess figures of the world in that *she lived and died as an ordinary woman.* Her gradual ascendancy over centuries of worship and contemplation came not only from considering the goddesslike qualities of her being that resembled earlier expressions of the divine feminine but also from acknowledging her role as a woman in conceiving and establishing a new vision of our relationship with God. Beyond embodying those qualities we associate with the divine feminine, Mary *manifested* those qualities in this world.

If we are concerned about becoming excessively preoccupied with one embodiment of the spirit, we might do well to consider what Rabbi Herbert Weiner, author of *Nine and a Half Mystics,* once said. When he was asked why he consented to speak for a Christian organization, he replied, "Deep talks to deep." He went on to explain that when we go deeply enough into our own *specific* religious heritage, we eventually tap into the one spirit that gave rise to the diverse traditions.[9] Consequently, he said he felt at home wherever individuals had committed themselves fully to a particular spiritual tradition. With this in mind, our concentrated focus on Mary may, paradoxically, take us beyond narrow religious perspectives to gain a broader appreciation of the universal experience of the divine feminine.

If, as Rabbi Weiner suggests, we can come to an appreciation of universal truths through devoting ourselves to a specific religious path, some of us may also come to honor the particular importance of Jesus, Mary, and other distinct spiritual beings through a consideration of universal teachings. Indeed, some notable thinkers have come to embrace the importance of Jesus and Mary in particular after pursuing an extensive open-minded search for meaning in the great sacred traditions. For instance, psychiatrist Carl Jung eventually concluded that Jesus was the quintessential example of psychological individuation in the West. Having previously considered himself a Gnostic—in the ancient "heretical" tradition of placing the *knowledge* of God above faith—Jung referred to himself as a Christian toward the end of his life, thus returning to his roots as the son of a Protestant minister. With regard to Mary, Jung referred to the Catholic church's dogma of the bodily assumption of Mary into heaven as one of the most significant events in the entire history of Christianity.

Andrew Harvey, modern mystic and author, also discovered the significance of Mary—not at the beginning of his search, but after an in-depth spiritual journey. Born in India, Harvey has made pilgrimages around the world to explore the mystic traditions of the great religions. For a period of several years, he even devoted himself to Meera, a Hindu guru known simply as "the Mother," who currently resides in Germany.[10] More recently, however, he has turned to Mary as the supreme embodiment of the divine feminine. In acknowledging the *universal* being who expresses herself through a variety of spiritual teachers, mystics, and mythical figures, Harvey asserts, "There is only *one*

Mother."[11] Yet he feels that Mary stands above the rest as the *specific* person who most fully unites a complete responsiveness to spirit with a willingness to live and love fully as a human being.

꙰

Most of the experiences included in the following chapters occurred as waking visions during meditation or prayer, in vivid dreams, or during out-of-body experiences. A few were auditory locutions, in which Mary manifested to the recipient as a clear inner voice.

In the course of researching Marian encounters, my partner, Mickey Lin, and I obtained accounts from three sources.

First, we interviewed or corresponded with dozens of individuals who were willing to share their previously undisclosed encounters with Mary. The contributors contacted us originally in response to letters and notices where we asked for such accounts. We have pursued word-of-mouth leads from the friends and relatives of possible contributors and from organizations that have been founded to study Marian phenomena and apparitions. The fortunate timing of the publication of a magazine article about my work,[12] as well as my book about encounters with Jesus,[13] brought us even more reports of such encounters. Ultimately, we received well over one hundred stories, about half of which we have included in this book.

As we began to research Marian encounters, Mickey Lin and I engaged in daily meditation and prayer work. Almost immediately, she began having dreams, visions, and meditation experiences with Mary. Eventually, I found out that Mickey Lin's deep connection with the divine feminine had begun early in her life. Her stories galvanized my own interest in Mary and drew me into contemplating her in my own daily spiritual practice. Our own experiences thus provided an unexpected secondary source of Marian encounters; and since both Mickey Lin and I are therapists, our collaboration has given us many psychological and spiritual insights into Marian encounters and the people who have them.

I recount in chapter 2 my own steps leading up to this project, and I have interspersed some of Mickey Lin's encounters with Mary throughout the book. These rich, intimate, heart-opening experiences appear more or less in the order of their occurrence in her life, thus allowing the reader to view the dynamic unfolding of her relationship with Mary alongside the presentation of numerous accounts of anonymous individuals.

Third, since this project began, Mickey Lin and I have befriended several people who, it turns out, have had encounters with Mary. We did not always know ahead of time that this was the case, but we were drawn to them for inexplicable reasons. Mickey Lin in particular has known intuitively on many occasions to ask people she hardly knows about their encounters with Mary. Many of the accounts have come to us because of her sense of immediate kinship with individuals who only later admitted having a close relationship with Mary through their own direct experiences. This circle of Mary's "friends" continues to expand, and the affection we have shared continues to deepen. For more than a year now, we have met together on the first Saturday of each month to meditate and pray the rosary for world peace. As the reader will see, a few of the visionary experiences that I report herein occurred during our monthly meetings. Mickey Lin and I believe that these "visits" from Mary were meant to be shared with readers of this book.

In presenting the accounts we have obtained, I have endeavored to allow the experiences to speak for themselves and have sought to amplify their meaning rather than to impose arbitrary interpretations on them. No matter how impartial I have tried to remain, however, some readers might wonder if the approach I have taken is objective enough to produce valid conclusions about the phenomenon of encountering Mary.

Even if one wished to pursue a more scientific approach to the subject, one would still have to differentiate between the open-minded, objective attitude that scientists have always idealized and the skeptical stance that questions anything that cannot be measured by the senses.

When I first began my research on Christ encounters, I told a friend—an engineer by training—about my initial success in obtaining so many moving accounts. Without evidencing any curiosity whatsoever, nor venturing even a single question, he expressed immediate skepticism. How did I know, he asked, if the recipients were *really* encountering Christ? And how did I know if they were telling me the *truth*? He became increasingly agitated over the idea that I was researching such experiences without knowing the answer to his questions. While he could immediately identify the weaknesses of my research, his cynicism and arrogance betrayed his lack of impartiality. My friend was arguing for the superiority not of science but of a *belief system* that for him was just as compelling as the belief that Christ or Mary can come to us today.

Understandably, most recipients of encounters with Christ or Mary shy away from exposing themselves to this kind of scrutiny and judgment. Their experiences are simply too sacred to them to risk sharing them with an unsympathetic audience. Indeed, many of the contributors shared their accounts with us only after ascertaining the spirit with which we would present their treasures to the world. Because we have been respectful and open-minded, we have made it possible for the contributors to submit experiences for publication that they have previously shared only with their most trusted intimates.

Because one cannot directly *observe* spiritual experiences, *predict* their occurrence, or *control* them, we can only *describe* secondhand what people tell us about their experiences of the sacred. Obviously, the experiences we report are subjective, but we have made every effort to encourage honesty and full disclosure. Beyond these efforts, however, I believe that we face a simple choice: to allow the shared experience of the sacred to move us toward a greater understanding and a deepening faith or to ignore these experiences altogether.

As Jung once said, "I believe only what I *know.* Everything else is hypothesis and beyond that I can leave a lot of things to the Unknown."[14] And so, if these encounters resonate with our experiences, and inspire us to go deeper in our search for meaning, then they are perhaps as true as anything can be. The rest we might leave, as Jung said, to the "Unknown."

The Common Theme of Love

In researching encounters with Christ for my book *I Am with You Always,* I found to my amazement that one can summarize the experience of meeting Christ face-to-face with a single word: *love.* The love Christ reveals to those who witness his presence is unconditional. His love encompasses a complete knowledge of the person's history—including strengths, weaknesses, and what might be considered unredeemable characteristics and behaviors. In such encounters, Christ rarely offers advice and hardly ever expresses any judgment toward his witness. His messages are typically brief, if he speaks at all. Indeed, he remains largely silent except in regard to the bigger issues in life, such as loving more and serving more. Concerning these larger matters, he remains firmly and lovingly uncompromising. But he almost always leaves the person with the twofold experience of being *completely known* and *completely loved*. This experience, in turn, affects each person in different ways, depending on what he or she needs at the time. Sometimes physical healing follows Christ's manifestation, sometimes a sense of emotional healing, and sometimes a realization of having been taught something profound and life-changing.

Similarly, an encounter with Mary reveals, often wordlessly, a simple communication of love, which, as with Jesus' message, depends on the person's needs at the time and affects the recipient in a variety of ways. There are notable differences between an encounter with Mary and an encounter with Jesus, however. I will point these out as I analyze and comment on the accounts.

Even though this book explores personal visions and dreams of Mary, such experiences often precede or follow encounters with Jesus. In some encounters, Jesus and Mary even appear together or refer to each other during the experience. I eventually came to realize that an adequate appreciation of either of these beings necessitates an acceptance of the relationship they share. This realization came too late, unfortunately, to incorporate Marian encounters into my book about encountering Christ. But in this book, I have included some examples of Christ encounters reported by recipients who also experienced Mary's presence.

To assist you in appreciating the dimensions of the Marian encounter, I have grouped the encounters according to discernible themes that unfold in the course of the experience. In addition, I have ventured a perspective on the aim or purpose that the encounter evidently serves in the recipient's life. While by taking this approach I run the risk of inserting my subjective viewpoint, I believe it may help you to examine the deeper purpose and practical relevance of such spiritual encounters. Otherwise, the experiences might *inspire without informing* us about our own relationship with the divine.

How This Book Differs
from What Has Been Done

When I first considered writing about encounters with Mary, I knew that several excellent books on Mary or the Marian apparitions had been published. I also knew that there was no need to repeat what has already been accomplished by such writers as Sandra Zimdars-Swartz in *Encountering Mary,* Janice Connell in *Meetings with Mary,* or Annie Kirkwood in *Mary's Messages to the World.* To make a distinct contribution to this subject, I knew that I had to approach Mary from a different point of view—not as a scholar like Zimdars-Swartz, or a devoted Catholic like Connell, or a channel like Kirkwood. I elected to approach Mary as a non-Catholic, a psychotherapist, and, most importantly, a Christian mystic. In short, *breaking new ground meant coming to know Mary myself.*

One of Mickey Lin's first dreams about Mary underscored the importance of adopting this ambitious approach. She dreamed that she and I were in a beautiful library, looking for books about Mary. Mickey Lin then heard Mary say, "Books are fine, but he has to come to know me through his experience."

Since my first two books grew out of my own experiences,[15]

Mary's words to Mickey Lin confirmed what I already felt to be the only approach I could take. Therefore, when Mickey Lin suggested last year that we go to Conyers, Georgia, to experience the apparition of Mary there, I declined, saying that I wanted to complete this book first. "I want people to know that they can find Mary right *where they are*—in their dreams and in their prayer life. If I can come to know her where I am, then they can, too," I told Mickey Lin. I believe this approach will help readers who as yet do not know Mary or cannot travel to those sites where she has appeared.

In the book *Jonathan Livingston Seagull*, Jonathan discovers that one can achieve "perfect speed" only by realizing that *one is already there*. Once he discovered this truth, Jonathan only had to be still and to know that he was already there. Ultimately, I believe that no matter how far we travel or how many books we read, our capacity to commune with Mary comes down to the question of whether we can open our hearts and minds to her. Sacred sites may facilitate that opening, but few of us can, or will, allot the time and the resources for a journey to Lourdes or Medjugorje. If we wish to know Mary, we must find her where we are. If we can do this, then all of the books on the apparitions—and all of the pilgrimages that we might make to the sacred sites—will serve as external confirmations of what we have *already* found by opening ourselves to her.

Who Is It, Really?

In the movie *Anastasia*, the woman who believes she was the daughter of Nicholas and Alexandra of Russia finally manages to arrange a meeting with her grandmother, who has assumed for years that Anastasia was assassinated along with her parents. At first, the dowager empress expresses only cynical disbelief at the young woman's allegedly fraudulent claim. But then, as she observes the woman's obvious affection toward her and learns of Anastasia's intimate knowledge of the family's past, the grandmother's defensiveness melts into the conviction that, incredibly, her granddaughter is alive. As she embraces Anastasia tearfully, she says, "If it's not really you, please don't tell me!"

Of course, the question, Is it *really* Mary? will occur even to the most ardent believers as they read these accounts. For some, it will be hard to believe that these experiences have anything to do with a woman who lived and died two thousand years ago. It is difficult enough for some of us to accept that Jesus appears to individuals today; but at least his promises to manifest himself to those who love him are clearly stated and reiterated in the Gospel of John: "I will not leave you comfortless: I will come to you. . . . He that hath my commandments, and keepeth them, he it is that loveth me: and he that loveth me shall be loved of my father, and I will love him, and will manifest myself to him"(J14: 18 and 21).

Clearly, the Scriptures do not lay the same claims or foundation for an ongoing relationship with Mary. She remained largely silent in the scriptural record: She made no promises to commune with us and left us very little that might help us know her as she was then. For better or worse, we must come to know the woman who was "the first of the believers of the new covenant"[16] through the growing body of experiences with her, including—if we are so fortunate—our own. Instead of seeing this as limiting, we might regard it as an opportunity to embark on a personal quest to behold the feminine face of God through our own experiences. Given the abundant devotional writings about Mary over the course of Christianity's history, we can see that Mary is as knowable as the heart is open to her.

Who *is* the Mary that these visions reveal? Since this book focuses on individual mystical experiences, the Mary that the reader can come to know through this book may or may not resemble the popular view of the elusive historic person of Mary. Further, the Mary of these accounts may differ somewhat from the Mary of the church, an image that has arisen in the course of two thousand years of church-sanctioned veneration of the mother of the Lord. The Mary of these accounts is the mystical Mary, revealed entirely through our personal experiences of her. As the mystical Mary, *she is more the source than the product of everything we know about her.* She is the direct interior experience of the feminine face of God, in which all speculation about Mary is, perhaps, ideally rooted.

Can these experiences add anything to what we know about God? Some say that if we are made in God's image, then the search for meaning produces dreams, images, and concepts that, while filtered through our own experiences and beliefs, unerringly spring from the divine, thus revealing its true nature and intent. Jung referred to the internal representations of enduring truths as "archetypes," but this abstract word fails to convey just how personal the divine can be. In the experience of the divine, God manifests in surprisingly personal ways. While we tend to think that the closer we get to the divine, the *less* personal it becomes, the reverse may be true. *God may be more personal than we are willing to admit.* In the absence of any proof to the contrary, we are entirely free to think that we can know God *best* by first examining our own experiences of the personal embodiments of the divine that arise in the course of our search for meaning.

Of course, any private spiritual experience bears the imprint of the visionary's cultural heritage, beliefs, and expectations, and one cannot easily subtract these conditioning factors from the encounter. But if one examines a number of such encounters, the individual variations become increasingly apparent, and the enduring reality behind the subjective experience emerges more and more clearly. Rather than considering the individual variations as mere distortions, however, we can appreciate the myriad ways in which individuals perceive the divine feminine and come to understand her significance in their lives.

In the final analysis, the nature and identity of the being who appears in Marian encounters poses a mystery that one can never conclusively resolve. Because individuals experience the divine in a variety of forms, it is tempting to conclude that the identity of a particular spiritual being is merely a function of the witness's own beliefs. I think this is only partly true. Just as the divine might manifest to us in a variety of ways, so on a subatomic level, an electron can be in many places at once, as a particle *and* as a wave. It seems strange, but on the subatomic level, only potentialities exist for the electron's location—that is, *until one actually observes what is there.* In the act of observation, the potentialities collapse into an actuality, and the electron appears in one place only.

Similarly, the divine apparently manifests to us in many different forms, depending on the needs, beliefs, and expectations of the recipients. For instance, when the archangel Michael appeared to the four girls in Garabandal, Spain, he eventually announced that Mary would appear to them as our Lady of Mt. Carmel—one of many familiar ways that Mary has been depicted in the Roman Catholic tradition. In essence, the angel implied that the *form* of Mary's appearance was only one of many possible ways that she could manifest to them. Another apparition of Mary has appeared over a period of several years to a small group in the St. Maria Goretti church in Scottsdale, Arizona. When she manifests, she appears to several young people at the same time, but she appears *differently* to each one.[17] As Father Faricy has noted, "In each of her comings, Mary appears in such a way that the people to whom she comes can relate to her. To black people she is black. To Koreans she looks Korean. . . . She comes as their Mother because that is what she is. Ours, too."[18]

Rather than considering the individual variations as distortions, we can come to appreciate these differences as creative approximations of a complex truth that cannot be reduced to a single form. We can treat the myriad ways in which individuals experience the Holy Mother as partial but invaluable information about a being who, ultimately, can be known *only* through the eyes and hearts of human visionaries.

I am reminded of a Christ encounter that I reported in *I Am with You Always*. A woman encountered an orb of light in the woods one afternoon. She asked, "Who are you?" It answered, "Some call me Buddha, some call me Christ." She then said, "I don't know Buddha." And the light replied, "Then I am Christ." Significantly, the being did not say that *any* name would do, only that more than one name was equally fitting. This suggests that within the potentials inherent in an encounter with a spiritual being, more than one correct identification may be possible.

Of course, it is difficult to conceive of how higher beings—or various personal aspects of the divine—can "co-inhere" in the eternal light and yet appear to us in such personal, distinct ways. Perhaps the light is not as amorphous as a wave, but more like a gemstone whose facets all reveal, in unique ways, the beauty of the one who unites them. From this point of view, the particular being we encounter may be the living facet of the divine who can best answer to our particular needs, beliefs, and aspirations at the time. Of course, even though there may be an "identity of best fit" for each of us, one cannot determine for someone else whom that might be. And yet, for some reason, our collective needs at this time call forth a manifestation of Mary more often than most any other being. Clearly, Mary is a "constellated" archetype: She embodies many emerging facets of our spiritual natures and awakens us to the urgent need to reintegrate the feminine into our conception of God and our own spiritual natures.

One night, I dreamt that I was outside and that everything I looked at began to glow around the edges. Knowing that this was impossible, I realized that I was dreaming, and then I set about to see through the form of the images and commune with the eternal light. But as soon as I concentrated on the images around me, hoping to perceive the radiance behind the forms, they lost their luster and again assumed the appearance of ordinary objects. I became frustrated because I could not figure out why the light continually eluded me. Then a woman walked up to me and said, "If you wish to commune with the light, you must first learn to love the form in which it comes."

With this in mind, let us consider the notion that by loving the form in which the divine feminine manifests to us, we may enter more deeply into a personal relationship with God and gain knowledge of the unifying spirit that expresses itself in a myriad of forms. By suspending our need to separate fact from fiction and subjective from objective—and, above all else, by *feeling* her presence—we may draw closer than ever to the grace-filled being who impels us forward on our journey and forever awaits us.

In practice, of course, as Father Pelletier says, "the degree of our devotion to Mary will be a matter of discerning the authentic promptings of the Holy Spirit. The same Spirit will attract some people to honor and pray to angels; others, this or that saint. And so, too, it is in regard to Mary." But, as he goes on to say, "We must not be afraid of loving Mary too much."[19] C. S. Lewis agreed that it is far more important to worship God in whatever form suits us than it is to quibble over his or her degree of personhood. As he asserted, "No soul has ever perished by believing that God the Father has a beard."[20] Or for that matter, I might add, a mother's touch.

Last June, before our monthly prayer and rosary group meeting, Mickey Lin went outside to cut roses to decorate the altar. She gathered all the available blossoms except one—a large yellow rose, which just seemed too beautiful to pick. She went back and forth until she finally decided to include it with the rest. Later that evening, during our meditation, Mary appeared to her in a vision.

First, Mickey Lin saw a glowing ball of light turn from a bluish white to a golden yellow. From the center emerged the Madonna's profile; she was smelling the bouquet of roses that had been picked from the garden. As Mary bent her head to appreciate fully the last yellow rose that had been picked, Mickey Lin knew without a doubt that she was really enjoying this perfect rose. Mary turned, smiled at Mickey Lin, and said, "I like this one the best! Thank you for honoring me."

I sincerely hope that this book is like Mickey Lin's yellow rose—the very best of what I can give to Mary, and the best of what Mary wishes for us to know. All of the encounters and commentary included herein are intended to honor her and the one she brings to us.

1

My Coming to Know Mary

> He has to come to know me through his
> experience.
>
> *Mary's words to Mickey Lin*

Coming to know Mary in a profoundly personal sense is by no means easy for people who were either underexposed or over-exposed to her in early religious training. By the time we are old enough to consider for ourselves the question of how she might fit into our spiritual lives, our adult minds may have become overly rational and resistant to the idea of grace, spiritual guidance, and the redemptive capacity of love. Finding Mary as a living mystical presence cannot come merely from an act of will or from intellectual exploration. She must be found in the center of our being, where the prompting of the divine is *felt*. Perhaps this is why Mary has often chosen children as her messengers, for the sweet openness of childhood remains relatively untouched by theological argument, and she can more easily be heard and felt in that central place that, for the lack of a better word, we call the human heart.

As a man who was raised in a Protestant church, I was twice-removed from a natural appreciation of the feminine face of God. A Methodist who was entirely ignorant of Mary's position in the Catholic tradition, I was not predisposed to develop or pursue such a relationship. So I do not think I would have discovered Mary on my own. However, I have been blessed by numerous mystical experiences since my late teens. Through this open channel, the divine feminine has come to me in deep dreams and visions and ushered me into a relationship with her that is still unfolding in a beautiful and mysterious way. Every day, she seems to come a little closer—living in and through me as a heartfelt presence who brings love and assurance as well as the urge to serve others in a world that seems simultaneously closer to God and further from God than ever.

For the benefit of readers who might find themselves as yet unfamiliar with Mary, I have retraced my steps to her—or hers to me—in order to convey to readers how someone like myself can come to a point where Mary occupies a central role in his spiritual life and the rosary a prominent place in his prayer life. My story may also serve to introduce readers to the heart of this book—to the importance of the mystical relationship that we can enjoy with Mary and the devotional practice that she urgently advocates.

About ten years ago, I went up to the Blue Ridge Mountains to fly-fish for trout. Usually, a friend goes with me, but every once in a while I go alone for the communion with nature that only seems possible when I do not have to talk or listen, and to be in a place where I can quietly make and unmake every little decision about where to go and what to do.

A builder had just begun construction on a log cabin that I'd dreamt of having for years. I arrived late at night, set up a cot and sleeping bag on the rudiments of a front porch, and went to sleep thinking about the brook trout that I would stalk the next morning with my tiny homemade flies. Instead of waking up refreshed, however, I awoke feeling anxious and unsettled. The memory of a disturbing dream was fresh in my mind.

The last part of the dream still is vivid and unforgettable. An unknown woman stood before me, holding a large, ancient book, which I understood to be my soul record. She looked at me and said, "I have followed you through all of your sojourns. And I am *angry!*" Then she reached out and scratched my face. That is when I woke up.

I could not shake an eerie sense of vulnerability as I ate my breakfast and dressed for the day. Fighting a tendency to leave for home, I drove a few miles north, toward several streams that flowed clear and cold out of the upper elevations of the George Washington National Forest. Looking back, it is obvious by the names of the streams that I was unconsciously approaching the threshold of a new realization. I passed my old friend, Big Marys Creek—a stream that most fishermen would not give the slightest glance, but one in which I had caught and released many little brook trout. I passed Little Marys Creek, a mere trickle of a stream that I'd never fished but had often wondered about. And I went on to visit one of the legendary gems of the Blue Ridge— the St. Marys River.

I parked my car and hiked up the stream on the national forest trail. The month of May had brought out everything; spring had arrived in full force. But the beauty was undermined by my knowledge that the small, brilliantly colored trout were rapidly disappearing in the St. Marys due to the cumulative effects of acid rain. Tragically, this pristine stream had become a casualty of the unrestricted burning of coal hundreds of miles away. This was insidiously eroding her capacity to sustain the life that had been hers since the Ice Age.

I had been fishing for a while with little success when the anxiety from the dream became intense. I couldn't escape the sense of being found out and condemned by the woman in the dream. I stopped to pray. It was my practice in prayer to commune with Jesus, who had become very personal and real to me after years of daily meditation and dream work. While such prayers usually had exerted a calming influence on me, they fell short on that occasion of stilling my deep foreboding.

I do not recall why I thought of praying to Mary, but this was the first time in my life that I turned to her. She somehow became—not because of any prior belief or accepted doctrine—the answer to my dilemma. As I began my open-eyed prayer, casting my fly upstream to the next pool, I felt a sense of immediate comfort and caring coming from her. My mind tried to convince me that this could not be true—that Mary was nobody to me and that she was just a convenient fiction for me to cling to. But something in me prevailed over these arguments. In that moment, I *knew* somehow that Mary would be my advocate with the women in my life, and with the feminine aspects within myself which I had neglected, misunderstood, or alienated. I also *knew* that I had to do my part, which was simple to define but hard to do: I had to stand up before their assessment of me, knowing that my healing depended on facing willingly what I'd run from so many times before—feelings, needs, intimacy, and dependency. I felt the beginning of a long process of inner and outer dialogue that would not be easy but whose eventual fruition would surely justify the struggle.

My experience on the St. Marys River served as a wake-up call to me in my practical and spiritual life and deepened my spiritual practice through my attempts to emulate the responsiveness of Mary. Although the experience then seemed to come from out of the blue in response to my prayer for understanding my distress, as I look back now, I realize that earlier intimations of this awakening had been clearly evident in the momentous dreams of my early twenties.

The Early Stage: Encounters with Light

At nineteen, I first experienced what Christian and non-Christian mystics alike have referred to as the divine or eternal light. Of this universal mystical experience, Carl Jung said: "The phenomenon itself, that is the light-vision, is an experience common to many mystics, and one that is undoubtedly of the greatest significance, because in all times and places it appears as the unconditional thing, which unites in itself the greatest energy and the profoundest meaning."[1]

My first experience of this light began as an ordinary dream in which I was walking home from my college classes, carrying my books. For some reason, I realized that I was dreaming. I stopped to look at my hands and my body, noting the vividness of every aspect of my experience. It seemed not only real but *more* real than any waking experience. I concluded that my physical body was sleeping but that I was nonetheless fully awake. Marveling at this paradox, I walked up to large black double doors, reached for ornate brass handles, and pulled opened the doors. As soon as the doors parted, bright white light streamed through and filled my vision.

The sense of love and purpose was staggering as I felt the light course through my body with an authority that was at once undeniable and comforting. I felt I had come home once and for all.

The interior seemed to be a small chapel with large vertical windows that looked out onto barren land. I walked about, asking myself what it all meant. I thought that someone would surely appear at any moment to tell me why this was happening. At one point, I carried a crystal wand, at the top of which a spinning crystal circlet was hovering. The light passed through the crystal and was exquisitely beautiful.

While the room remained full of light, no one came to me. As such, this first of many encounters with the divine light left me asking, From whom does such light and love come? As D. T. Suzuki once said of the highest state in consciousness, it is not an abstract reality; to the contrary, it implies a personality.[2] In support of this idea, of which I knew nothing at the time, I felt an instinctive need for someone to be there. And yet I had no sense of whom that might be. But the experience of light left me wondering.

After several similar experiences, the encounter with light began to include a more personal touch. While it eventually became associated with Jesus more than anyone else, there were several experiences in which the embodiment of the light was clearly feminine. As I reflect back on these early encounters, I see now that the divine feminine served as a forerunner and companion experience to my first encounters with Christ, as well as a foundation for an eventual relationship with Mary.

After one of these early experiences of the eternal light, I naïvely remarked to a friend, who had also experienced this light, that we were probably close to enlightenment. Richard looked shocked and said, "Don't talk that way!" Since that time, I have discovered that the experience of the eternal light does not ensure one's fulfillment anytime soon; it comes to awaken a new view of oneself and one's overall purpose in life. Rather than consolidating an unshakable confidence, it leaves one feeling more exalted *and* faulted, such that two contrasting and equally compelling views of oneself begin to exist alongside of each other. This intensified sense of internal division gives rise to what Christian mystics have referred to as "the dark night of the soul"—a meaningful but painful period during which the less lofty aspects of oneself are cast in stark relief against the growing impulse to serve God. This period of inner conflict can seem interminable. The following dream illustrates how the inner division became dramatically evident in my life.

In the dream, I was a prisoner of the devil. I was outside at night with a group of other prisoners. The devil was a powerful, brutish man who remained close so that we could not escape. But at one point, while he was talking with some of the others, a woman and I decided to escape. She and I began running across a lighted lawn, hoping to reach the shadows before he realized that we had fled. As we ran, we became separated in our individual efforts to flee to safety.

As I ran, I heard a voice say gently, "If you go any farther, you will fall into a well." I stopped, not knowing what to do. As I hesitated, I saw the devil's shadow creep past me. He had seen me and was approaching from behind me. Feeling hopeless and terrified, not knowing what he would do to me, I prayed, "God have mercy," then turned around to face him. But the devil was gone! In his place stood a beautiful woman dressed in white and surrounded with white light. She walked up to me, bent over, and touched me gently on the forehead. Immediately, my vision was filled with white light, and once again I felt an almost overpowering energy and love. As I floated into

> waking awareness, I knew without doubt that she had
> healed me—but of what, I did not know.

If I'd been raised a Catholic, it would have been natural for me to identify the woman as Mary—if not in the dream, then surely in the waking recollection of the dream. And if I had been a Buddhist, I might have called her Quan Yin or some other female embodiment of the divine. *Faced with the ambiguity of an unidentified spiritual being, we tend to speculate in the direction of our existing beliefs.* We too easily forget that the experience itself often leaves the issue of identity in question. At the time, however, my belief system did not include a feminine embodiment of God; hence, for better or worse, the being remained unidentified.

❧

In my search for someone who could help me along on the spiritual path, I briefly considered in the early 1970s devoting myself to an Eastern guru. One night, after spending an inspiring evening with a friend—who was at the time a devotee of Charan Singh, a Sikh master—I went home wondering if perhaps I, too, should consider seeking initiation from this teacher.

That night, I had a dream in which I went to see Charan Singh in India.

> *A*fter waiting in line, I was admitted to a small house,
> where I found him sitting in his turban and robe on a
> divan. His face was radiant and smiling, seeming to wel-
> come me. But I didn't know what to say! I struggled for
> words, then told him my name. He nodded and smiled.
> Then, as I began to ask him a question, I said, "Mas-
> ter—" He promptly interrupted me and said, "Who is

master?" in a gently admonishing way. With only these words, I realized that he was telling me he was not my master and that I should know who my master was. I concluded that he was referring to Jesus. Just then, a woman came into the room to give me instructions in yoga. As we sat face-to-face on the floor practicing the cobra asana, I experienced the white light. As it coursed through my being, filling me with a deep sense of love, I looked at Charan Shingh through a white haze and saw that he was laughing joyously.

Charan Shingh surprised me by refusing my attempt to honor him as master. His refusal made me consider the possibility that a relationship with Christ was preferable to one that I might have with any physically incarnate being. The dream also suggested that this relationship already existed even though I was still largely unaware of it.

It is also possible that Charan Shingh was referring to someone else whom I failed to acknowledge at the time. After all, he didn't specify whom I should serve. Maybe he was referring to the "master" *within*—that is, my own potential for enlightenment, or the potential indicated by the inner light. Just as likely, he was referring to the woman who assisted me in opening myself to the light. And yet I don't think these positions are contradictory. Indeed, I believe they represent equally valid facets of the whole truth. To say that Charan Shingh was referring exclusively to Jesus, *or* to the woman, *or* to my own capacity for enlightenment is to engage in a fruitless kind of either/or thinking. Ultimately, it would allow God to reside in one place only—which was perhaps a problem in my own thinking that Charan Shingh was encouraging me to overcome.

Soon afterward, I began to see Jesus in the light. For a few years, he appeared in several deep dreams and meditations to confront me about unfinished work, to heal me of old wounds and fears, and just to let me know that he loved me. The divine feminine presence who had preceded him largely ceased to manifest in my dreams.

One day, after it seemed that my encounters with Jesus had ended, at least for a time, and that I would be on my own for a while without the consoling influence of his presence, I was surprised when he appeared once again in a dream.

In the dream, I was working on my computer on a writing project. Suddenly, the screen opened up like a stage curtain. There was Jesus only a few feet away, bathed in an indigo light (which I have since found in my research on Marian encounters to be often associated with experiences of Mary). He asked, "Do you love me?" I said yes. Then he asked me, "Do we love Mary?" Surprised, I said yes. Then he said, "Then you are my father and my brother." I was confused by his words, and he laughed gently at my consternation.

I had no idea what this dream meant, but it seemed clear that he intended to point me to the next step in my growth. Having little familiarity and affinity for the ways that Mary was worshiped in Catholicism, however, I lacked a natural avenue of approaching her. So, except for an occasional prayer in her direction, I did nothing, and more time passed. After all of the experiences pointing me to the feminine face of God, I still hadn't gotten the message. Or perhaps the need had not become great enough.

Crisis and the Opening of the Heart

About a year later, I experienced a major new development in my own spiritual journey. This all happened at a time when things in my life became intensely difficult. First of all, I had been sued with two other therapists in a frivolous suit. (It eventually came to nothing.) The continual lack of resolution in this slow-going legal matter undermined my confidence as a therapist. Shortly thereafter, I became a father; my mother became ill and died after a three-year battle with pancreatic cancer; and my wife's father developed terminal cancer, requiring her to be away for weeks at a time. My marriage began coming apart. All of the premises that had once governed my life now seemed unreliable. I was smack in the middle of a midlife review, and I felt I couldn't do anything right. God seemed far away from me, and for the first time in my life, I did not believe that I deserved his love. Even so, I continued meditating and praying for up to two hours every morning. One day, I simply let go. I knew that life was bigger than I was and that I could not reverse the forces at work in it. I was afraid, but I was somehow relieved that it was, perhaps, a battle I wasn't supposed to win.

While meditating one day during this time, I felt as if my heart were expanding to the point where it seemed to be leaving my body. I had meditated for more than twenty years on a daily basis, and this was new! It was pleasant but startling. Although I knew that this was not actually happening to my heart, I felt an expansion and vibration of what might be called a subtle or finer body, especially in the area near the heart. Having experienced the eternal light on so many occasions, I knew that it was often accompanied by intense electriclike energy, called the kundalini in the East. But these sensations were gentle.

A few days after this began, I had one of the most beautiful dreams of my life. In the dream, I was meditating and saw a flash of light. Then I got up and began walking toward a garden that I knew lay to the northeast. As I approached the garden, I saw a light shining in the middle of it. Intrigued, I went to investigate. As I got closer, I could see that the light was coming from a large egg-shaped crystal object that was floating above the ground and was protected by a blue canopy. The whole arrangement looked like a tiny gazebo with the light in the center. The closer I got to the light, the brighter and more intense it became. I knew that the light loved me completely and unconditionally as a mother might love a child and that it was responding to the quality of love within my heart. *I walked away from the light and then returned to it. Once again, the closer I got, the brighter the light shone. Then I walked down a path with an unknown woman beside me. A dove flew up and landed on my shoulder. I knew that the dove was also responding to the quality of love within my heart and that its fearless attention was a great confirmation. Then I looked up ahead and saw a man who was the master of the garden. He looked at me without speaking, awaiting our approach.*

The dream about the radiant egg told me that somehow, even though I found it hard to believe, I was still loved for what was within my heart. I had inadvertently entered a period of my life when I ceased to look upon spirituality as something one could attain once and for all and instead began to see it as a continuous process. I had begun to emphathize with people who had struggled a great deal, and who had matured through embracing their ordeals. I became an adult, I believe, when I finally began to accept that the only thing by which I am measured is *how much I love*. Honesty—speaking from the heart—became paramount in importance to me as I strove to act on this empathy and love. The quality of the heart became for me the new criterion by which I related to people, to the world, and to the divine. With this new orientation, it was only a matter of time before a conscious devotion to the divine feminine emerged as one phase of my life resolved and a new phase began. This was intimated by another wondrous dream of light.

I was at my childhood home. It was late at night when I went out in the backyard and looked eastward toward the Gulf of Mexico and, more specifically, in the direction of the Laguna Madre (or Mother Lagoon)—a shallow, clear bay between Padre Island and the Texas mainland that remains my favorite place in all the world. A warm wind blew from the southeast, and I knew that it would be calm by the next morning, making for ideal conditions for fly-fishing in the Laguna Madre. As I looked up at the sky, I saw a full moon through the trees. Then I saw another orb of light beside the moon. How could this be? I wondered. Was it the sun? Was it another moon? I was puzzled. Then I realized that I was dreaming. As I came to this awareness, the two orbs started moving together. I lay down on the grass and meditated on the celestial light, knowing that I was perceiving the eternal light, not the actual moon or the sun.

As the two lights joined, they became a larger orb of white light, upon which a more brilliant white star was superimposed. The new singular body of light now appeared behind thick clouds, but a tunnel through the clouds gave me a clear view of the light.

Then, to my surprise, the combined light pulsated and a shimmering light came down through the tunnel—all the way down to where I was—and entered my chest. As it did, I went into an ecstatic, intense state of love. Then I heard a man's voice say, "You have done well with this."

Then it was morning in the dream, and it seemed that I had awakened from it. I was with my sister and my wife, who were sitting in the grass close to where I'd received the light. I told them about the dream, then realized that it was late in the morning and that I had to leave for the Laguna Madre. I considered asking if it was okay, but then I realized it was my choice to make. So I said nothing more and then left alone.

Just as Jesus passed me on to Mary, the dream indicated the beginning of a solitary journey "later in the day" of my life—a journey toward the East and the Mother, and into the heart.

A Guide and Companion

The most recent phase of coming to know Mary began with the completion of my book about dreams and visions of Jesus. I had the opportunity to write a similar book about Mary but felt unqualified to explore experiences that were ostensibly about her. I have always found that I can write and speak only about those things that I have experienced. I struggled for weeks over what to say.

One thing alone convinced me to go ahead: my then new relationship with Mickey Lin, who, I came to find, knew the divine feminine in a profound way. I was drawn to Mickey Lin from the time I met her, but I was puzzled as to why she supported without question my suitability to research and write about Marian dreams and visions. She seemed unrealistically optimistic about this work, and she even offered to help me locate contributors. Then one night, as I struggled with the decision about whether I could do the book, a dream came that helped me understand why Mickey was so confident.

In the dream, a man told me that a woman who was in the spirit—that is, not embodied—was coming to visit me. He said that this woman was half Mickey. *He went on to say that Mickey had known this woman before and had once helped her. And he said that on one occasion this woman had given Mickey water.*

As I awoke in my bed, I lay quietly, puzzling over this dream. Then suddenly, I heard what sounded like a powerful wind. I opened my eyes, startled by the sound. I knew *that the female spirit mentioned in the dream was present. Anxiously, I closed my eyes again, only to hear the powerful wind once more. I opened my eyes, expecting to see someone there, but I saw nothing unusual in my bedroom. The same phenomenon repeated itself again before I sat up to pray. I'd had enough, and I was alarmed about what might happen.*

I work with dreams every day in my counseling practice, but this one stumped me. I knew that when Nicodemus, a Pharisee, asked Jesus if a man had to be born again, Jesus said, "Verily, verily, I say unto thee, Except a man be born of water and *of* the Spirit, he cannot enter into the kingdom of God. That which is born of the flesh is flesh; and that which is born of the Spirit is spirit" (John 3:5–6).

Considering how Jesus used the phrase "born of water" to represent physical birth, I thought that the woman's gift of water to Mickey could represent the gift of birth. Could this woman have been Mickey's mother? I wondered. Carrying this thought beyond the literal, I wondered if the woman the man referred to was, by chance, the Divine Mother, or Mary.

I was still puzzled when I told Mickey the dream two days later. Did she know who the woman might have been and what the water could have meant? I asked. I was surprised when tears came to Mickey's eyes. She said that there was something she'd never told me about. She *had* told me about falling into a well when she was three years old. She had not mentioned, however, that someone had ministered to her during her two-day ordeal.

The incident had occurred more than thirty years ago in the hills of Taiwan. Mickey had been playing outside on her father's estate, apparently without her nanny's close supervision. She does not recall falling into the abandoned well, nor does she remember how she ended up at the bottom of the narrow shaft. Yet she still wonders whether she fell or whether she was pushed by someone who was perhaps jealous of her mother's relationship with her powerful father. All she can remember of her ordeal today is a pervading sense of comfort and love, and a bluish lavender light.

Soon after she fell in, Mickey's cries were heard by someone passing near the well. She would have been rescued without delay, but the adults could not get to her. The well shaft had a bottleneck through which a normal-sized adult could not pass. They were understandably afraid of suffering Mickey's fate. Finally, after almost two days, Mickey's mother, who was a tiny woman, insisted on trying to force her way through the narrow opening into the lower portion of the shaft. Her attempt was successful.

As she was lowered into the darkness, she held out desperate hope that Mickey would somehow be okay after such a fall and two days of exposure. As she passed the bottleneck successfully and entered the darkness, she was startled to see a bluish violet light shining beneath her. As she inched downward, she perceived a beautiful, luminous woman standing in the midst of the light, comforting the little girl, who had somehow climbed onto a dry ledge above the water's edge. Mickey's mother watched the being gradually disappear as she reached down and touched her child for the first time in two days.

This event was hailed as a miracle by those who came to know about it. The local Buddhist priests even wanted to take Mickey to the temple and train her, believing that her miraculous survival indicated a spiritual depth that needed to be nourished by a life of spiritual practice. However, her mother refused them, knowing that she would no longer see much of her daughter if she consented to the priests' request.

No one around Mickey claimed that she'd had an encounter with the Virgin Mary, even though she was being raised as a Buddhist *and* as a Catholic. Years later, after immigrating to the United States, Mickey saw this being standing in the midst of a storm outside her bedroom window. It was a particularly difficult time in her life, and the being appeared again as if to say, I am still with you. Since that time, Mickey has come to identify this presence as Mary.

After Mickey told me about her experience in the well and her other, more recent experiences with Mary, I realized that we had come together, in part, to work on this book and that with her I would enter into a deeper relationship with the divine feminine. Sometimes I have felt as if I was a blind man whom Mickey was leading through a maze toward something I could find on my own only with great difficulty. And sometimes I have felt that I have given Mickey water when she has stumbled and fallen.

Our journey together into this dimension of spiritual practice and unfoldment has become a major source of inspiration to me. It has made the difference between writing about Mary from the outside and writing a book that springs out of communion with her.

Our encounters over the last year and a half—together with the accounts of others—will, I hope, assist you in gaining a sense of how accessible Mary can be to those who sincerely seek to know her *directly* as a mystical reality. We feel that we have been blessed by her presence, and we feel we have been called to speak of her interventions in our lives.

Several months ago, Mickey and I were wondering whether we should continue our relationship. After a long night of insomnia, Mickey fell asleep and had the following dream.

I was crying in my dream—sitting on my knees, with my hands covering my face. In the midst of streaming tears, I noticed a blue cloth whispering by, flowing. I took the cloth in my hands to absorb the tears, then realized that the cloth was attached to something else. I felt very embarrassed that I was so engrossed in my own pettiness, I was not conscious of using something that belonged to someone else without asking. With blurry vision, I sheepishly looked down and saw sandals just below the blue hem. A sweet, gentle voice urged me to look up, but I could not. I felt very unworthy and shameful. Then I heard the gentle voice say, "It's okay. I will be here when you are ready."

That very night, at about the time when Mickey had her dream, I was awakened by an influx of energy and light. I tried to be open to the healing that the light seems to bring me. I saw no one, but I felt a great presence behind the gift. A while later, I got up to pray and meditate. Toward the end of my meditation, an amazing thing happened: I had a vision! It was simple and vivid. My whole field of sight was suddenly filled with what was clearly a cloth of a blue color. The image was so distinct that I could see every thread. Then it was gone as abruptly as it had come. I didn't know what to think until I spoke with Mickey later that day. Mary, it seemed, had reached out to both of us with a symbol of her caring.

I believe that my relationships with others somehow depend on devoting myself to a mystical relationship with Mary. Communing with Mary can be, for me and for others like me, the way to deepen a capacity to *sustain a commitment to God and to loved ones* and to overcome the obstacles that prevent the open exercise and expression of that capacity. Mary has become the perfect example of one whose commitment sustained her through a life of unparalleled purpose, joy, and anguish.

Mary's Manifestations and Her Secrets

There are mysteries which man is called
upon to unveil, and there are others which
are meant to be felt, but not to be touched,
whose secrecy must be respected.

Lama Anagarika Govinda

As a non-Catholic and a psychotherapist, I felt rather strange when I first began studying the historic manifestations of the Virgin Mary. The sense of strangeness came from a fundamental difference between my own religious heritage and the worldview shared by the authors of the well-known books on the apparitions. Most of these writers had grown up in a richly symbolic, complex religious culture that was far removed from my own austere Protestant background. As Thomas Kuhn might say, these Roman Catholic authors shared a religious *paradigm*, or view of the world, that differed from mine.[1]

Operating from *within* a paradigm, one possesses an unquestioning acceptance of certain underlying premises that from the outside might seem strange or even arbitrary. Operating from *outside* the paradigm, however, one can sometimes ask new questions and offer a fresh perspective that may change the way one looks at mysteries that might have been too conveniently explained away by the prevailing worldview.

For better or worse, I realized that I was on the outside looking in. Once I got past my discomfort, however, I found myself asking questions and receiving answers that I believe have not been considered—or at least emphasized—in books on the historic apparitions.

The overview that I present in this chapter will assist the reader who as yet is unfamiliar with the major apparitions; it will also benefit the reader who is already familiar with these events. For in this chapter, I introduce some previously unarticulated ideas about the encounter with Mary, which I develop more fully in the later chapters and which I sincerely believe may revise or deepen our understanding about the purpose and importance of these events.

Today, we have come to associate Marian encounters with the apparitions that began in Europe during the middle 1800s and which continue to this day in various parts of the world, including Bosnia, Venezuela, and the United States. Yet the encounter with Mary is by no means a recent development: Many well-known religious figures reported private visions of Mary prior to the era of modern apparitions. From the first century of Christianity, Mary has intervened in countless lives. To date, reports of these manifestations number over 21,000.[2]

According to St. Gregory of Nyssa, Mary appeared to St. Gregory the Wonder-worker in the third century. Accompanied by the apostle John, she appeared to him in the night, more than life-size, surrounded by light, "as if a brilliant torch had been lit." In Gregory's vision, Mary told John to make the mystery of the true faith known to Gregory. John was heard to consent because such was her wish.[3]

Centuries later, on returning to England from the Crusades in 1261, St. Simon Stock experienced a vision of Mary now well-known to Roman Catholics. In his vision, Mary urged St. Simon to wear a small piece of brown wool—a token piece of her mantle, which would, she said, guarantee its wearer immunity from eternal fire at death. Since then, countless people have worn the brown scapular as a visible sign, like a wedding ring or a locket, of their devotion to Mary and her virtues.[4]

In spite of Mary's appearances to such individuals over the centuries, David Blackbourn, author of the scholarly work *Marpingen—Apparitions of the Virgin Mary in Nineteenth-Century Germany*, points out that the apparitions and visions seen by early saints "were incidental features in the lives whose legends they embellished: it was the saint who was the object of the cult."[5] Because the church treated the encounter as secondary to a famous person's religious life, neither the visions nor the miracles frequently associated with them became the focus of widespread devotion.

But starting in the early 1800s, the emphasis began to shift away from the seer to the messages conveyed by Mary, and to the miraculous healings that took place around the apparitions. This shift may have occurred because Mary's messages were changing to include statements about the world as a whole or because the church and the public found it difficult to establish a cult around the recipients of these new apparitions—women and uneducated children. Blackbourn says that:

> Something new clearly was happening in the nineteenth century. For all the changes that took place in the idiom of Marian apparitions from about 1400, it remains true that there was no period before the nine-

teenth century in which children were more favored than adults, or female visionaries outnumbered males. Both were distinctively modern developments.[6]

Because Mary's appearances began to favor individuals with less religious and social status, the church and the public may have been more inclined to look beyond the seers and focus on the wider relevance of the apparition.

Sister Catherine Labouré

Catherine Labouré, a novice nun in the convent of the Sisters of Charity in Paris, served as a transitional figure in the development of the modern apparition. As a cloistered nun, she was protected from the public scrutiny that was to plague later visionaries. Indeed, people only learned her name years later. At twenty-three, she was older than most of the later apparition visionaries. As a child, she was also better-off than many have believed, having become the mistress of a large farm at the age of twelve.[7]

In July 1830, Catherine was awakened in the middle of the night by a child dressed in white standing at the foot of her bed—a being Catherine later identified as her guardian angel. He beckoned for her to follow him. She rose from her bed and followed him down the hall into the chapel of the convent. On her way there, she was amazed to find candles lighting her way down the hallway. As she entered the chapel, she encountered Mary for the first time. She heard a sound like the "rustle of silk," then saw Mary enter the room and sit in the father director's chair. Catherine fell on her knees and knelt before Mary, experiencing the "sweetest moment of her life." Meanwhile,

Mary spoke to Catherine about the tragedies that would befall France in the years to follow, and of a mission that she wished to entrust to Catherine. When Catherine looked up later, the child was still there, but Mary had disappeared.

Interestingly, Catherine's first experience bears the earmarks of what modern dream researchers refer to as a "false awakening." This is when a person *believes* she has awakened, when in actuality she is having a special type of dream that starts when the person *apparently* awakens from sleep. When the person actually awakens later, it is tempting to believe that the dream events actually took place in physical reality. In Catherine's first experience, the anomalous presence of the candles in the hallway strongly suggests that she was dreaming or "out of her body." By accepting the anomaly as factual, the dreamer succeeds in sustaining the belief that she is in a normal state of awareness. Even if Catherine's experience was a false awakening, it should not diminish the importance of her initial encounter for us. But by acknowledging this possibility, it keeps us cognizant of how such apparitions often begin—in the state between waking and sleep, where "reality" mimics the waking state but includes phenomena originating in psychic or spiritual realms. Many of the encounters in this book clearly occurred in this in-between state of consciousness. Typically, because people experience this state as in no way inferior to waking awareness, they will often report it as a waking experience, even though they are not sure whether they were awake or not. The bedside visitation in particular should serve as a cue for us to question whether the person was awake in the ordinary sense or if she was conscious in that fertile in-between realm where vision and what we call reality overlap.

Later that year, Catherine saw Mary again, this time while meditating with the other novices in the chapel. Catherine again heard a sound like the rustle of silk, and she looked up, to see Mary standing beside a picture of Joseph. Mary was surrounded by light, and gem-colored beams of light shone from her fingers as if to represent her gifts to the world. Mary slowly turned in an oval frame, and the reverse side showed itself to Catherine. On this side was the letter *M*, a cross, two hearts—one encircled with thorns and the other pierced by a sword—and this inscription: "O Holy Mary, pray for those who have recourse to thee."

During another vision two months later, Catherine saw the entire scene again. But this time, Mary told Catherine to have this image struck as a medal that people could wear. After a canonical inquiry, permission was granted in 1832 to have the medal produced. At that time, an epidemic of cholera was gripping Paris. When the medal was distributed, those who wore it exhibited a remarkable immunity to the disease. Today, millions of Miraculous Medals have been produced, and countless miracles credited to them.

Sister Justine and the Green Scapular

A similar series of private visions of Mary—which produced yet another devotional object that has been widely used ever since—took place ten years later in another Paris convent. In January of 1840, Mary appeared to Sister Justine Bisqueyburu, a novice of the Daughters of Charity. The first several visions with Mary seemed to have no other purpose than to deepen Justine's relationship with her. However, shortly after she had received her habit and had been sent to serve the poor, she witnessed another apparition during prayer. She saw Mary holding in her hand a type of scapular, surrounded by flames. Similar to the one received by St. Simon, this piece of wool was green. On one side was a picture of Mary and on the other side was a heart aflame with rays more brilliant than the sun, and the heart was pierced with a sword. Further, the heart was surrounded by an oval inscription, which read, "Immaculate Heart of Mary, pray for us now and at the hour of our death." Sister Justine understood that this scapular and the prayers of those who would wear it would assist God in ministering to those who had no faith or who had strayed from their faith. Apparently, the green scapular would assist in the *conversion* of the unfaithful, whereas the brown scapular would serve to bring its wearer Mary's protection and her love.

Unlike later apparitions, those experienced by Catherine and Justine never became the "malleable product of an interaction between the seer and the public."[8] Instead, they produced only static devotional objects. Their visions marked the beginning of Mary's wider influence, however, as evidenced by the individuals to whom she appeared. Mary, it seemed, intended to reach beyond the visionaries to enter into the hearts and minds of people everywhere.

La Sallette and Lourdes: The Modern Era Begins

Six years later, in 1846, the modern era of apparitions began. A beautiful woman appeared in a cloud of white light to two children, aged fourteen and eleven, in a meadow near the alpine village of La Sallette, France. The two unlikely seers—Melanie Calvat and her fellow cowherd Maximim Giraud—described a single experience of encountering a woman who emerged out of a cloud of white light and sat on a rock to speak with them tearfully about God's displeasure with the region's inhabitants, and about coming crop failures.

Since the two children hardly knew each other and lived some distance apart, people found their identical story credible and soon concluded that the woman had been Mary. The church authorities, however, spent a great deal of time and effort evaluating the apparition, and they interrogated the children on numerous occasions before declaring it an authentic manifestation of Mary.

Sisters Catherine and Justine never faced the kind of scrutiny that Melanie and Maximim did. Unprotected by religious vows or convent walls, the two innocent children quickly found themselves caught between two worlds. They wished to remain loyal to the woman who was clothed in light and they wished to satisfy the church's and the public's need for information. But they could not do both.

The problems associated with a mediational role are by no means unique to apparition visionaries. They also plague any individual who claims publicly to have had direct contact with the divine. What does one share, and what does one keep back? How does one preserve the accuracy of the experience as opposed to what people want to believe, or what the church deems acceptable? In such cases, the visionary faces ongoing pressure from those who are deprived of ongoing contact with the divine and yet yearn to know everything the visionary has experienced. Not only does the visionary's experience position him or her between the public and God as a conduit of information and blessings; it also places the visionary alongside, and in competition with, existing religious authorities whose function is to mediate God's will to others.

Bernadette Soubirous's encounter in 1858 with the apparition of a beautiful young woman near the grotto of Massabeille at Lourdes remains the most famous of all Marian apparitions. Indeed, Lourdes became the standard against which all subsequent apparitions have been compared. As Blackbourne states, "At Lourdes, all the elements of the classic modern apparition fused: the simplicity of the humble visionary, the delivery of a message, the initial skepticism of the parish priest, the hostile reaction of the civil authorities, claims of miraculous cures, and finally the purposive creation of an official cult by the church."[9]

Bernadette's story is well-known to Catholics and non-Catholics alike. Bernadette went gathering firewood and bones on a cold, wet day with her sister and a friend. When the two other girls waded across a shallow stream, Bernadette stayed behind, apparently not wanting to get wet and cold, since she suffered from a chronic asthmatic condition. Then she felt a gust of wind, and something white in the shape of a very beautiful girl appeared. Appearing to be around sixteen or seventeen years of age, the girl wore a white dress with a blue cape, carried a rosary on her arm, and had a yellow rose on each foot.

After this first encounter, Bernadette witnessed Aqueró's presence in the grotto on seventeen subsequent occasions. The girl remained silent during the first few encounters, but later on in the series of apparitions, the girl taught Bernadette a prayer that she was to recite daily for the rest of her life. Following the pattern set at La Sallette, in which a woman gave children secrets for the first time, Aqueró revealed three secrets, then made Bernadette promise not to disclose the secrets to anyone. Unlike many of the visionaries who were to follow her, Bernadette carried Mary's secrets to her grave.

During all eighteen appearances of the girl, Bernadette never referred to her as Mary or the Blessed Virgin. She merely called her *aqueró*, a local word meaning "it" or "that one." At first, people were of the opinion that the girl was the ghost of a recently deceased local girl. It was only later that the public came to believe that the young woman was the Blessed Virgin.

At first, Bernadette was the only one who could see the girl when she appeared, thereby undermining her credibility with many of the onlookers and the local religious and civil authorities. However, two aspects of Bernadette's visions eventually ensured their acceptance by the church and the public.

First, after Bernadette had pressed the girl to identify herself to no avail, the girl finally revealed her identity in one of her last visitations. She assumed the well-known posture of Mary on the Miraculous Medal (the one given to Catherine Labouré) and said in the local dialect, "I am the Immaculate Conception." Only four years earlier, Pius IX had declared the dogma of the Immaculate Conception—a widely held Catholic belief that Mary had been conceived without the stain of original sin. For young Bernadette to hear these *of all possible words* profoundly enhanced the status of her visions. Indeed, the local head pastor, who had remained skeptical up to that point, quickly reversed his stand on the previously controversial visions and wrote to his superiors at once to urge a formal inquiry.

Second, the girl instructed Bernadette to ask the local priests to have a church built at the grotto, establishing what was to become a pattern of Mary advocating the construction of shrines and other tangible reminders of her presence. Coming from a mere fourteen-year-old girl, this message to build a new church greatly irritated the priests; however, the church authorities eventually complied with the request once the authenticity of the apparitions had been established.

During the eighth of the eighteen visions, the girl also told Bernadette to dig with her hands into the muddy ground of the grotto. Complying with this strange request, Bernadette shocked the people around her by dropping to her hands and knees and digging in the mud. Many people promptly left the scene in disgust, concluding that Bernadette was surely deranged. But to everyone's surprise, Bernadette uncovered an underground spring, from which now flows 27,000 gallons of water every day. Just as the church obtained what it needed theologically, the public got something, as well—a concrete focal point for the abundant miracles that subsequently flowed from Bernadette's visions. By satisfying the disparate needs of the church and the public, Bernadette's visions at Lourdes became the most famous and accepted example of Mary's manifestation to the world.

A Gift Too Precious for Words

In most of the major apparitions, Mary eventually spoke to the visionaries about coming calamitous events and ways to prepare spiritually for such upheavals. However, in one famous case—the apparition at Knock, Ireland, in 1879—Mary never spoke. She appeared only once, remained entirely silent, and yet renewed the waning hopes of the Irish people.

The Irish had suffered for more than thirty years from recurrent devastating potato blights, which had left the population of Ireland decimated. Out of desperation, tens of thousands had immigrated to America on crowded, unsanitary ships. Many died in transit. The soul of the nation had been shaken by this protracted tragedy.

In 1879, the final year of the potato blight, Mary appeared to a group of people in the village of Knock. On a windy, rainy August evening, the local archdeacon's housekeeper, Mary McLoughlin, set out to visit some friends. As she passed the outside of the beautiful church, she saw what she believed at first to be three statues. She thought that Archdeacon Cavanaugh had ordered them and then had left them outside until a suitable place could be found for them. With other things in mind, she went on past and visited for a while with her friends.

Later, when she headed home by the same route, Mary was startled by the sight of the luminous figures, even from a distance of several hundred yards. As she approached and examined the scene more closely, she could see that the figures were not statues at all, but ethereal images floating about two feet above the ground. The Virgin Mary, clothed in a white robe and wearing something resembling a crown, stood in the center of the scene with her arms stretched out in front of her and with her eyes turned heavenward as though in prayer. She was flanked by two men, who people later decided had been Joseph and the apostle John. To one side could be seen a simple altar, upon which a lamb stood facing Mary.

Mary McLoughlin ran off to call others to see what was happening. Before the figures disappeared about two hours later, fourteen people had visited the supernatural scene. A fifteenth witness viewed the scene from a half a mile away but could see only a large globe of golden light. Unlike other major apparitions before and since, neither Mary nor the other figures spoke a word, and no one reported receiving any interior messages, or locutions. Further, the figures were incorporeal: When one woman tried to kiss Mary's feet, her lips were greeted only by the wet brick wall of the church.

Ironically, when the housekeeper went about notifying people of the miracle, she urged Archdeacon Cavanaugh to go out and see the miracle. But he misunderstood her and thought that the apparition had already ended. Widely known for his charisma and his profound devotion to Mary, Cavanaugh may have been the human catalyst of the apparition. He said afterward, "I have regretted ever since that I omitted to do so. God may will that the testimony to His Blessed Mother's presence should come from the simply faithful and not through his priests."[10]

The Relationship Between Spiritual Intervention and Faith

The archdeacon's lament echoes the feelings of innumerable priests, nuns, and other religiously committed persons who have puzzled as to why Mary appears to ordinary folk and not as a rule to those who have devoted their lives to her and the church. If one studies the major apparitions, a case can be made that a single factor—which might simply be called "openness"—increases the likelihood that a person will see Mary. Given how the well-known Marian visionaries tend to be unsophisticated children, we might assume that our degree of openness diminishes with age—unless, perhaps, we strive to preserve or restore this faculty through intentional prayer and meditation. Paul's statement, "I die daily" (1 Corinthians 15:30), conveys a sense of the radical and complete surrender that we, too, might foster through the intense devotional practice that Mary herself repeatedly recommends in her messages.

In the absence of such efforts, most of us must await an unwanted crisis to break down our barriers and create—through the painful relinquishments of our attachments—an openness through which we might experience a direct encounter with the divine. However, the interpersonal and spiritual crises that typically create such an opening to spiritual intervention may be largely ameliorated by one's faith. Indeed, faith alone might eliminate a need for an abrupt and dramatic spiritual intervention.

If this is true—and it does make sense—a religiously committed individual may be spiritually open, but his faith may supplant the need for dramatic remedies. Surely, there are many complex and interrelating factors that determine who perceives the presence of Mary. In some cases, Mary has obviously appeared to persons—such as Italian stigmatist Padre Pio—who exhibit extraordinary piety and devotion. But a case can be made that Mary intervenes to awaken and deepen one's faith, not to reward the recipient. If a person possesses sufficient faith already, then an intervention may be wholly unnecessary. At least one of the accounts included in a later chapter supports this notion: When a recipient felt Mary's presence and asked why she was still unable to see Mary, she clearly heard in reply, "Because you already believe."

A friend of mine who has encountered Jesus on several occasions but who feels undeserving concurs with this idea. She believes that Jesus and Mary manifest to those who are struggling in their faith—in other words, to those who are remedial students on the spiritual path. Since many of us fit this category, then perhaps we, too, might reasonably expect to be visited by higher beings who minister to those who are, by comparison, rather lost. Those who already possess sufficient faith, however, may never experience such dramatic interventions. Like the prodigal son's brother, they may seem conspicuously unrewarded for having persevered in their faith; thus they must decide if they will join the Master in welcoming their brothers and sisters with open arms.

The Phenomenon of Mary's Secrets

Secrets have figured prominently in several of the most famous Marian apparitions of the last one hundred years, including La Sallette (1846), Lourdes (1858), Fatima (1917), Garabandal (1961–1963), and Medjugorje (1981 to the present). In the case of Medjugorje, Mary has revealed a series of ten secrets according to a different schedule for each of the six young visionaries. Interestingly, the visionaries who have received the full complement of ten secrets have ceased witnessing regular apparitions of Mary, as though Mary's influence or teaching has now been sufficiently "sealed" within the recipient in the form of the secrets.

Melanie and Maximim of La Sallette were the first visionaries to receive secrets from Mary. At first, people did not realize that the seers were keeping information back. But under subsequent questioning, the children admitted that the beautiful woman had also given each of them messages that they were told not to reveal. When she spoke privately to each child, the other child was unable to overhear the conversation. So neither child was able to confirm or deny what the woman shared with the other.

For months, everyone assumed that this information had been personal in nature. Without the children's input, however, some people seized upon the idea that Mary had given them prophetic information. As this belief took hold, the children still refused to comment. In the context of their silence and the public's unbridled speculation, their secrets eventually became the focus of intense controversy. Withholding this information put the young seers at odds with every priest and parishioner who wished to know more. In the face of all of this, the children valiantly protected the secrets through grueling interrogations.

It is significant to note that Melanie and Maximim initially failed to mention that they had been given privileged information. Only as people questioned them later did they admit that the woman had provided additional information—some of which was personal and some of which pertained to future events of general interest. Historians now find it difficult to assess how much importance the children originally attributed to these private messages. Further, there is some speculation that the secrets grew more elaborate as the public's interest in them increased. Researchers of Marian apparitions should examine this historic moment carefully, for it set in motion an expectation that Mary would thereafter confer secrets as part of any manifestation.

Even if Mary had not given Melanie and Maximim secrets per se to bear, they would have doubtless faced pressure to reveal more, anyway. For the very experience of seeing Mary or Jesus creates a problem, regardless of whether the vision bestows any secrets on the seer. Obviously, any encounter with an otherworldly reality leaves the witness in sole possession of something that cannot be verified by anyone else.

Whatever the person experiences, then, becomes secret or privileged information—if for no other reason than because we can know of it only through the visionary's willing disclosure. Our need to know what a person witnessed places any visionary, who may wish to maintain some degree of privacy, squarely between ourselves and what we seek to know. If the visionary hesitates at all, suspicions may naturally arise about the possibility of secrets. This is how the tradition of Mary's secrets developed to such a fever pitch: The public's needs and the church's authority collided with the visionaries' fierce loyalty to their private experiences. And a predictable escalation of tensions ensued in most cases. Zimdars-Swartz says:

When people become convinced that a seer harbors
secrets, speculation about their nature and content becomes inevitable, and the seer is pressed for anything
and everything that might be of public relevance. Indeed, the seer's ability to withstand such pressure has
often been understood as evidence of the authenticity
of an apparition.[11]

It is easy to understand why seers might wish to keep something back from the intrusive public. After all, a personal relationship calls for some degree of privacy. It is also easy to
understand why the public might suspect that there could be
more to the story. For Mary's messages have never ventured very
far from the familiar spiritual truths articulated by Jesus himself.
As Father Pelletier says about Mary's messages, "The spoken
message in its essential parts is never more than a reminder of the
Gospel, of things that we already know or should know."[12] Mary's
emphasis on traditional spiritual practices—on praying the rosary,
repenting, and fasting—leaves many of us hoping for something
new that will grant us a sense of control over our lives and knowledge of what is to come. And so *an understandable escalation of
mistrust naturally ensues between a seer—who alone experiences the
divine manifestation—and the public—who cannot believe that Mary's
reason for manifesting is only to reiterate familiar spiritual truths.*
Whatever Mary originally communicated to the children at La
Sallette, we can be assured that the apparition experience became a "malleable product" shaped by the intense pressures
placed on the seers by the public and the church. Not surprisingly, the La Sallette seers eventually succumbed to pressure,
recorded their secrets, and sent them in sealed envelopes to Pope
Pius IX. But by then, the secrets may have been altered by the

seers due to external pressures and the passage of time. Melanie in particular was accused of embellishing the authentic secret with popular ideas that occurred to her before she finally wrote down her full account. While she emphatically denied the charge, many people who believed in the authenticity of the La Sallette apparition were relieved when church authorities declared that the mission of the seers had ended.

Once a visionary announces publicly her encounter with the divine, she inevitably finds herself in the middle of various competing interests. Unable to satisfy one source of authority or need without betraying or disappointing another, the visionary's integrity—and even her judgment—can easily be undermined by the various triangles in which she finds herself.

Understandably, writers have been reluctant to address the possibility that the apparitions—and the subsequent recounting of them—have been molded by the seers' expectations and beliefs, as well as by the relentless pressures to accommodate the requests of those around them. Although the Marian apparition seems to represent an emerging spiritual archetype that is developing independently of the visionaries, it also seems that the visionaries have, to some extent, unwittingly molded the experiences to accommodate widespread expectations engendered by popular beliefs and earlier apparitions. We can never know, for instance, whether Bernadette of Lourdes knew of the concept of Immaculate Conception before the girl in her vision identified herself as such. Most believers assert that the apparition supplied the words, but others have pointed out that Bernadette could have heard of the concept beforehand, as well. Of course, the seer's contribution does not invalidate the apparition. For, if the apparition is a malleable, cocreated experience, then both subjective and objective forces interact from the first moment of the first encounter to produce any well-developed apparitional phe-nomenon. Assuming this is true, we can never separate out the respective contributions of the seer and the seen. What we do know is that the phenomenon seems to be evolving: Virtually every successive major apparition has lasted longer than its pre-decessors, has appeared to more witnesses, and has conveyed richer and more detailed information about how we can assist in the fulfillment of God's plan for these challenging times.

The Secret of the Secrets

As far as I know, no one has asked the obvious question: Why would Mary impart secrets that would put the young seers at odds with a clamoring public and a skeptical church hierarchy? Not surprisingly, instead of enjoying this privileged position, many of the seers have felt burdened by the responsibility of keeping Mary's secrets. After finally writing down the secret that Mary gave him years before, Maximim said wearily, "I am un-burdened, I no longer have a secret, I am as others. One no longer has any need to ask me anything, one can ask the Pope. . . ."

If we look beyond the content of the secrets, we can see that Mary has elected to depend on human beings much in the way that she might depend on a friend. After all, in human relationships, sharing secrets is something that we do only with intimate friends: We give them our secrets—and thus the power to betray us—in exchange for an intimacy that can only be purchased by making oneself vulner-able to the other person. The sharing of secrets also establishes a relationship that is *distinct* from any other relationship. So by imparting secret information, Mary effectively establishes a re-lationship with the visionary that is surprisingly personal and distinct from the relationship that she has with the world *through* the visionary.

The bestowing of secrets establishes Mary's vulnerability to the seer, who, in turn, depends on Mary for spiritual sustenance. As such, Mary enters into a personal relationship of mutual dependency.

Why would Mary do this? The key to this unusual gift, I believe, lies in Mary's own role in the incarnation of Christ. As a young woman, she was approached in the privacy of a vision and invited to take part in the conception and the birth of the new covenant. Upon consenting to her role, Mary faced the skepticism of those who doubted the possibility of the angel's visitation and a virginal conception. We know very little about what she faced; but it must have been a trying ordeal. The New Testament record does allude to Joseph's own struggle to accept the improbable story.[13] However, her private encounter with God's messenger must have made the inevitable suspicion more tolerable. Indeed, Mary's own "secret" conception marked the beginning of her own lifelong passion in bearing, loving, and losing a son who would remain beyond the world's capacity to understand him and love him as she would.

What Mary accomplishes by imparting secrets is, then, to invite individuals to do what she did: to bear inwardly the promise of God's unfolding plan and to accept the consequences thereof. This is never an easy thing to do, which is perhaps why Mary said to Bernadette of Lourdes, "I do not promise to make you happy in this life, but in the next." And she said to Conchita of Garabandal, "You will not be happy in this world, but in heaven."

The challenges that a seer faces in protecting a covenant with God from the world's destructive scrutiny parallels many of the stories in the New Testament: the Holy Family's flight into Egypt to escape Herod's soldiers, and Jesus' own puzzling refusal to provide simple answers to the Sanhedrin and to Pilate. Indeed, the tension between the seer and the world reenacts the drama of both Mary's and Jesus' own ordeals.

The gift of an apparition in general, and the bestowal of a secret in particular, sets up an initiation through which the visionary is called upon to place a spiritual calling above everything else, and to have faith in the face of the world's ignorance and mistreatment. History indicates that the best one can hope for, in most cases, is to be tolerated.

What is surprising is how well the visionaries have done in protecting Mary's secrets. Even Melanie and Maximim, who reportedly exhibited obvious weaknesses of character, demonstrated remarkable integrity and strength of mind whenever they were interviewed about their encounter with Mary.

> It should be noted here that while many of those who interviewed Melanie and Maximum were not impressed with their general demeanor, finding them lacking in manners and refinement, it was often reported that when they spoke about their experiences, they were transformed and seemed to speak with simplicity, seriousness, and a "certain religious respect." Certainly, the children were acquiring the aura of the age-old motif of the humble shepherds blessed with a holy visitation.[14]

The strength with which Melanie and Maximim, as well as more recent visionaries, weathered interrogation indicates that much more than confidential information is conveyed in the encounter with Mary. Apparently, one can say that *the encounter awakens, or instills, the necessary strength of faith with which to bear up under the scrutiny of others. To be set apart from the world by a relationship with the divine is not the same, therefore, as being deserted.*

And so, Mary's dependence on the visionary mirrors God's dependence on her in the conception and birth of Jesus. As Catherine Halkes says, "Mary freely and actively says yes as an autonomous person who in believing receptiveness is open to salvation from God and responds to that. If people want to talk about dependence, they should recognize that here God made himself dependent on a human being, and the human being was responsive to God."[15]

Mary was, as Halkes points out, the first of the believers of the new covenant and the first to enter so completely into a cocreative relationship with the divine. She willingly bore a promise that set her apart from those around her. Her plight is clearly reenacted by the meaningful ordeal of those who have witnessed her presence and who bear her secrets today. Given these parallels, we can see that *Mary manifests, at least in part, to implant or activate the potential of a divinely conceived new being. But this time, God conceives the new being in spirit—through the agency of Mary—as a promise that must be carried in one's heart. And the "birth" that we might expect from such a conception is the "incarnation" of Christ-like qualities in us and through our lives.*

The reader will observe in the ensuing chapters that many of the personal visions and dreams of Mary resemble the historic apparitions in many ways; however, these previously undisclosed accounts rarely include the bestowal of secrets. We might ask, Why the difference? One answer that comes to mind is that *there is no need for secrets when a relationship is already private; the whole relationship is sacred and inviolate.*

Mary's wish to secure a personal relationship with her witnesses is rendered unnecessary by the visionary's ability to remain discreet about the encounter.

The conception in spirit remains secreted from the onslaught of the world—and the birth of a new being is, presumably, a matter of time and of sustained commitment on the part of the visionary.

The Ascendancy of Mary

To Catholics, the apparitions fit into a worldview that allows for Mary's special role as our advocate to Christ, whose love for Mary predisposes him to consent to her wishes. She is the natural bridge between this world and the next, at once a human and a mother, as well as Christ's partner in the redemptive process. As Luther said, Mary "points ever to Jesus."

The non-Catholic world has been slow to recognize and appreciate the manifestations of this being who has been known as the Mediatrix of Grace, the Queen of Heaven, and even Co-Redeemer. After all, there is virtually no scriptural foundation to support Mary's presumed position in a divine hierarchy. We owe her ascendancy to several factors. First of all, the early church fathers were confronted with the problem of how Christ could incarnate through an ordinary woman. The more the church felt it necessary to underscore Jesus' divinity, the more his mother was logically elevated, as well.

But more than philosophical debate about Jesus was at work in the elevation of Mary: The perennial yearning for an immanent and caring God played an equally important part in sustaining devotion to Mary through the centuries. Unfortunately, perhaps, Jesus ceased to be seen this way as the church fathers increasingly asserted his divinity over his humanity. Gradually, Mary came to be seen as the mediator of grace—a role once assigned to Jesus alone. In turn, he took on the role of mediator of justice. Ironically, the Old Testament God of judgment reentered through the man who had proclaimed a new covenant of love; and this toughness had to be mitigated, in turn, by his mother's clemency. Not everyone consented to this framework, but they eventually lost out. Indeed, virtually every heresy that the church refuted in the first few centuries of Christianity was a movement against the arguably simplistic solution of equating Jesus with God. These heresies sought to preserve, if not emphasize, that Jesus was also a man like the rest of us. The more the orthodox gap between Jesus and the rest of us widened, the more people turned to Mary as the accessible bridge between God and man.

One might protest that fond hope does not a religion make—that Mary's ascendancy has no other basis than in mere human yearning. Recognizing this, Protestants have remained separated from Catholics by a doctrinal abyss that has been widening to a startling degree. With the pronouncement of the twin dogmas of the Immaculate Conception (1854) and the Assumption of Mary into heaven (1950), the differences between Catholics and Protestants with regard to Mary have become more pronounced than ever. In spite of these doctrinal differences, however, there is widespread recognition of the need to incorporate the divine feminine into the spiritual life. From the Catholic side, many Catholic theologians have become silent about Mary, believing that the church has gone too far in translating public veneration for her into church dogma.[16] At the same time, the public's devotion to her has ascended to even greater heights because of the evidence of the apparitions and other miraculous phenomena. As Marian devotion continues to break free of the church's dogmas, many Protestants are being drawn into this appreciation for the Holy Mother: They are discovering Mary for the first time.

Charles Dixon writes that it is time for Protestants to consider Mary's importance to them: "The development of a mature Mariology in Protestant thinking could do much to temper the harsh portrayal of a God of judgment and provide it with a healthy (and I might add a scriptural) concept of God."[17]

If the visions and apparitions of Mary had remained within the walls of the Catholic church, then the non-Catholic world might have continued to dismiss such things as uniquely Catholic events. But starting with the early French apparitions, Mary began appearing in the pastures, in the skies, and on the hillsides around the world—mostly to children, who, while being Catholic, possessed an innocence that transcended religious differences. Further, Mary's messages often contained information that deviated slightly from, or became critical of, that of the church hierarchy and church practices. Indeed, her criticism of the church accounts for why some of the apparitions, such as Garabandal, await acceptance by the Catholic church. On the other hand, non-Catholics can more easily feel at home with a being who while resembling in most ways the image of Mary held dear by Catholics also speaks her mind concerning changes that urgently need to be made.

While modern Marian visionaries remain Catholic as a rule, Mary's stated message at such famous sites as Medjugorje are, we are told, explicitly for the world as a whole. Given Mary's outspokenness in many of the apparitions, and her desire to reach people of all religions, it is not surprising that non-Catholics have begun to see and hear her, as well. One Protestant woman, Annie Kirkwood, through whom Mary has presumably disseminated messages to the world, initially protested when Mary came to her for the first time. "I'm not Catholic!" Annie said. She then heard Mary reply, "Nor I."[18]

The Value of Previously Undisclosed Encounters

As we shift our focus away from the content of messages to the *relationship* between Mary and those who have experienced her presence, we can learn a great deal from visions and dreams that have never been publicized, and in which no discernible message has been given. Indeed, we may even learn *more* about this kind of relationship from individual dreams and visions—regardless of the content of the communication—than we can from the more publicized apparitions, which quickly become vulnerable to, and potentially degraded by, intense scrutiny and controversy.

I have mentioned already that the exposure of an apparition to public need and church scrutiny typically places the Catholic visionaries under tremendous pressure to conform to various conflicting expectations: to reveal more to the public, to refrain from politically controversial pronouncements, and to respect the church's authority in such matters. In several cases, the seers have been threatened, punished, or made ill by the stress imposed by the conflicting reactions of their families, the community, the government, and the church.

In the case of the Fatima seers, "It is clear," says Zimdars-Swartz, "that they . . . suffered great physical and emotional strain . . . as great numbers of people began to intrude on their formerly very private world."[19] Two of the three seers—Jacinta and Francisco—contracted flu and died during an epidemic, probably because they had become so weakened by the lack of sleep and the incessant invasion of their privacy.

Not surprisingly, Conchita—the primary visionary at Garabandal—expressed a preference for a private, interior relationship with Jesus and Mary. She seemed relieved when the inner voice, or locution, replaced the apparitional phenomenon: "I prefer the locution to the apparitions, because in the locution I have her within me.... Oh, what happiness when I have the Blessed Virgin within me. What a shame to be so bad! But this is the way the world is.... I prefer to have Jesus in me.... Here is the prayer I say to Jesus: 'Oh, my Jesus! *Ay, Jesus mio!'* "[20] Conchita's childlike prayer conveys the visionary's weariness of having served as a conduit for the apparition's messages, and her relief in finally securing a personal, interior relationship with Jesus and Mary.

To circumvent the effects of publicity—both upon the visionary and the experience itself—I have elected to examine the visions and dreams of those who have previously kept their experiences private and who prefer to remain anonymous in sharing their visions. Although my emphasis on previously undisclosed visions of Mary may seem inferior to a consideration of the major apparitions, even the best-documented apparitions have their critics. Indeed, one can say that every major historic apparition has its advocates and detractors, its strengths and dubious aspects. As Blackbourn says, "Unless we are prepared to see divine intercession at work in separating a small number of cases from all the rest, there is not good reason to narrow our inquiry to the hallowed few."[21]

If one is prepared to accept Blackbourn's view, then it is only a small step further to include private, heretofore undisclosed visions of Mary alongside the well-known apparitions. By so doing, our base for making comparisons widens, and our ability to clarify the consistent truths associated with the Marian encounter arguably increases.

With this in mind, we will now examine a series of heretofore unrevealed and uninvestigated encounters with Mary. Except for slight editing for readability, they are presented as the recipients

first reported them to Mickey Lin and me. My analysis of the
encounters focuses on parallels with major historic apparitions,
explores the similarities between these experiences and encounters with Jesus, and looks at each account as information about
the nature of the mystical relationship that unfolds from these
encounters.

I believe that these encounters will convey to the reader how
profoundly available the divine feminine is to us today and will
reveal the kind of life-changing relationship that awaits anyone
who can suspend the skepticism that undermines the evidence of
things unseen.

3

AWAKENING TO MARY'S PRESENCE

O Ark of the New Covenant, clad on all
sides with purity in place of gold; the one
in whom is found the Golden vase with
its true manna, that is the flesh in which
lies the God-head.

From a sermon on Mary by
Athanasius of Alexandria
(295–373)

When I first began my research on Marian visions and dreams,
I felt obliged to explore the roots of devotion to Mary in the early
church. I read about the different beliefs and religious debates
about her nature and her role in the redemptive process, and I
immersed myself in the imagery that grew out of centuries of
veneration of her. As I journeyed through history, Mickey Lin
began having dreams that paralleled my study, even though I had
not discussed my research with her.

In one of her first dream visions, Mickey Lin came face-to-face
with Mary before the Ark of the Covenant.

In a dream, I saw a triangle with six flames along each
of two sides. As I counted the flames, I wondered why there
were only twelve. For some reason, I thought there should

be more. Then I noticed that a thirteenth flame was in the center of the triangle. Looking into the heart of the central flame, I felt myself drawn to a room that was empty except for an altar and a rectangular sandstone object that I knew to be the Ark of the Covenant. The ark stood just in front of the altar, between two windows through which an orangish light poured into the room. I realized that most bystanders would overlook the ark because of its humble appearance. However, its lid was removed and great energy and light shown from it. I was aware that the power within the ark was such that it could destroy anyone who was unprepared for it. I felt unworthy and unclean to be in its presence, so I chose to remain at the threshold of the room.

Then, from the right side of the sacred room, Mary approached and stood in front of me. She looked powerful and stern, and yet she was gentle at the same time. She told me that "he"—the one inside the ark—was the thirteenth and she was the keeper. She then moved to the side for me to approach the ark, but I refrained because I felt unworthy and afraid. Nonetheless, I was drawn—I did not walk; I was simply moved—into the room to stand in front of the ark. As I approached the ark, a gilded sarcophagus tilted upward out of the ark. It was made of pure gold and shaped in the figure of a man. An indigo blue and violet light radiated from it. I knew that I was in the presence of the Almighty—that I stood face-to-face with the essence of life itself. I was ashamed and fearful of mistakes I'd made along the way. Yet I did not feel judged, and this confused me. There is no way to express all I felt and observed in that moment. But then I let my conscious

> *mind interfere and I woke up analyzing how the golden*
> *sarcophagus could stand up on end without more space.*

I was astounded by Mickey's dream because I had just read how early Christians drew comparisons between Mary and the Ark of the Covenant—even to the point of referring to Mary *as the ark itself,* since she carried God's new covenant within her womb. Along these lines, the visionary nun Catherine Emmerich, who lived in Germany in the early 1800s, observed in one of her many visions that Mary's conception involved a transmission of a luminous, most secret presence from the Ark of the Covenant into the womb of Anna—Mary's mother—at the moment of Mary's conception. About this mysterious force, Emmerich said, "This holy thing, concealed in the Ark of the Covenant in the fear of God, was known only to the holiest of the high priests and to a few prophets. . . . It was the work of no man's hands, it was a mystery, a most holy secret of the divine blessing on the coming of the Blessed Virgin full of grace."[1]

As such, Emmerich envisioned the Ark of the Covenant becoming flesh for the first time in the conception of the mother of the Lord. While the ark had symbolized for previous generations the containment of the covenant, Mary came to represent its next stage—an unassuming human vessel who not only contained the new covenant but issued it forth in the form of a divine person.

Mickey knew nothing consciously about Mary's association with the ark. But recently, Mickey had become aware of her own capacity to manifest much more of her latent intuitive and healing abilities. Thus it makes sense that an image of great promise like the ark would appear at this time and that Mary—its human equivalent—would appear to intimate Mickey's own capacity to enter into a deeper relationship with her own spiritual calling.

Since that dream, Mickey has sought to overcome her fears and low opinion of herself and to accept the opportunity to embrace her spiritual calling more completely. Just as the angel appeared to Mary to announce her role in the new covenant with God, Mary announced to Mickey the emergence of her own latent abilities to serve the divine.

With the help of Mickey's experiences, and the many other encounters with Mary that grace these pages, I have come to realize that Mary resides within each of us as a pattern of complete responsiveness to spirit that can alone bring us into a cocreative relationship with the divine. Becoming consciously aware of this latent capacity is, no doubt, a necessary first step, but surrendering to it may involve a protracted struggle with fears, feelings of unworthiness, or conflicting religious beliefs. Thus, between the awakening and full acceptance, one may experience years of denial—and even forgetfulness.

The following stories all involve a childhood encounter with Mary that, for various reasons, the recipients set aside until later, when crisis or unrequited yearning caused them to reach into the past and find her—the ark of a new covenant within themselves, ready to be opened.

Last year, I had what may prove to be my final session with a woman, Rachel, who first came for counseling four years ago.[2] She came into therapy originally to deal with the effects of being raped ten years earlier, and because of the progressive erosion of her self-esteem from having been married to an alcoholic for twenty-seven years. Our work together proved to be intense and difficult, but she was eventually able to heal the pain of her rape and overcome the fear of asserting herself in relationships. She was almost ready to leave therapy about a year ago, but she elected to stay a while longer, attending a weekly therapeutic dream group and scheduling an occasional one-on-one session. As it turned out, recalling and relieving the earlier pain was not enough; Rachel also had to reclaim a vision of herself that had been lost to her. The event that signaled the end of our work was Rachel's recall of a memory that she'd long forgotten—a memory of seeing Mary when Rachel was only sixteen.

The catalyst for Rachel's recollection was a lecture that I had recently given on modern-day encounters with Christ and Mary. Rachel wanted to attend but had been out of town. So she obtained the tapes of the morning-long presentation and played them in her car's tape player. She admitted to me later that she had been somewhat critical of my interest in these traditional religious topics. And yet as Rachel drove down the road, listening to the lecture, she was moved in spite of herself by a forgotten memory that came back to her after forty years. She pulled over by the side of the road and wept.

Rachel explained to me that when she was a child, her parents urged her to stay out of the swamp next to their property. But she was drawn to go there and decided, in this case, to ignore their wishes. One tree in particular called to her, so she often sneaked away to climb it. There she found the sense of freedom that eluded her in a family where she was often misunderstood. So Rachel escaped to the swamp and to her special tree—not so much to run away from home as to find a home for herself.

One day, she went into the swamp and climbed her tree. Peering through the woods to the other side of the swamp, she could see the new Catholic school that was almost finished. And there she could see, out in the courtyard, a statue that had not been there before. Wanting to get a closer look, Rachel climbed down, crept through the woods, and walked out into the clearing where the new statue stood. It was made of cement, all grayish white, but it was adorned with wreaths of fresh roses. A ceremony must have just taken place, Rachel thought. The stone figure was of a girl about Rachel's age. Although Rachel had been raised a Southern Baptist, she knew that the girl was supposed to be Mary, and yet she was surprised by Mary's youthfulness. As she marveled at this, *Rachel was startled to see the face of the statue gradually transform into the living face of a young girl.* The girl had deep blue eyes, and she beamed down at Rachel a most loving smile. Stunned, Rachel thought to herself, You're like me!

And then the girl said, "Yes, Rachel, I'm just like you."

Rachel never told anyone about the experience, and she quickly managed to forget about it. Why would anyone forget such a momentous event? Through my experience, I have discovered in my work as a psychotherapist that this is commonplace. Indeed, I have found that we typically forget two types of extraordinary experiences: traumas that are too painful to bear and uplifting experiences that exceed the upper limits of what we consider possible for ourselves. It is easy to understand why people suppress the memory of emotional and physical trauma. But too often, it seems, we also suppress the good news about ourselves that we simply cannot accept as true.

As Rachel told me of her recollection, tears of relief and gratitude ran freely. She admitted that she had rejected the gift from Mary. She had rejected Jesus, too, because Jesus was whom her family worshiped, and she couldn't accept much of what they stood for. So as an adult, Rachel turned to the East and found her guru. But after remembering her encounter with Mary, Rachel said she realized that Jesus and Mary had always been there for her. "I am so happy," she said, "that I have found them again."

Carl Jung once said that the healing of the psyche inevitably involves a spiritual cure. Rachel's recollection of Mary's surprising assertion of their essential sameness was the spiritual intervention that Rachel needed to begin her life anew: It effectively restored her sense of unsullied goodness—something that had been lost for half a lifetime.

Since the modern Marian apparitions began 150 years ago, the principal witnesses of Mary's presence have been children. We know of their encounters because they went public with their experiences—either because they wanted to or because their friends and family refused to keep the experiences confidential. But in spite of the many stories that have been told, others have never been revealed. Indeed, at least some young visionaries have managed to keep their encounters from public scrutiny—either by remaining silent as Rachel did or by telling people who, in most cases, simply dismissed the stories as childish fabrications.

It might seem that the encounters that have been kept secret—and then often forgotten—amount to a wasted resource that could have served the needs of others, as well. If the purpose of every encounter with Mary—and other spiritual beings, for that matter—is to communicate to the masses through the visionary, then this assessment makes perfect sense. But if the purpose of the Marian encounter is, first and foremost, to establish a relationship with the divine or one's deepest spiritual nature, then the dissemination of messages can be seen as merely one way that this relationship might bear fruit in the visionary's life.

Even though the recipients of these quiet, isolated encounters with Mary often forget about them until much later, the experiences seem to represent a kind of early spiritual conception that germinates slowly in the dim recesses of unconscious memory. It makes sense that the vision breaks through early in life, because most of us are more open to such experiences then. The divine enters through the portals of childhood innocence, sinks into forgetfulness, and then resurfaces later in the midst of a crisis to redirect and deepen the course of the person's life.

So many mystics have reported that the awareness of the divine breaks through when we are least likely to expect it—when we are quietly musing, thinking of those we love, or expressing our joy over simple things. The German mystic Jakob Boehme (1575–1624) experienced his first spiritual illumination as he contemplated the beauty of sunlight reflecting off of a burnished pewter dish.[3] Similarly, the following account tells the story of a little girl who was surprised as she celebrated the beauty of springtime in her backyard, and her love for Mary.

> *It was in the early 1950s and I was between the ages of six and eight. Our family lived in a small central Texas farm town where the majority was Catholic, and I was enrolled in the local parochial elementary school.*
>
> *One day, my father gave me a wooden apple crate he had gotten from the local grocer. I was delighted with the crate and placed it on a small table in our backyard. There I decided to build a shrine, or grotto, to Mary. Each afternoon after school, I joyously played by creating my shrine. Laying the shrine, or crate, on its side, I placed inside an old plastic statue of Mary—about eight inches in height—that was white and had features painted in black. Each day, I searched for old containers that would*

serve as vases surrounding the statue, such as jar lids and cans. While today it seems all this could have been accomplished in mere minutes, I remember it taking me days. It was my mission to search each day to find just the right items, and I recall discarding things I deemed unsuitable. At last, all seemed ready one day. I gathered a few flowers from my mother's gardens and even some small wildflowers, added water to my vases, and placed this in the shrine around the statue. Then I began singing some songs to Mary and about Mary that I had learned in school. I recall even dancing to the songs—which I had not *learned in school. In the midst of a dance, I glanced at the shrine and became transfixed. I dropped into a sitting position while staring at the shrine.* The statue had taken on colors! *The face had real skin tones, as did the hands; her dress was white, but now a crystalline white, and the mantle on her head was blue—quite soft in color. She held a crystal rosary that reflected soft rainbowlike colors. She seemed real and very humanlike. She looked very calm, serene, and peaceful. And although she first looked down toward her bare feet, she lifted her eyes slowly without moving her head and smiled sweetly at me. There were no words, but I knew without being told that she liked the shrine.*

I don't know how long we gazed at each other, but I then received a strong compulsion to get pencil and paper. I dashed into the house and retrieved them, then returned to sit cross-legged in front of the shrine. I drew the lady as I saw her. She remained perfectly still as I did so. Know that then and now I could draw only stick figures—yet I drew then as easily as if I was an artist. I was using a

*pencil on a scrap piece of paper, but the picture was col-
ored—flesh tones, white, blue—in exactly the same hues
as she appeared. The drawing of her was about two and
a half to three inches. She, by the way, was appearing
about the same size as the shrine statue and had a cloud-
like gauze or a film around her. It never occurred to me
during this entire time that this was odd or strange. I felt
no fear, nor questioned any of it. After I finished the
drawing, we looked at each other for a while and then she
melted away. I was left staring at the plastic statue. I
looked at the drawing and I saw it in colors. Days passed,
and I continued to play at the shrine, although not each
day, as before. I never saw her again, but strangely I felt
no urge to want to—as if that once was sufficient. I had
hidden the picture and told no one about it or the visit.
This was not from fear, nor lack of sharing. I simply never
thought about telling anyone—as if it was a highly personal thing. Many months later, winter came, and in our
preparation for it, my family and I cleaned out the backyard. I put the weather-beaten crate in the trash/burn
pile, along with the dead flowers, jars, and lids. The statue
I stuck in a drawer where we kept broken religious items.
One winter day, I showed my parents the drawing, but I
did not mention the colors I still saw it in. I was quite put
out when they said, "Oh, you traced a picture of the
Immaculate Mary. Go color it." It was then that I saw it
in pencil and not in colors.*

*I kept the drawing tucked away for many years; yet
whenever I looked at it, it was a sketch done in pencil. As
I grew up, I even began to doubt that I had ever drawn it.
One day, I threw it out. My life has proceeded on a*

crooked route, and at one point I turned my back on my religion. Surprisingly, though, I always kept a rosary by my bedside even if I did not pray it. Four years ago, something happened in my life that turned me back to my God. Before seeking him, however, I turned to devotion to Mary—who I feel led me back to him. That is when I recalled vividly *my Lady's visit from youth. As I write it now, I can see mentally the entire scene as clearly as I view this pen and paper. It is a scene of utmost peace, serenity, and simple beauty.* (S.O.)[4]

S.O.'s experience never made the headlines. It never impressed her parish priest or her congregation, nor did it produce documented healings in those around her. And yet her encounter differs from Bernadette's initial vision at Lourdes in only two insignificant ways: It occurred only once and no one else found out about it. In other, more important ways, it bears a great deal of similarity: The woman in her vision never spoke and she remained unidentified, and yet a profound relationship was established in the course of the brief encounter. As we shall find, this silent, ambiguous introduction is by no means unusual. Something of great significance is conveyed without a single word. Like the historic Mary who left us her life—not the written word—as a testament for us to contemplate, these encounters offer a silent invitation to join her in a cocreative relationship with the divine. If, as the Eastern meditation text says, "all methods take their source in quietness,"[5] then Mary exemplifies in these subtle encounters what may be the pinnacle of spiritual practice—that is, the dynamic stillness of mind and openness of heart through which the divine can reveal itself in all of its splendor.

Those familiar with the series of apparitions at Lourdes will detect a similarity of *feeling* between Bernadette's first encounter and S.O.'s experience. Bernadette exhibits a shy but openhearted wonder as the apparition acknowledges her without a word. According to Bernadette's own story, she heard a loud rustling in the hedge above the grotto called Massabeille. She saw the hedge moving, then saw something white in the shape of a young girl. Bernadette stared at the girl for a moment and then knelt to pray the rosary. The girl showed Bernadette that she, too, had a rosary on her arm, then walked into the grotto, disappearing from view.

In this first meeting, the two parties are not, as yet, fully acquainted: The relationship points to the indeterminate future. Even so, it is hard to imagine the relationship proceeding without this quiet experience of shared mutual regard and common spiritual practice. Indeed, Bernadette's introduction to the girl may have seemed relatively rushed and impersonal without this period of quiet mutual contemplation.

In Saint-Exupéry's classic, *The Little Prince*, there comes a time when the shy fox consents to the Little Prince's request to be his friend. But before that can happen, the fox tells the Little Prince that he must first tame him:

> "What must I do to tame you?" asked the little prince.
>
> "You must be very patient," replied the fox. "First you will sit down at a little distance from me—like that—in the grass. I shall look at you out of the corner of my eye, and you will say nothing. Words are the source of misunderstandings. But you will sit a little closer to me, every day . . ."[6]

This passage captures a profound truth about how we ideally come to know others—through nonverbal, purposely indirect encounters. Most of us, if given the chance, rush headlong into personal disclosure and wholesale verbal exchanges. By so doing, we may miss what might transpire between two persons who willingly suspend their verbal exchanges for a quiet communion in spirit. There is an old Buddhist saying, Know ten things and say nine, which again alludes to the power of the unspoken. From our own tradition, the allure of Jane Austen's fiction can be attributed, in part, to our fascination for relationships that unfold through subtle, understated exchanges between individuals who come to love each other, often without intending to do so.

Whenever more than one person experiences the presence of Mary, the likelihood that the experience will become publicized greatly increases. When Lucia and her cousins, Francisco and Jacinta, witnessed their first apparition of an angel at Fatima, Lucia urged the other two not to tell anyone. Lucia had learned to be discreet the hard way: When she went for her first confession, she emerged from the confessional, to find several people laughing at her for what she had said. Fearing that people would again ridicule her, Lucia hoped that she and her cousins could keep their experience among them. But the other children talked anyway; and Lucia proved to be right about the ordeal that ensued.

In the following account about an apparition of Mary, we learn that two sisters encountered her together. Unlike the Fatima seers, these children agreed to keep their vision a secret.

When I was about ten and my sister eight, we had a vision of the Blessed Mother.

It was a beautiful summer day. The sky was blue—no clouds. It was very quiet—no other people, animals,

cars—nothing. *Then we looked in the sky and there she
was. She was in dark clothes. She had dark hair.*

*We knelt and prayed. We walked home, agreeing not
to talk about it or to tell anyone.*

*About five years ago, my sister and I were at a dinner.
My sister and I sat across from each other. She said, "Do
you remember, when we saw the Blessed Mother near
Nannie's house?"*

*I started nodding my head and I said, "Yes, I remem-
ber."*

*After that dinner, my sister and I were able to recall
and share with others that experience of long ago.* (J.A.)[7]

Like so many of the visions in these chapters, J.A.'s apparition
resembles an abbreviated form of one of the major historic apparitions. Among others, J.A.'s experience resembles the apparition at Pontmain, France, in 1871. It was there that Mary
appeared in the evening sky above a snow-covered landscape to
a farmer's son, Eugene Barbadette, aged twelve, who had gone
outside into the barnyard to see what the weather was like.
Eugene's brother, Joseph, who was ten, soon joined him, and he
was able to see the apparition, as well. Above them they saw a
smiling woman dressed in a deep blue star-spangled robe and
wearing a golden crown. Over the course of the next three hours,
many people gathered in the barnyard as the boys reported what
they saw and the changes that took place in the apparition. Three
other children from the town joined the gathering later and were
immediately able to see the woman, as well. However, none of
the adults—including two nuns and the local priest—could see
anything except what appeared to be three stars that remained
visible only for the duration of the apparition.

During the three-hour barnyard vigil, the children observed letters appearing on a broad streamer that lay at the woman's feet. The children slowly spelled out three messages: "But pray, my children"; "God will soon answer you"; and "My son allows himself to be moved." Toward the end of her manifestation, she held a red crucifix upon which Jesus was hung. Her grief was profoundly evident, but her original state of joy returned again just before she disappeared from the night sky.

At that time, the whole region was under the threat of take-over. Napoléon III had declared war on Prussia in July of 1870, and thirty-eight of Pontmain's five hundred inhabitants were immediately conscripted. Within weeks, the French had suffered terrible defeats; by January of 1871, the Germans had advanced to a point only miles away from Pontmain. A takeover of the area seemed imminent. The apparition appeared on the eve of a sudden reversal: The soldiers withdrew within days, and peace was declared.

Some people believe that Mary manifested to urge the people to intervene with their prayers in a situation that could still go either way. If so, the prayers of a few people figured heavily in the outcome of the war. Regardless of whether the group's prayers served to turn the tide, Mary's celestial appearance coincided with an unexpected turning point in what seemed to be a hopeless situation.

❧❦❧

The purpose of the Pontmain apparition seems clear on the surface: to awaken hope and faithfulness in a despairing people and to urge them to make a difference through their prayers. But the particular details of the Pontmain apparition remain universally relevant. Indeed, the lack of specificity in the Pontmain message actually increased the applicability of the vision in the context of later times and places. Even though a general message might frustrate our desire for more specific responses to our particular needs, it withstands the passage of time more easily than a message that concerns only immediate problems. The more *general* the message, the more it transcends the original context that gives rise to it.

And so we can see that Mary's characteristic terse or nonverbal intervention style in these initial encounters enhances the meaningfulness and widens the applicability of the experience. Like Jesus, who often frustrated his audience by his silence and brief, enigmatic responses, Mary says a lot by saying a little, thus ensuring the relevance of her manifestations for years to come.

We have seen how Mary manifests to individuals early in life as if to implant an idea that only later flowers into its full expression. Understandably, this initial manifestation can provoke a variety of responses. In the accounts we have examined thus far in this chapter, the children have welcomed Mary's presence. But if the purpose of Mary's manifestation is to prepare a person for a later spiritual awakening, the response of the recipient at the time of the original vision probably does not matter very much. Apparently, *whenever* the person acknowledges her, Mary comes forth at that time as a potent memory to affirm the presence of God in the person's life.

The following account supports the notion that a person's initial response does not prevent the vision from exerting a positive impact at a later point. Initially, the recipient may be frightened by the vision, but the person may reclaim the experience years later, when its value becomes more apparent.

I was five years old and lived in Grove City, Pennsylvania. My grandparents were going to take me to Florida for a vacation. We spent the night in Pittsburgh so they could visit some other relatives. The room I slept in was on the third floor, a converted attic at the front of the house. When I woke up in the morning, the room was filled with white light. I just lay there looking at it, when I heard a voice that said, "Turn around and look at the window." Although I had never heard such a voice before, it didn't scare me, but I also didn't turn around. The voice repeated the statement a second time and then a third time before I turned to look at the window. There, three floors up, on the front window, was the most beautiful woman I have ever seen. She was wearing blue and white—a long veil and gown. She never said anything, just smiled the most beautiful smile.

I had just been fitted for glasses and I can remember thinking she wasn't real, so first I rubbed my eyes, and she was still there. Then I picked up my glasses and put them on, and she was still there. Of course, I didn't need the glasses. She was just as perfect a vision without them as with them.

She was still there when I ran, hysterical and crying, for my grandparents to take me home. I wanted to go home. I never told anyone about the experience until I was an adult.

I never forgot the experience, but I did put it on the back burner through my youth. I was in my thirties when I really started questioning why it happened. Since then, I've turned into a serious seeker, always trying to do better and to be closer to God. I've still not figured the vision out

*yet. However, it's likely that the experience was supposed
to stick in my mind to nudge me on to the spiritual path.*

*One thing I've often thought about is that in all the
different pictures I've seen of the Blessed Virgin Mary,
none captured her beauty and none captured her light.*
(1st M.F.)[8]

In M.F.'s encounter with Mary, she witnessed her indescribable beauty. This corresponds with virtually every reported sighting of Mary to date. Invariably, the witnesses say that she is exceedingly beautiful, even beyond words. Two seers of well-documented apparitions—Vicka from Medjugorje and Gianna Talone from Scottsdale, Arizona—have thought to ask her why she was so beautiful. In both cases, they heard her say, "Because I love."[9]

❈

As we approach death, the barriers separating us from spiritual realities apparently dissolve. People who recover from life-threatening illnesses or injuries often attribute their healing to the luminous beings who appear to them as they hover between this life and, presumably, the next. But the healing may not originate from outside of ourselves; it may spring from the hope and faith released in encountering these loving presences who have been there all along. As these beings lovingly mirror to us our true natures, they may awaken in us our languishing capacity for healing and rejuvenation. Take, for instance, the following encounter with Mary.

*I was about eight years old and my mother had kept me
home from school because I wasn't feeling well. I had slept*

most of the morning and was running a fever, which was steadily rising. Just before noon, I remember getting up to use the bathroom, as I had diarrhea. I don't remember much until my mom came into the room to check on me. I recall her exclaiming, "What in the world!" and then she came and laid her cool hand on my forehead to assess my fever. Apparently, I had become so delirious with fever that I had used the bathtub instead of the toilet to do my business. Mom knew this was getting serious. She cleaned me up and put me back into bed. My temperature had gone up to 104 degrees.

We lived in a suburb on the outskirts of Minneapolis. The doctors were a forty-five-minute drive away and Dad was at work with the only vehicle our family owned.

Mom tried to soothe me and get me as comfortable as possible. She left my side to call Dad to come home to get me and take me to the doctors as quickly as possible. While she was gone telephoning Dad, I had the most beautiful experience.

Beside my bed, the Virgin Mary appeared. She just stood there about two feet off the floor and smiled at me—the most beautiful smile, which penetrated every cell in my body. Her skin was milky white, her eyebrows were very thin and arched, and she wore a light blue cloth draped over her head. The cloth either had a white lining on the inside or she had a second white cloth draped beneath the blue one atop her head. Her garment was a robelike style of light blue and white. Everything about her seemed to be emanating this peaceful, complete trust and love feeling. As she smiled at me, it was as though she spoke to me telepathically. I remember hearing her say,

"Everything is going to be all right." Then I closed my eyes and dozed off, feeling totally at peace.

As luck would have it, Dad was out to lunch when Mom called, so she left a message for him to call home as soon as he returned. I remember telling her, "It's okay, Mom, Dad doesn't have to come home. The Virgin Mary was here beside my bed and she smiled the most beautiful smile and told me everything would be all right. She was so beautiful, Mom!" I said.

Mom at first thought I was still delirious and went to get the thermometer to take my temperature again. I told her I was sure it would be back to normal . . . and sure enough, it was. Some people, I know, would argue that diarrhea will often help reduce a fever, and I agree that that may have helped. But I know what I saw and felt. It is still as vivid today as it was over forty years ago, and I am very thankful for having been given such a beautiful memory.

I am also thankful for a very loving mother who has always been very open-minded and has loved so uncondi-tionally. (L.D.)[10]

We can never know if Mary manifested to heal L.D. directly or just to mobilize L.D.'s own capacity to restore her health. If we see Mary, or any spiritual being, as an external agent of healing, then we see ourselves, in contrast, as passive recipients in the process. From this perspective, Mary becomes an allo-pathic healer—like a traditional physician—who restores us to health by introducing the necessary medicinal agent to destroy or offset the intrusive, debilitating illness. If, however, we see Mary as a spiritual catalyst who awakens our own dormant inner healing processes, then we in turn assume a more active role as we *respond* to the awakening power of her presence. Speaking metaphorically, Mary becomes, in this case, a homeopathic healer whose role is to elicit *from* us what we need to reestablish health. This distinction may seem trivial when all we care about is getting well, but actually, it defines two distinct worldviews that affect how we interpret God's role in our lives. From one point of view, we are errant children forever in need of rescue; from the other, we are divine beings who are merely asleep—unconsciously endowed with all of the spiritual attributes we associate with Jesus and Mary, and other spiritually advanced beings.

※

The greeting that Mary extends to a child can assume many forms, but in virtually every case she affirms her love for the person—then and always. In the account that follows, Mary gave a potent message that has reverberated throughout her life and ever since.

I've had many spiritual incidents in my life and the most special ones happened when I was attending St. Elizabeth's grade school in Wilmington, Delaware.

I had two concerning Mary, and I'd like to tell them to you. It was another heavy homework assignment, but this time I had to write two poems, on top of all my other homework. One poem was to be four or five stanzas long and the other three to four lines. Mine was a dysfunctional family, and I couldn't start my homework until my father went to sleep. I was still struggling with the poem while the clock ticked away. It was after ten P.M. and I was tired and in tears. I asked God to please help me. I told him I couldn't go to bed until I had my poems because I was afraid to face Sister Julia if I didn't have my homework assignment completed.

The next few minutes I started writing, and it sounded beautiful. I asked God for a title, and I wrote out "The Ivory Tower." Happy now that I was finished, I started to pack my books away, when I remembered I still needed the three- or four-line poem. Almost falling asleep, I prayed again, and this poem I remember.

> All the flowers are in bloom,
> If more come there's plenty of room,
> But the one that is the fairest of all
> Is the Blessed Mother.

As I put the poems in my binder, I remember thinking the writing was not like my writing: My writing was rounded and bigger, while these letters were smaller and looked different.

The next day we took turns, one at a time, putting our poems on Sister Julia's desk and returning to our seats. Sister Julia looked straight at me and ordered me to her desk immediately. I was puzzled by the redness of her face—something that happened when she was angry. She pushed the poem at me and said she didn't want me to copy the poems from a book. I quietly told her that I didn't copy them, that I wrote them myself. This caused her to lose control. She accused me of lying and said it was possible that the short poem was mine but that since I lied about the other one, I was probably lying about that one also. She was furious that I also would let someone else

write them for me. I told her that I had written them.
That was the last thing I said, because she ripped them in
pieces and threw them in the wastebasket, and I had my
knuckles rapped, after which she ordered me back to my
seat and she left the classroom, slamming the door after
her. I heard the whispers of the other children, but I could
only look down at my desk. I wanted so badly to retrieve
the pieces from the wastebasket, but I was afraid that she
would enter the room and reprimand me again. I have
thought over the years about being hypnotized to try to
remember that poem, but I have so many terrible memo-
ries in my childhood that I have always been hesitant to
pursue that.

The other incident with Mary happened in first or
second grade. My classmates were putting their names
into a box to see whose name would be picked to be Mary
in our May procession. Well, I asked God and the Blessed
Mother to please make sure that my name was not picked.
I was ashamed of my old clothes and my hair, which was
poker-straight. Then right before they picked a name, I
heard a woman's gentle voice say, "I choose you." This
was upsetting to me, and I hoped that I just thought I had
heard it. They picked a name and it was mine.

These were two very special events that took place in
my childhood, but it was many, many years before I re-
alized just how special they were. (J.C.)[11]

J.C.'s second experience with Mary resembles the experience
of a woman who saw Christ appear to her at a prayer meeting.[12]
Moved to tears by the honor of seeing him, she thought, Why
me? only to hear him say, "Why *not* you?" Obviously, his words

conveyed much more to her than a simple answer to her question: With his question, he challenged her to disqualify herself in the light of his vast and timeless acceptance of her. Similarly, Mary's simple statement about choosing J.C. obviously goes beyond the context of her involvement in the May procession: Mary chose J.C. in that moment—and for all time.

At the beginning of our lives—before we have embarked on any conscious search for meaning—Mary exists within us as an inherent, unconscious potential to become a handmaiden to the process of the divine working through our lives. Like the humble appearing Ark of the Covenant in Mickey Lin's dream, the Mary within us is easy to overlook. Her power derives from being in *relationship* with God and carrying the divine seed to fruition. Until we recognize the importance of fully entering a cocreative relationship as she did, our own responsiveness may shrink in comparison to the qualities more often valued by the world.

Mary's manifestation in a childhood vision or dream provides recipients with a foretaste of their own capacity to serve God as she did. As a living ark, Mary exemplifies the release of the virginal potential that so often remains dormant until we desparately need it. In the midst of adult crises, we might find her waiting for us in our dreams, if not also in the distant memories of childhood.

The Lessons of Mary's Silence

> Then many times she remained silent;
> we were silent and she was silent. . . . She
> said she was looking at her children.
>
> *Conchita of Garabandal*

We have observed that when Mary manifests to children for the first time, she often says very little, or remains silent altogether. Even so, her silence in the initial meeting does nothing to mute a profound sense of presence that the recipients feel then and later, even though years of forgetfulness may lie in between. In the accounts that follow, the reader will again observe that when Mary manifests to adult visionaries, she often says little to them, as well. We might ask, Why would Mary remain silent during an encounter that the recipient may never experience again? Surely, it makes sense that she would take advantage of the fleeting moment to leave the recipient with something specific that might positively influence life choices thereafter.

Although a verbal exchange between ourselves and Mary might seem more desirable and more evolved than a silent encounter, it is by no means clear that such an exchange is better. In other spiritual traditions, spiritual teachers often avoid speech altogether as they work with followers for whom language has become more of an impediment than an ally in their understanding of deeper spiritual truths. One modern teacher of note, the female Indian guru Amritanandamayi Ma, refuses to deal with Westerners in particular on a verbal level. "Ammachi's tactic of refusing to deal with Westerners on a verbal level is brilliant: It forces us to come to her as she comes to us, from the heart. It strips us bare of our manipulative strategies; we're inarticulate children again, at the feet of our mother."[1]

Like Ammachi's silence, Mary's silence may represent the most effective form of communicating to those of us who might concentrate on her specific words and miss the bigger picture. Perhaps the appearance of Mary accomplishes all that is needed to stimulate and deepen one's relationship with God. In support of this view, we would do well to consider once again the famous apparition in which not a single word was spoken—the apparition at Knock, Ireland, in 1879.

The reader may recall that throughout the apparition at Knock, Mary remained entirely silent and unmoving while fourteen people weathered the wind and rain to marvel at the luminous figures of Mary, John, and Joseph floating just above the ground. Yet the absence of a verbal message did not deter the populace from attributing the greatest significance to the event: Our Lady of Knock became immensely important to the Irish people, and she has been credited with numerous miraculous healings. The church also accepted the apparition as authentic. Despite her silence, Mary's presence worked its way into the imaginations of those who saw her or learned about her appearance afterward. Like a painting that permits the beholder to arrive at his own interpretation, the apparition at Knock left the Irish people free to discern Mary's message for themselves in the context of their own personal and collective concerns. No matter how far removed we are from that time and circumstance, her silence still frees us to do likewise, even though a century has passed since then.

The encounters in this chapter resemble the apparition at Knock in one significant way: Mary remains silent throughout. While many of us would gladly exchange the ambiguity of her silence for the guidance that her specific words might bring to us, her presence wordlessly communicates a profound meaning to the visionary—a meaning perhaps more subtle and complex than words could ever express. In the final analysis, it may be true that words are often a poor substitute for what silence alone can convey.

Indeed, we will observe in the following encounters that Mary's quiet presence accomplishes several things at once: It allows for a communication that is beyond the capacity of language to convey adequately; it models the state of quiet receptivity that we may need to emulate if we hope to become channels of the living spirit; it evokes an awareness of those things that may stand in the way of a continuing relationship with her; and, finally, it serves as an invitation to a relationship that may, as yet, require more preparation on our part.

Silence is the highest language of love. The deepest exchanges between people typically occur in silence. Experience informs us that words too easily trivialize the complexity and richness of love in its deepest forms. We often stop talking and become very still when we feel profound love for someone. Or we may talk about other things, choosing to preserve the sanctity of the relationship by avoiding mention of what matters to us the most.

For instance, my spiritual mentor, Hugh Lynn Cayce, and I

said very little to each other about the love and respect we shared. We played bridge and talked about other things instead. But every once in a while, one of us would say just enough to let the other one know that our friendship was based on the deepest soulful connection. Known to be deeply spiritual and psychic, he rarely alluded to what he knew about me. On one occasion, he merely said that he'd dreamed of us fighting in the Crusades. Concerned, I asked him, "Were we fighting against each other?" He laughed and said, "No, we were on the same side." He never said much more about such things.

When I elected to leave my position at the organization where he was president—the Association for Research and Enlightenment—and to pursue my career as a counselor, he asked me to go to lunch with him. I was afraid that he would pressure me not to leave my job and would express concern about my overall direction in life. The prospect of his judgment was always on my mind, even though he never made the slightest criticism of me. I sat nervously while he did most of the talking. Compared to me, he was completely at ease. Then I couldn't resist asking him if he had anything to say about my leaving. He looked at me with a puzzled expression, and then he realized the nature of my concern. He laughed heartily and said, "*You?* I am not worried about *you!*" Then we resumed our talk about less weighty matters.

Sometimes silence is about a love so deep and so accepting that it goes without saying.

To illustrate the power of silence to communicate an almost overwhelming love and sense of peace, let us consider the following waking vision of Mary.

*A*bout twelve years ago, I went to my first healing Mass led by Father Kellerher. I got there at seven P.M. The church was already crowded, and I took a seat over on the right-hand side. I knew that Father Kellerher would appear at eight P.M. Meanwhile, we were being led in the rosary and in charismatic singing.

As I prayed, suddenly I had a vision of Mary. She was standing about seven rows up on the right-hand side, just above the pew. The bottoms of her feet were about three inches from the top of the end of the pew. She was dark-skinned and had very thick eyelashes. Her dress was blue, and she wore a long outer jacket that had gold stars on it, all of which were shimmering. The jacket also had a gold border all around it. Her hands were joined as if in prayer and there were golden stars around her head and shoulder area. She kept her eyes almost entirely closed. The peace that she emanated was lovely. I don't know how long she stayed. As I breathed in her essence, I felt overwhelmed. Then I heard a rustle and Father Kellerher came out. He walked over to the very spot where she manifested, and she disappeared as Father Kellerher began talking. He would go sideways or a little forward, but he always returned to the spot where Mary stood, as though he was being drawn there. I could feel that she loved him. (T.P.)[2]

In her vision, T.P. witnessed an image of Mary similar to what the children saw in the sky above Pontmain, France, in 1871—a woman dressed in dark blue with gold stars adorning her garments and surrounding her head. T.P. has had two other waking encounters with Mary, and two with Jesus. In every instance, they remained totally silent as they manifested to her. And yet in every case, T.P. understood the reasons for their appearances without having to be told. Apparently, much can transpire between the seer and the seen in the virtually unlimited medium of silence.

A silent encounter with Mary may not involve ponderous issues at all. Indeed, she may appear simply to convey her love to one who may or may not need a special intervention in her life.

> *I* dreamed this about twenty-five years ago, when my children were small.
>
> I was in a theater on Forest Park Boulevard here in St. Louis where they showed wide-screen movies. I heard a hubbub at the rear of the theater. People were running into the street in great excitement. I left the theater to see what was going on. People were gazing up at the sky, but a tall building seemed to cut off my view, so I walked up the street, where I beheld a large vision of Mary in the night sky. It looked like a white chalk drawing on black paper, but the draperies were moving and blowing somewhat. I was thrilled to see this and continued walking toward it. Suddenly, the vision changed to full color in a bright blue daylight sky! The clothing was in pleasing but muted shades of red and green and blew softly in the breeze. There seemed to be grass and shrubs around her. The Blessed Mother smiled and waved. I had no doubt at all that she was Mary. And I have never had such a beautiful and memorable dream, before or since. (M.O.)[3]

Such dreams and visions suggest that Mary's blessing lives beyond the momentary encounter as a presence felt within that can perpetually activate and reaffirm one's faith. In such experiences, we come under her mantle, and thereafter we feel a deeper sense of her personal presence and regard for us. In the East, devotees of the great masters refer to this experience as *darshan*. Beyond words to express, it is the treasured experience of receiving the silent and undiminished blessing from the master. From the standpoint of the ego, one might experience this blessing as a *personal* gift. However, the master's presence awakens this experience in anyone who is open to it. Indeed, one modern spiritual teacher, Da Lovananda, says that the master is like a light in a room. Whoever enters the room might say, The light shines on *me*. But the light, says Lovananda, shines equally on each and every one who enters the room.

Experienced as energy, radiance, love, and knowledge, a single moment of *darshan* can become the sustaining force in the life of the serious spiritual seeker. In an instant, the disciple receives the master's essence, and through spiritual practice, he may retain it for all time.

Silence may be Mary's principal message. In addition to providing a powerful medium through which the deepest love and blessings can be bestowed, Mary's silence may also represent her central message to the recipient—that is, *to be still and become a vessel of the living spirit.* From this standpoint, her nonverbal presence intimates our own capacity to attain that state of expectant stillness in which the divine might find its greatest pleasure. As a model for us, her silence subtly challenges us to nurture a quiet yearning that remains entirely receptive to the spirit.

I have encountered this lesson in many of my most memorable dreams, including a recent dream about Mary herself.

I dreamed I was looking at a statue of Mary similar to the one Mickey Lin made that stands upon the altar in our family room.

I was studying the statue's face closely when, to my surprise, it began to come to life! Her head moved and she smiled at me a most joyous smile. I let out a cry of surprised delight, and the statue promptly resumed its lifeless appearance. But then, as I sat quietly again, her face moved and she smiled down at me, as if to say: If you will remain still, I will come to life in you.

This dream brought to mind other dreams from my past that, while differing somewhat in content, conveyed the same essential message about the importance of quietly allowing the spirit to have its way with us.

In one, I was outside in a nighttime setting. I looked up and saw an orb of brilliant white light approaching. Knowing that I was dreaming and that I was seeing the eternal light, I cried out in anticipation, only to see the light retreat, as if awaiting a quiet, more receptive response. I bowed my head and turned my eyes away from it. Then the light came down upon me, awakening a painfully intense sense of love and ecstasy.

In another, I dreamed I was lying awake in my bed and the light came again. As it coursed through my body, I gave myself to it as much as I could. The energy grew more intense and the light more brilliant. I realized in that moment that when the spirit comes to us, *we must remain entirely quiet and receptive* if it is ever to consummate its purpose within us and through us. It is what Mary did when she accepted her role in the advent of the new covenant; and perhaps it is what she invites all of us to do now.

In the following account, Mary appeared to the dreamer—literally out of the clear blue—in the midst of a power outage. M.J.'s encounter with Mary came to her only after everything familiar had failed her.

I dreamed that I was standing in the doorway at the office and someone came up behind me and said, "The computers have all quit working!" I looked at the computers, and just as I did, they quit working and the lights went out. I looked around and saw that the entire suite of offices was dark. It was so still and quiet—not a sound. A storm must be coming, I thought.

The office is at a corner and there is a window on each corner wall. From the doorway, I looked toward both windows but could not see anything. I walked over to the window on the right. I looked up at the sky (I was on the sixth floor of a seven-story building). The sky was a beautiful blue, with a couple of small fluffy clouds. Then I walked over to the window on my left. I looked up at the sky and saw again that it was a stunning blue. Just then, a big fluffy cloud moved into sight. It was hovering just above the seventh floor. I thought, That cloud is really low and beautiful. As I was looking at it intently, it opened up and Mary, the mother of Jesus, appeared as if in a picture. But then as I looked closer, I could see she was not a picture. I thought, Is that a statue of her? Just then, she moved and looked right down at me, right into my eyes. I was so startled to realize she was alive that I jumped about two feet back from the window. At the same time, she moved from the cloud into the office window. We were face-to-face and I was speechless. I was awestruck, as well, by the intense sensitivity and compassion in her eyes. Love emanated from her. I understood that she was projecting her love to me without having to say it.

I then began to move, as if gliding backward, away from her. I wanted to stay with her. I knew she wanted to

say something more to me. I started to cry and pleaded
with God not to make me wake up, but God told me I
had to wake up now but that there would be more later.
(M.J.)[4]

The collapse of the usual hubbub of activity left M.J. open to
encountering Mary in what was perhaps the only climate condu-
cive to her coming: complete silence. In this dream, we can see
how the divine enters our lives through the quiet openings created by the unexpected.

As M.J. stood face-to-face with Mary, she knew that Mary
loved her *without having to hear the words*. She felt this deeply,
and she lacked for nothing in that precious moment of profound mutual regard. She wanted one thing—for the experience never to end. But when it did end, she found that she
could bear the anguish of separation, for she knew that a relationship had been established and that they would be together
again. This promise of a future reunion is, perhaps, the only
thing we have to cushion the pain of separation from such a
presence. This yearning—activated or intensified by such encounters—keeps us in a state of anticipation, and it keeps us
forever wondering if what we do and what we think takes us
closer or farther away from the promised reunion. It gives our
life new meaning and intensity, even though we might never
be quite as contented as before.

Like M.J., most of us never find God through our own efforts.
We have to be caught unawares during emotional and spiritual
"power outages"—when unexpected changes or setbacks leave
us quietly open to surprises. This is one of the paradoxes of the
spiritual path: The search itself gets in the way of the openness
we need to allow the spirit to enter our lives. Consequently, we

may ultimately have to abandon the search and be taken by surprise.

To illustrate this point, my friend Walter Starcke, who is a modern Christian mystic and author,[5] is fond of telling about his first breakthrough experience in meditation. He was concentrating intensely and doing all the right things but was getting nowhere. He felt that it was hopeless, so he finally gave up trying. As soon as he did, the eternal light burst upon him for the first time, and he was overwhelmed by its sheer power and love. Consequently, he thought that he had found the secret! It was in letting go, he realized. So the next day, he proceeded to repeat the process, but to no avail. Finally, he decided that it just wasn't going to work. And then the light came again! He realized later that there is simply no way to orchestrate letting go and that the moment of illumination always comes as a surprise—and often on the heels of a genuine sense of failure.

The following meditation encounter with Mary closely resembles M.J.'s dream.

Mary came to me while I was meditating. Her face appeared right in front of me and she looked at me without speaking. I felt that there was no separation between us, and I felt a great sense of quietness and humility, knowing that my true nature was as her own—that is, spiritual.

I remember especially the colors. Her eyes were clear blue, like the drape around her head and body—a beautiful sky blue. Her hair was yellow, like the glow I saw around her head. She held out a pink rose to me, which I understood to be her gift of love. I could smell its sweet fragrance.

But then I began to doubt what I was seeing, and I

thought that perhaps I was making it all up. At that point, she began to fade from view.

When I let my judgmental mind go quiet again, she returned in full, brilliant color—blue, yellow, and pink. (M.W.)[6]

In her vision, M.W. experienced Mary approaching her and bringing an intense, almost overwhelming sense of love and presence. But, like my friend Walter, M.W. discovered that Mary's coming depended on her remaining open and suspending intrusive analysis and judgment. M.W.'s encounter also resembles my own experience in which the statue of Mary came to life only so long as I could suspend my excitability (see page 103). M.W. faced a similar challenge—that is, to hold in abeyance the intrusive doubt and analysis that so easily shatter our moments of deepest intimacy. To this end, Jesus said that we must become as little children to enter the kingdom of heaven. "Verily, verily, I say unto you, Except ye be converted, and become as little children, ye shall not enter into the kingdom of heaven" (Matthew 18:3).

Indeed, in considering M.W.'s experience, one can observe that the whole experience hinges on a singularly open state of mind, which for most of us remains elusive—if not entirely buried in our memories of a more innocent time.

Silence is a powerful intervention. When a person who is important to us remains silent without explanation, all kinds of feelings may stir to life—such as curiosity, self-doubt, and intensified yearning. We may spend a lot of time trying to interpret the silence, and we will inevitably learn more about ourselves than about the other person in the process.

It is easy for us to overlook the evocative power of intentional silence in relationships. Talk is everything in our culture, and silence typically connotes indecision, passivity, or downright dislike. As a psychotherapist, however, I know that one of the most generous things I can do is to remain silent and noncommittal at important junctures in my work with my clients. Silence may not be what they want from me, but it causes them to consider *how they are seen* from a more objective viewpoint and *what they might do for themselves* in the absence of external feedback and assistance. Of course, they may imagine many true and untrue things about me—that I judge them, that I care for them, or that I am bored. But whatever a person experiences in this ambiguous context will usually reveal the work that they still need to do. Indeed, silence from those who matter to us stirs feelings and memories that otherwise remain untouched by the small talk of day-to-day human contact. In the midst of the experience of intentional silence, one learns whether fear or trust, passivity or initiative will fill in the spaces created by the people one cares for the most. Without saying a word, the presence of a silent witness can awaken us to the presence of unfinished business or neglected duties that may have prevented further spiritual development. And out of all of this can come a life-reorganizing question, What do *I* need to do *now*?

From this standpoint, Mary's silence can be seen as a form of intervention. By silently revealing herself to us, she creates an opening into which we can pour our thoughts and feelings about what lies, as yet, between ourselves and a more complete relationship with the spirit.

Silence prepares us for a deeper relationship. Building on the above idea, Mary's silence may indicate that the recipient is in the early stages of a relationship that can eventually sustain a fuller exchange with her when and if additional growth takes place. Mary's silence may, therefore, testify to the recipient's unreadiness, while mobilizing the recipient to do whatever is necessary to enjoy a more complete exchange.

Some of the most famous Marian apparitions evidence this process of silent preparation for a more direct and dynamic exchange. Bernadette encountered Mary several times at Lourdes before Mary spoke to her; thereafter, a period of instruction ensued, whereby Bernadette received personal guidance as well as information that was intended for others. The seers at Garabandal, Spain, witnessed the coming of a silent angel on several occasions before Mary appeared for the first time. Similarly, the seers at Fatima, Portugal, experienced the presence of an angel on three occasions before Mary herself appeared to them. The angel, who identified himself as the angel of Portugal, guided them to pray unceasingly and gave them Communion on the occasion of his final visit. In each case, these initial visitations served as a clear preparation for a more complete relationship with Mary. The implied message throughout was: You must be prepared for a relationship with me.

Thus we can see that initial encounters with angels—or silent visitations from Mary herself—prepare the visionaries for a relationship that may eventually develop into an ongoing exchange between Mary and the seers.

I have stated previously that I believe Mary manifests in our lives to activate a potential within us that is similar to the greatness that was hers as the mother of the Lord and that her silence in these encounters conveys the spirit of openness and surrender required for such an undertaking. She comes to awaken in us our capacity to *contain* the spirit, to *carry its promise* to term, and eventually to *give it a life of its own* through service and love. Other than her presence itself, there are many symbols of this latent capacity within us, including the Ark of the Covenant and the Holy Grail. In the following dream, a man witnessed this capacity as a dazzling container that held the Host.

> *I had a very powerful dream last year here in Nova Scotia. I was staying in Halifax at the time and wondering whether I should schedule some presentations on Edgar Cayce's prophecies, a subject that had long fascinated me.*
>
> *In the dream, I was looking up at a beautiful pastel cloud-covered sky. Then suddenly, as if with a wand, the clouds parted and the image of Mary holding the infant Jesus appeared. Then the clouds closed and opened again and the Host appeared in a dazzling golden container shaped like the sun. The clouds closed and opened again and a large angel appeared. He held a sword in his hand and said he was the "guardian of the schools." I looked around—it was a city scene—and I saw people running away, as if frightened. I called out to them to look up at the sky. I was very excited and elated.* (2nd M.F.)[7]

In each of the three scenes of M.F.'s vision, he saw an example of the capacity *to carry and protect that which is most precious*. Mary carried the infant Jesus, the dazzling sun-shaped container carried the Host, and the angel carried the sword of protection. Each of these riveting images involved submitting to the service of God in order to ensure the survival of the highest good. Beyond the imagery, one can hear the question, Will you? Apparently, the great opportunity for M.F. at this time had to do with giving himself fully to mothering and protecting the incarnating spirit. One gets the sense from the uncompromising imagery that there is no provision for halfway measures. Given the commitment required, it is no wonder M.F. saw people running from such a sight. Whether the people represented the attitudes of the world or his own lingering reservations, or both, M.F. faced the loneliness that such a commitment brings. The presence of the sword-bearing guardian angel informs us that the path of development intimated in this dream is not for everyone.

The following account was submitted by a woman who had also had a childhood encounter with Jesus.[8] Obviously blessed with a lifelong openness to mystical realities, she experienced her initial encounter with Jesus when she was only fourteen. She was walking through the woods on the way to her bus stop. While singing the hymn "In the Garden," she turned and saw Jesus walking beside her. Today, she is a writer who is disabled and in chronic pain. Her monthly newsletter on spiritual subjects conveys an optimism and generosity that one would expect to see as an outgrowth of a closer walk with the spirit. Recently, she wrote to me about a vision that she had in which she saw Jesus and Mary together, wordlessly expressing an immense sorrow.

I have grabbed the first pen I can find so that I can record what I have just seen. At approximately 9:40 A.M., I was thinking of my long-ago vision and dream of Jesus and of the unconditional love I felt coming from Christ. This has been a dark, dismal morning, but a few cumulus clouds have drifted in. I looked out the eastern window and, to

my amazement, saw a likeness of Mary and Jesus im-
printed in the clouds. Both looked infinitely sad as they
gazed down at the earth, and though no words were spo-
ken, I somehow knew they were thinking, Did God's only
son die for this? Then a bright rosy glow suffused a frosted
window, also on the east end of our mobile home. It was
the most beautiful light I've ever seen. I watched until it
disappeared. It came from no visible source. When I looked
back toward the clouds, the images of Mary and Jesus
were gone. These images were like photographs projected
against the clouds. This may have been a "waking
dream," but the terrible sorrow of the Blessed Mother and
Jesus was unquestionably real. I felt that same sorrow
until I looked at the other window and saw the rosy glow,
which I interpreted as infinite love and hope.

Regardless of the source, I may forget the exact details
of the visualization in days or years to come, but I'll
never forget the sorrow, which was all-pervasive, nor the
beautiful rosy glow. (M.H.#1)[9]

From M.H.'s experience, we can see how a silent vision may
come not so much to convey information as to provoke a response
that may carry over into a person's everyday life. When we treat
such experiences as oracles, then we may be easily disappointed
by the absence of information or guidance. But when we consider
these visions as *interventions to awaken a new or deeper response to
life*, we analyze the experience from a different viewpoint altogether. We begin to see that its value lies in the recipient's
response entirely. Instead of asking, What did Mary tell the person? we ask, Does the recipient's *response* allow for the spirit to be
expressed more fully in the person's life?

What response does such a silent vision come to awaken in M.H. or, for that matter, in any one of us who imagines witnessing such sorrow? Virtually any witness of such a scene would ask, Do *I* cause them sorrow, or do I bring them joy? Such an ambiguous vision would naturally prompt us to consider how *we* can give God less cause for sorrow and more cause for delight. By reviewing what *we* can do to make a difference, we also come into a closer relationship with the two persons in our Christian tradition who best exemplify a path of selfless giving for the benefit of the greatest good.

Another woman witnessed a silent Mary with Christ in a waking vision.

Very recently, this year, I was in prayer and an incredibly intense beam of light came to me. My eyes were shut. I know that light. *For me, it is Christ. It is very laser-like and cuts clearly and sharply, and it has a message for me when it comes. Usually, I focus on the light and attune myself to its message, which I did on that particular night. But this time, my eyes shifted, and behind the light I saw Mary in her own light. Her light was very soft, almost orange in color. She was on the plump side, and very, very motherly. I felt so much love—so much unconditional "I love you just as you are" kind of love. She had her arms wrapped around her plump body, as if her body were the entire cosmos.* I knew her love was for absolutely all of creation. *I knew that I was surrounded by those loving arms and was completely in her care and protection.*

Looking back, I think the intense male light of Christ was being balanced by the round, full, gently feminine love of Mary. It was as if I were seeing two levels of conscious-

ness manifested side by side. They were different, but each
a part of the greater whole. (A.T.#1)[10]

As she gazed upon a silent Mary, A.T. understood something
that eludes the descriptive power of language. She apprehended
a *way of being* that assured her of Mary's love for her and all of
creation and provided subtle encouragement to embrace life in
the same fashion. So much was communicated in that moment,
and nothing of importance was left open to question. A.T. knows
that Mary loves her and loves all of creation. She knows that this
warm, loving presence stands behind and quietly supports the
discriminating and expressive power of the Christ spirit. And she
knows, as well, that what Mary did, she can also do.

From the preceding consideration of Mary's manifestations, we
can see that her silence does not limit the importance or the
meaning of an encounter with her. To the contrary, it accomplishes several important things at once. It allows us to receive
her love in an undiminished and unburdened form. It intimates
our own "virginal" capacity for receiving the spirit in a state of
expectant stillness. It catalyzes an unassisted review of our personal lives and of our readiness for a relationship with her. And it
invites us to do the things necessary for a more complete relationship with her and the Christ spirit.

Silence may also be Mary's distinctive way of bringing our
relationship with her—as an externalized, tangible presence—to
a close. At Lourdes, for instance, Bernadette encountered a silent
Mary at the beginning *and* at the end of her appearances. Joseph
Pelletier suggests that Mary's silence in these initial and final
encounters at Lourdes was a particularly meaningful aspect of

these apparitions. He believes that her silence underscored the importance of two aspects of Catholic religious observance—the rosary and the scapular. About Bernadette's final vision, he says:

> It was a silent but obvious preaching of the scapular, just as her teaching of the rosary had been silent but eloquent. . . . This silent message was like a last testament, something she kept until the very end because she wanted to impress us with its importance. . . . Her last visit . . . was an invitation to wear the scapular as a symbol of placing ourselves under her protection.[11]

By remaining silent, Mary directed Bernadette's attention to how she could continuously experience Mary's presence even after Mary had gone—in particular, through the use of the rosary and the wearing of the scapular. Beyond the uniquely Catholic connotation of these two symbols, the rosary signifies for all of us the *practice* of Mary's principal teaching—that is, to pray unceasingly. And the scapular, which represents a piece of Mary's mantle that she first gave to St. Simon Stock in 1261, bestows upon its wearer the continual *presence* of her motherly protection.

Both of these religious symbols—when embraced as ongoing practices and attitudes—give us the means *to do the work* and *to evoke the presence* of the divine through our own self-directed efforts. They thus serve as sufficient substitutes for the externalized presence of the divine—freeing us from the dependency upon such phenomena. Perhaps this is as it should be, for eventually we are bound to discover that any external demonstration or message—no matter how dramatic and evidential—leaves us wanting more. In our search for something ultimately fulfilling, we may even come to doubt the authenticity of what once inspired and moved us. In the end, we will probably discover that anything that is only "out there" cannot feed the soul for long.

If Mary spoke eloquently to our every need, then we might never engage in the spiritual practice that we need to do, nor awaken to the subtle motherly presence that can embrace us from within. In time, like the visionaries who have seen Mary appear for a season and then leave them, we discover that the true measure of her presence becomes not so much what we can see or hear but how fully her spirit lives within us. As our spiritual practice matures and our internalization of Mary's essence progresses, she apparently recedes from view, quietly beckoning us to find her within ourselves through spiritual practice and a constant invocation of her motherly embrace.

5

MARY'S TANGIBLE GIFTS

*This is my precious gift that I leave
to you.*

*Mary's words to St. Dominic
upon giving him the rosary*

Some time ago, after I had just begun researching Marian encounters, I was taking a break from my studies and sitting on the sofa. I closed my eyes for a moment to think, and suddenly I lost track of where I was. For a few moments, I found myself in a place I'd never been before—a Catholic church where apparitions of Mary were known to manifest. It seemed to be the St. Maria Goretti Church in Scottsdale, Arizona, where Mary began appearing to a group of young people in 1987. A priest spoke to me about the places in the church where Mary often appeared.

Then he said, "To worship Mary is to worship the unmanifest."

As I emerged from the brief experience, I found the priest's words puzzling, for they seemed to contradict the traditional view of Mary as the bringer of healing and other tangible gifts. But then as I pondered his words more deeply, I realized that Mary represents our capacity to carry and issue forth the very best of what we yearn for, but which remains, as yet, unborn—that is, the Christ within. However, Mary also meets us where we are, intervening in ways that from one standpoint might seem, at times, trivial. One might ask, Why would she stoop so low to help us?

I am reminded of the story of a Tibetan king who asked a yogi to teach him how to meditate.[1] Knowing that the king loved his collection of precious jewels above all else, he told the king to meditate on his jewels. Rather than resisting the king's desires, the yogi knew that the beauty of gems could serve as the best means to focus the king's attention and to inspire a deep yearning for enlightenment. As the king followed the yogi's surprising advice, he attained enlightenment, and he went on to become a famous teacher in his own right. In so many of the great stories of enlightenment, we learn that the path to wholeness is through, not around, those things we yearn for the most.

We know that from the beginning of Christianity, people have petitioned Mary for assistance in resolving every human problem great and small. And, as countless testimonials indicate, such petitions often produce tangible results. For instance, a woman who attends our rosary group experienced what was clearly a miraculous healing as a child, apparently through Mary's intervention.

Kathy was born with a congenital condition that rendered her arm totally useless. Apparently, the nerves that normally control the arm muscles were simply nonexistent. The doctors at Johns Hopkins even recommended amputation, since the limb would remain forever unusable. Indeed, Kathy's brother was born with the same condition, and to this day, he cannot use his arm at all.

Despite the doctors' assessment, Kathy's grandfather turned to Mary for help. As the little girl slept in the bassinet, he placed a small statue of Mary at one end of her little bed. He was not much of a believer, but he loved his granddaughter. If he had been the Tibetan king, then Kathy would have been his jewel; and he was willing to do anything to preserve the beauty he saw in her. The next morning, Kathy woke up and began moving her previously limp arm! When the doctors examined her later, they found the limb normal, which they declared to be impossible. To this day, she is normal in every way.

The mind may resist the obvious, but innumerable testimonies tell us that calling upon Mary makes one's prayers especially efficacious, and their results particularly concrete. For instance, Nancy Fowler—a visionary who has witnessed a series of monthly apparitions at her farm in Conyers, Georgia—relates the story of how Mary assisted her in finding just the right car for herself.[2] It might seem odd that the Holy Mother would get involved in that level of mundane detail, but it appears that the more we open ourselves to Mary, the more she participates in every dimension of our lives, helping to bring into our experience whatever good that has been previously lacking or unmanifest.

In my own practice as a psychotherapist, I only recently asked Mary for assistance in my work. The first time I asked for this form of intervention was less than a year ago.

I had been working with Barbara for eleven years, and still she needed medication and psychotherapy. Tragically, she had remained totally resistant to medical treatments for her lifelong clinical depression. She had been treated unsuccessfully by a foremost expert on depression in this country, Nathan Klein, before his death. She had taken every kind of antidepressant available but had not obtained any lasting relief. She had then undergone electroconvulsive therapy; then she tried to kill herself. Finally, she came to me when I was fresh out of graduate school. Daunted by the challenge that she represented, I tried many therapeutic roles and interventions before finally just settling into a caring, supportive role with her. That is when things started to get better, for no one, she said, had done the incredibly simple thing of just listening to her. Thereafter, we worked well together; she made modest progress as we explored the story of a tragic past that included rape, betrayal, and parental desertion. She was always willing to share her dreams, no matter how hopeless she felt. Her dreams clearly suggested that she would someday recover, but I did not know how or when it would happen.

I often prayed for Barbara, for there were many occasions when I felt deeply concerned about her state of mind, fearing that she would finally decide to kill herself. Then one day last year while Barbara was in my office, I silently asked Mary to intervene. It felt especially appropriate, for Barbara had lacked nurturance all her life. I never told Barbara, who was a Baptist by upbringing, that I had asked Mary to intercede on her behalf. Anyway, within a couple of weeks, Barbara returned to my office. She looked and sounded better than ever before. Neither of us could account for the improvement. She chose to terminate her therapy at that point. That was eight months ago, and Barbara has since experienced her longest period of sustained relief from depression since childhood.

The most famous instances of Mary's manifestations suggest that her love becomes especially concrete as we petition her for help. Legend has it that Mary handed St. Dominic the first rosary during a time in the early 1200s when he was working diligently to convert the Albigenses in southern France. Mary gave him something to hold on to—not merely some idea or a message—that would organize and anchor his spiritual practice, as well as provide a practical method of praying that he could teach to others. In other encounters, she introduced scapulars and religious medals—objects whose concreteness gave their wearers a sense of reassuring closeness to her and Christ. It is easy to dismiss such artifacts as unnecessarily primitive, but Mary has become known for bringing about measurable changes that give our faith a foundation we can see and touch.

Even today, Mary's impact is often felt in very tangible ways. Well-known Marian phenomena include spontaneous physical and emotional healings, the fragrance of roses, a silvery sun spinning in the sky, colored lights around religious shrines, rosaries that turn to gold, and weeping statues. Further, these signs of her presence frequently manifest without an attendant visual apparition: People *feel* Mary behind the phenomena, even though they may never see her.

The weeping statues in the St. Elizabeth Ann Seton Church in Lake Ridge, Virginia, are a good case in point. For several years in the late 1980s and early 1990s, a single wooden statue of Mary wept intermittently. Later, many other statues of Mary were also seen to emit tears whenever associate pastor Father James Bruse blessed them or was merely in their vicinity. During this time, Father Bruse also developed painful wounds on his wrists and feet that were reminiscent of Jesus' own wounds. Father Bruse became the second priest in Catholic history, after Padre Pio,[3] to bear the wounds of Christ.

The incidents involving Father Bruse left Catholic authorities in an awkward position. To be safe, they decided to restrain him from talking with reporters. When Mickey and I visited Father Bruse privately to have our own statue blessed, we could sense that the imposed silence may have frustrated him, for so many people had been converted on the basis of learning about the miracles. Nonetheless, he was humble and discreet about the whole matter.

The Lake Ridge phenomena manifested in the absence of an

apparition or any other unambiguous signature of their source. As far as I know, Mary never appeared to a visionary at Lake Ridge. And yet the miraculous phenomena and numerous conversions left most of the parishioners convinced that the Holy Mother had overseen the process every step of the way. When one woman jokingly suggested that "the tears were prompted by the presence of sinners," Father Bruse responded, "That may be." Even so, the same woman said her experience of seeing the weeping statue gave her a renewed faith in God and confidence in herself. "I sing like I never could sing before," she said.[4]

In the following accounts, the recipients tell about experiencing many of the ways that Mary has been known to manifest her love in tangible ways. While they did not actually see her, they emerged from their experiences having been given something tangible to indicate, without doubt, that they had been blessed by her loving presence.

G.W.'s miraculous experience came as an answer to her need for help. Suffering from a paralyzing fear of driving an unreliable car, she received a surprising blessing.

When a dear friend decided to move to Florida, she gave me a twelve-inch statue of Mary flanked by two kneeling angels. It was one of two statues given to her by her deceased mother.

I placed the gift on my carpeted bedroom floor—upright against the wall and under my sewing machine cabinet— until I could find the perfect place to hang it. As busy as I was at the time, the gift remained there for longer than I had intended.

In the meantime, my automobile was giving me a bit of

trouble. It seemed to hesitate whenever I turned a corner. I complained to my husband and he exchanged cars with me for a couple of days, but he did not experience the same problem.

We exchanged cars once again and the car's hesitation was still evident to me. That night as we were preparing to go to bed, I confessed that the car was making me very nervous and that I was afraid it would die as I turned onto a major highway. He assured me that it would not do that. And since he was a service manager and former mechanic at a Cadillac dealership, he said I could take his word as being reliable. I finally fell asleep, still worrying, despite my husband's assurance.

I don't know what woke me in the middle of the night, but I raised myself up and turned around. I had been sleeping on my right side, with my back to the bedroom door. I was amazed to see a beautiful golden light surrounding our floor-length mirror, which was situated in the corner near the door and next to my sewing machine cabinet. The light then slowly expanded to cover the entire corner. It was, without a doubt, the most beautiful sight I had ever seen. I was so awestruck that I failed to wake my husband. When I finally thought to do so, the light had disappeared.

When the alarm woke us the following morning, I told my husband of my experience and he agreed that it could not have been a light from outside, since our blinds were tightly closed to keep any light from disturbing our sleep. Therefore, it had to have had a supernatural source. But what was the light's message? I wondered.

The answer came as I was standing in front of my dresser mirror combing my hair later that morning. Some-

thing told me to turn and look at the statue under my sewing cabinet. There, situated between Mother Mary and the angel on her left side, was a small object that had not been there previously. I walked over and removed the object. It was an old, worn medal from the Sacred Heart Auto League, blessed to protect the owner while driving his or her automobile. Needless to say, I went into a state of euphoria. This was a gift from Mother Mary to ease my troubled mind and heart. I felt that I need not worry any further about driving my car.

Still, I felt the need to phone my friend in Florida to be certain that the medal had not been placed there by her mother. She assured me that her mother had not put it there and that she had never belonged to the Sacred Heart Auto League. Further, she insisted that no one in her family had ever owned such a medal. She also told me that she had thoroughly dusted the statue before giving it to me. I was then convinced that it was a gift from the Virgin Mother and that the golden light was the aura of her presence in our bedroom.

I carry this medal wherever I go. Since it appeared, I have had many spiritual happenings in my life. But I must confess that even before this blessed event, I received many other blessings, including a visit from Jesus. I've also witnessed many visits from my guardian angel. I could go on and on, but it would take up too much of your time. (G.W.)[5]

While the mind may balk at the idea that Mary would, or even could, materialize a worn Sacred Heart Auto League medal, G.W.'s experience brings to mind well-documented accounts of individuals who have visited spiritually evolved beings in the East who apparently have the power to materialize physical objects. Currently, such stories abound concerning the famous living guru Sai Baba. From childhood, Sai Baba has reportedly materialized innumerable objects, apparently out of thin air. My Buddhism professor at the University of Texas, Radjah Rao, who was himself a Hindu Vedantist, once reportedly visited Sai Baba. Apparently, Sai Baba was impressed with him, for the guru materialized a ring for him to wear. Radjah allegedly took the ring and threw it away, saying that it was not his master.

With this gesture, he affirmed that the only thing worth serving was his master, who happened to be someone other than Sai Baba. But even if his own master had given him the ring, Radjah may have thrown it just as far. It has been said that when someone points to the moon, the fool looks at the finger. When my teacher threw away the ring, he resisted the temptation to settle for something less than the attainment of enlightenment itself.

By insisting on such an austere approach to the spiritual path, however, we can perhaps deprive ourselves of the evocative power of supernatural events and sacred objects. The Protestant tradition was founded, in part, to do away with the devotion to intermediaries of all kinds. Like my professor, Luther and his followers threw away the tangible symbols of God's immanence in our lives. Reacting to the substitution of images and priestly authority for the ultimate source of our salvation—that is, God himself—the Reformers left the faithful to contemplate the divine without the help of time-honored symbols that had arisen in the course of centuries of worship. Jung frequently lamented this loss in Protestantism, saying that the Catholic church alone still possessed the living symbols capable of reconnecting us to our spiritual depths. He said, "The Protestant is left to God alone.

For him there is no confession, no absolution. . . . He has to digest his sins by himself; and because the absence of a suitable ritual has put it beyond his reach, he is none too sure of divine grace."[6]

Certainly, we should not base our faith exclusively, or even primarily, on tangible symbols, gifts, or intermediaries of any kind. And yet faith can be activated—and, perhaps, sustained—by observable symbols and inexplicable phenomena that temporarily arrest the mind's tendency to undermine everything that it cannot see or measure. For W.H, the medal in her pocket was obviously not the treasure itself; it only pointed to the loving being who cared enough to allay her fears during a frightening time. But its comforting physicality will doubtless serve as an important pointer again and again to that which truly matters to her.

I began collecting accounts of Marian encounters in early spring, and oddly enough, I found myself yearning to plant roses. It was remarkable because never in my life had I felt much interest in planting flowers. For almost twenty years, I had devoted all of my gardening efforts to growing organic vegetables and fruits, but never flowers. I knew absolutely nothing about growing roses. However, in response to this newfound desire, Mickey Lin and I purchased four rosebushes and planted them in early May, the traditional month of Mary. Within a few days, all of them were blooming. I thought myself lucky. But then when the yellow rose near the front door bloomed on the day of the meeting of our monthly rosary group, I realized that we were more than lucky. Further, that was the night when Mary appeared to Mickey and, as she smelled the freshly cut yellow rose, told her, "I like this one the best! Thank you for honoring me" (see page 23).

Each month through the summer and into the fall, the yellow rosebush—which grew twice as fast as the others—brought forth a new set of blossoms just in time to greet our friends as they came to our door for the rosary group. For some reason that we can never fully understand, Mary loves roses; and when we are near to her heart, the fragrance of roses may greet us as her way of acknowledging us. I used to think that such reports were embellished, if not fabricated. But that changed when I smelled roses that were not really there.

For months, Mickey had reported smelling roses when she was with me or with other friends—even twice while she was on the beach—but I had never smelled them. Knowing that the smell of roses is a well-known sign of Mary's presence, I was nonetheless skeptical. I am also a psychotherapist, and I know the power of the mind to create its own reality.

Mickey and I had scheduled a session with a woman, K.P.,[7] who had come to work with us—with Mickey for hypnotherapy and with me for relationship counseling. Complaining of various problems, she was most interested in obtaining relief from severe chronic pain from multiple surgical procedures, so Mickey spent many hours helping her to develop hypnotic strategies for pain control. She had already completed two lengthy and productive hypnotherapy sessions. Then, as planned, she wanted to explore problems in her marriage with me.

As I opened my office door and followed Mickey and the woman into the room, the smell of fresh roses greeted me. I knew that the smell could not be coming from my office, so I assumed that the woman was wearing some kind of strong rose perfume. But the odd thing was, the odor smelled *exactly* like roses.

Throughout the hour, the smell persisted. At times, it was so intense that I was distracted by it. Having recently planted several rosebushes and enjoyed their first blossoms, I had become familiar with the subtle differences in smell between various types of roses. I thought at one point that the smell was from a yellow or a white rose.

Later, I asked the woman if she'd been wearing a rose perfume. She said no. And she had not smelled the roses at all. But Mickey had also noticed the pervasive smell.

Although the evidence for a supernatural explanation was compelling, I kept looking—unsuccessfully, I might add—for ways to dismiss the phenomenon. Mickey simply laughed at my skepticism. "When are you going to start believing that Mary is with us?" she asked.

When we discussed this phenomenon in front of a friend of K.P.'s, he looked startled. He said that two days before K.P. arrived in Virginia Beach, he had come home one afternoon and found his apartment filled with the scent of roses. He did not know what it meant, but he was convinced that it signified the presence of some spiritual being.

The story culminated two weeks later back in Indiana. K.P.'s husband wanted to help her but did not know what to do, so he asked her what he might do to relieve the pain. She showed him some bodywork procedures that Mickey had employed along with the hypnotherapy. As he laid his hands on his wife, he suddenly felt overcome by an energy and a presence. Then he had a vision: He saw Mary's face before him, as clear and as colorful as if she were physically there. He was deeply moved by the shock of her presence and the intense love and energy that seemed to emanate from her and pass through him. K.P. said that it was as though the life had been put back into her. After the experience, her husband was in tears off and on for days.

In the following account, F.L. tells of smelling the fragrance of roses while meditating in a group. For her, it marked the beginning of Mary's influence in her life.

At the age of forty, and as a mother of two, I entered the depths of a marital transition and personal crisis. So I began to try various "therapies" to help myself. Not much worked until I began to go deep inside and listen to my heart instead of my mind. Gradually, as I surrendered to God and allowed the light of Jesus to fill me up, I felt the presence of the Divine Mother.

In the summer of 1994, I attended a meditation and healing group where the healing presence of the Divine Mother first came to me. At first, I did not know for sure if it was just my imagination. But while meditating with a group of women, I began to feel very relaxed and open. At this point, I began to smell a very strong fragrance of white roses. I remember thinking, Boy, Melissa sprayed a lot of air freshener around. This is unbelievable! Then I began to feel extremely warm from the inside out. Eventually, the outside of my body became very warm, but not uncomfortable. It seemed as though there were a glowing presence all around me.

As we ended our meditation, we went around the room to talk about what we had experienced. I discovered to my surprise that no one had smelled the roses—except my friend Barbara, who was sitting right next to me. She told us that she, too, smelled the distinct fragrance of white roses. Then, as I shared my experience, I noticed how wet I was. You could actually see moist droplets on my skin; however, the glowing warm feeling was no longer there.

About two weeks later, I visited a woman who does spiritual counseling. She knew only my name—nothing else. She began to meditate and call upon my angels to speak about my purposes, life lessons, and worthwhile goals. About halfway into the meditation, she stopped in the middle of a sentence and said she felt the presence of the Virgin Mary with me; and this had happened with her only a couple of times before.

At this point, she started sweating and said she felt very warm, just as I had during the group meeting. After that session, I felt pretty convinced something special had happened to me.

Then, about a month later, I was talking to a lovely old woman about her life. At one point, she said, "Excuse me a minute," and went into the other room and got some-thing for me. She said, "Here, I'd like you to have this. It's for you." I had told her nothing about my Marian experiences. I opened this small envelope she gave me and saw a beautiful silver medal of Mary with the Christ Child in her arms and accompanied by two angels above her. I almost started to cry, and I asked her why she had given this to me. She said, "I don't know, but it's yours now." I carry the medal with me now always and look at it from time to time and thank Mary for being in my life now and always. (F.L.)[8]

Unlike G.W.'s experience with the Sacred Heart Auto League medal, which happened all at once, F.L.'s experience of Mary's growing influence happened during a series of related events.

Nonetheless, her three experiences culminated in a similar way—with the gift of a physical reminder of Mary's love. Again, we see how our connection with Mary is symbolized and anchored by objects that we can hold, even as we may yearn for what we cannot see or touch.

Prayers to Mary often bring dramatic changes in people's lives. Like myself and many others whose accounts are included herein, E.M. did not turn to Mary until she was desperate. As a nonpracticing Catholic at the time of her crisis, she reached into her religious heritage and found the rosary. And through the rosary, she rediscovered Mary, who apparently catalyzed both a financial reversal and a spiritual reawakening for her.

On April 19, 1991, I received a layoff notice from a high-tech firm where I had been employed just over a year. Two years earlier, I had received a layoff notice from a similar firm, where I had been employed for over seven years. The first experience had been very traumatic, but this second layoff absolutely paralyzed me. I did not know what to do next, since the high-tech industry in the Northeast was in chaos and almost all companies in the area were downsizing their workforce.

The following Thursday, I went to a spiritual study group that I had joined a year before. For some reason, the Medjugorje experience of one of our members came up for discussion just before people began to leave.

John had visited Medjugorje the year before. When filming the sky at six o'clock in the morning, he captured on film cloud formations that looked like the Blessed Virgin and the head of Jesus wearing a crown of thorns. After sharing his experience with our group, John gave me sev-

eral things about the Marian apparitions to read and to share with others.

This new information came at a time when I had already begun to turn to Mary. At that time, my anxiety level was extremely high due to my increasing financial burdens. I carried a large mortgage on my home, a four-hundred-dollar-a-month equity loan, and an equally high car payment. All of this, and I had only been given a month's severance pay. It was a horrible time. So I began doing novenas on a daily basis.[9] When the fear escalated to the level of panic, I would turn to the rosary to calm myself down. I was also petitioning Mary for her help.

While I welcomed John's material, it was several days before I finally sat down to read it. As I settled onto my couch on a Tuesday afternoon around two o'clock, I felt a sudden stillness in the room. A stream of sunlight shone through the front windows, and I had a fleeting thought of perhaps adding sheers to keep the sun from fading the carpet. Slowly, but noticeably, the light coming through the window changed from yellow sunlight to a soft golden tone. The light also changed from a slanting position to a straight vertical shaft. I sensed rather than saw that someone else was in the room. I looked around the room to see whether or not it was my dog, but he wasn't there. I looked back at the light, and it was still straight up and down, as though someone was standing there.

Then, I heard a voice in my head gently say, "Don't worry. Everything will be all right."

I knew at once that it was the Blessed Virgin Mary. "Why can't I see you?" I asked silently.

"Because you already believe," she said. And the brief experience was over.

The light changed again, back to yellow sunlight that slanted through the window. I sat mesmerized for over an hour.

Four weeks later, I was hired at a higher salary than I had ever earned before. This firm was also in financial trouble, and I knew that the job would not last, but it paid the mortgage and other bills until I could sell the house.

The experience lifted my self-esteem, which was in the wastebasket by that time. I had always found it easy to get jobs before, and the experience of losing two jobs was one I had never dreamed of facing. Before the Marian experience, I felt worthless. After the experience, I felt that if Mary took the time to come to tell me that my life was going to be all right, I had importance "up there."

Not only did my experience make me feel better; it was also a spiritual awakening for me. I went back to the Catholic church, but I still felt something missing. The only pleasure I seemed to get from life was reading and discussing with other people ways in which we might get closer to God.

Since my encounter, Mary has not let me down. I have been supported financially, even though I've had to use my savings sometimes. I am still in the process of making the transition from my old life to a new one, but I'm happier than I've ever been in my life. I attribute my transformation to the Marian experience. That she took the time to reassure me still overwhelms me with gratitude. (E.M.)[10]

Many of us shy away from praying for specific positive changes in our lives. It seems too much like telling God what to do. "Thy will be done," we utter, asking God to direct the course of our lives. But in trying so hard to avoid telling the divine what to do, we may never consider what we want in the first place. In *Alice's Adventures in Wonderland,* for instance, Alice encounters the god-like Cheshire cat sitting in the tree at a fork in the road. She asks the cat for directions.

" 'Would you tell me please which way I ought to go from here?'

" 'That depends a good deal on where you want to get to.'

" 'I don't much care where—' said Alice.

" 'Then it doesn't matter which way you go,' said the Cat."[11]

Jesus said, "Whatsoever ye ask in my name, that will I do" (John 14:13). He never said that we had to be vague about it. After all, in teaching us how to pray, he did say, "Give us this day our daily bread," not "Nourish me if it suits you." I think that the preceding stories—of the king and his jewels, of E.M.'s career reversal, and of Alice and the Cheshire cat—appeal to us because they remind us that our desires, when combined with our willingness to submit to higher will, give the divine a place to start working in our lives. Without our expressing a clear wish—however trivial it may seem—the forces of healing and transformation may remain idle in our lives.

Of course, personal crises force us out of hiding to reveal what it is we want. Like E.M., we suddenly decide that saving a life, a job, or a precious jewel is worth petitioning the divine, without concern for the relative merits of our requests. Through such passionate prayers, we expose our weaknesses, yes; but we finally enter a relationship where we become fully revealed—which may be the point at which the divine can, in turn, become more fully revealed to us. In regard to this idea, Lewis says, "By unveiling, by confessing our sins, by 'making known' our requests, we assume the high rank of persons before Him. And He, descending, becomes a person to us."[12]

In the following account, L.H. tells of the evolving relationship she has experienced with Mary because of her own willingness to unveil her desires and to ask Mary for assistance with various practical matters.

Prayer has always been an important part of my life. However, most of my prayer time has been spent praying for others and not very much for myself.

Then, last year, my father and I began looking for some property in upstate New York. We had actually been looking for some time, and yet we possessed very limited funds. Consequently, we became very discouraged when we saw what we could afford. In July, my father announced that he was ready to give up hope and stop looking, but I begged him to continue looking with me. Without my father's help and partnership, I knew I would never realize my dream of owning my own property.

That night in a cry of desperation, I turned to a prayer that I hadn't used very often, although it has always been one of my favorites—the Memorare [see page 146]. It is a prayer that invokes the Blessed Mother Mary to intercede on our behalf and grant our petitions. I prayed to her and meditated for help in our quest for this property. Believing that if one should ask to receive, one should also make an offering, I promised our Lady I would make a shrine to her and my Lord Jesus if she would only help me in my quest. I also told her that I would be indebted to her for such a great blessing.

At that very moment, I was never more sincere in my prayer. Exactly three days later, I received a phone call from the broker and he told me about a property. From the description, it didn't sound like what we were looking for, and the price seemed too good to be true. Most properties in that range were far from our needs. The broker insisted that we should see it, and I told him I would get back to him. I called my dad, and though I wasn't that excited about it, he said maybe we should check it out.

That night, I had my first encounter with divine intervention. The previous days had been busy, and I had almost forgotten about my request to our Lady. Nevertheless, in a series of dreams it was revealed to me that this was the place for us. In one very intense, very vivid, almost lifelike dream, I saw the most beautiful face of a woman, whom I believed to be the Blessed Mother. Though I don't remember the words she spoke, I will never forget the impressions she put upon my mind. She revealed to me that this place was a very special place that was to be given to me, and that the shrine to her and Jesus should be located where others could see it. I knew she wanted it to be a special place for prayer and meditation.

Little did I know that this was only the beginning of my spiritual transformation at the age of thirty-three. The real estate closing went smoothly, and the first thing that I did was to set up the shrine.

During this time, I also set up some hunting blinds for the upcoming deer season. Another dream of mine was to hunt on my own land and to have a successful hunt. So it was on opening day at 9:00 A.M. that I was given a four-point buck. Immediately after the take, I raised my voice in thanks and prayer to God and to the spirit of the deer for his sacrifice for me. With the ease of the hunt, I knew that I had been truly blessed.

With all the physical work and strains of my job,

however, my body became racked with pain by the end of the year. I went to the doctor and he informed me that I had carpal tunnel syndrome in both wrists, a pinched nerve from a small fracture in my forearm, and softening of both patellae, the latter of which was the most painful of my problems.

On New Year's Eve, I didn't go out, since I could not even walk. I lay in bed, tortured by pain in my legs. In desperation, I prayed to my Mother Mary and invoked her help once again, all the while thanking and reminding her of the help she had given to me before. Again, I promised her in return for help and healing that I would do whatever she asked of me. The next day was Sunday, and after Mass, I spoke with my spiritual director about the Marian apparitions. He asked me to follow him to the rectory, where he gave me a rosary ring[13] and a scapular and told me about the Legion of Mary—a group devoted to the work of the Blessed Mother and our Lord Jesus Christ.

He explained that Legion members volunteer their services two hours a week, pray the rosary daily, and attend a weekly meeting. Well, right away I had doubts, and I told him my work schedule was very hectic and changeable. But that Sunday evening, I had another very intense dream.

In it, Mary made it known to me that this was the work she wanted me to do. She told me not to worry about my job, and she instructed me to tell them that I needed time off to attend the Legion meeting. She assured me that all would work out just fine and told me to put my faith in God.

The next day, I told my boss that I was going through this spiritual thing and that I simply had to attend the meeting! I encountered surprisingly little resistance, and I went to the meeting. Since our Lady asked for my service, I joined without further hesitation. Today, I volunteer in hospitals and nursing homes, where I visit the sick and elderly. I also assist at Mass and spread her message wherever I can—that through her we will be led to Jesus Christ.

Since I began all of this, my entire life has changed. And oftentimes, little miracles happen to me. My body is free of pain and suffering, except for on occasion, when I think it is to remind me of the blessings I have received from our Lady and our Lord. This new spirituality, this new path, has led me to helping and caring for the sick and less fortunate and doing what I can to bring God's love into the world. (L.H.)[14]

L.H.'s overall story conveys the rich interdependency among herself and Mary and nature, to the point where hunting and ministering to the poor coexist harmoniously in L.H.'s deepening relationship with the divine. As we follow her through her experiences with Mary, we see that her evolving relationship prepares her to serve others in a fuller way than ever before. The acquisition of the right property, the personal empowerment of successfully hunting on her own land, and the healing of her physical conditions obviously represented to L.H. desirable goals in their own right. But eventually, it becomes clear that Mary's interventions were designed to serve a greater overall plan—to activate a greater capacity in L.H. to serve the needs of others.

❧

As we have seen, Mary's love materializes in practical, concrete ways during times of crisis and the loss of one's faith. When we are unsure of our own worth, and when we doubt the meaning of life, what better gift can there be than a precious object, or a measurable phenomenon, conceived in spirit and manifested in miraculous form?

During an especially difficult time, M.H. found concrete reassurance of God's love for her.

In April 1975, I had a radical mastectomy. My doctor told me that I had a 30 percent chance of living as long as, but no longer than, two years. By August 1976, I had undergone two more surgeries, and I was still in bed recuperating from them when on the morning of September 10, 1976, Hurricane Kathleen's flash flood came roaring down the mountains into Imperial Valley. At first, it looked like a solid wall of water, with a crest of twelve feet as it came rushing toward our home. In the twinkling of an eye, our mobile home was inundated, the floodwaters destroying it and almost everything we owned.

I was too weak to survive in those powerful waters, which were debris-filled, stinking, and ice-cold. My legally blind husband towed me through those raging waters to safety on higher ground. Until that moment, I had not realized the depth of meaning of that beloved hymn of youth, "Higher Ground."

I had faced the diagnosis of cancer and prognosis of death with calm dignity. Never once had I asked, Why me, O God, why me? But now, with almost everything I had worked a lifetime to attain swept away, I plunged to the bottom of the slough of despond. Dear God, I wailed in the silence of my soul, I think you have me confused with Job. All of my life I've suffered pain, privation, and grief without complaint. But this time you have put on me more than I can bear! I could almost hear his chiding answer: You're alive, aren't you?

Although I am lame and my legs have caused me excruciating pain almost my whole life, my doctor advised me to take walks in the desert that bordered our rented home, to build up my strength. My three dogs and cat accompanied me on these walks. It was on such a safari that I found my healing stone.

When I looked at that stone and saw imprinted on it a beautiful image of the mother of Christ, I thought, This miniature could have been painted by a master artist.

But I knew the forces of nature had imprinted Mary's likeness on the stone. Some inner knowledge told me this stone was a treasure beyond price. So I pocketed it and began walking toward home, the dogs running ahead of me and the cat trailing along behind.

Whenever I touched my healing stone, I seemed to feel strength and spiritual healing surging through me. It was as if the stone were transmitting long-stored-up energy to me. Whenever I looked upon the likeness of the Blessed Mother, I felt comforted and consoled.

Gradually, I adjusted to and accepted our changed circumstances. I learned that when God takes something from us, or lets nature's rampaging forces destroy it, he gives us something far better in return. My gifts, I found, were strength to survive, a new zest for life, a spiritual peace, and a more creative lifestyle.

I am a retired photographer, but it never occurred to me to take a photograph of my healing stone. Perhaps I felt no need to do this because I thought the image on it was permanent. But as I grew stronger in spirit, the image on my healing stone began to fade, until only a few streaks of pink and blue were left. In time, these, too, disappeared.

But by then, the image of the Madonna the stone had once portrayed was internalized—imprinted forever on my memory, so that I would never forget the miracle my healing stone had wrought in my life. (M.H.#2)

As we have seen from M.H.'s earlier account in chapter 4, she enjoys a close mystical relationship with Jesus and Mary. While her life has been anything but easy, she has rarely felt abandoned or punished by her trials. When her once-strong faith was severely shaken, however, she found a physical reminder of God's love for her. Again, we see that the enduring quality of sacred objects can compensate for a person's temporary loss of faith. The impermanence of the image, however, is an interesting feature of M.H.'s experience. Perhaps it faded because the image was for M.H. alone, or perhaps it disappeared because she no longer needed a tangible reassurance of God's love.

M.H.'s discovery of the Madonna in the stone is by no means unprecedented. Indeed, stones bearing Mary's image were discovered two hundred years ago in a limestone quarry in Mexico. In 1792, a miner by the name of José Maria Galícia split apart a stone the size of his fist and discovered images of a Madonna and child clearly sculpted on the face of both halves of the stone. Following Galícia's momentous discovery, the residents of the nearby pueblo erected a church dedicated to the Virgin del Carmen. While these stones have heretofore been shrouded in mystery, a reporter recently obtained permission to examine and photograph the remarkable images.[15] In return for this rare opportunity, he promised to keep the location of the church a secret. The priest and the town residents are afraid that a church-appointed commission will take the stones away from their two-hundred-year-old home and house them in some far-off museum.

In the following account of her encounter with Mary, R.S. tells of receiving the assurance of Mary's protection during a time when she was worried about the well-being of her elderly mother. Again, we see how Mary consents to reach down to where we are and to show us the caring that one might expect from one's own mother.

During my life (I am fifty years old), I have had a number of encounters from Jesus, most frequently during meditations, and sometimes during special church services, such as funerals. Here, however, I wish to share my one and only encounter with Mary, which took place during the Christmas holidays of 1994.

I went home to Georgia to be with my children, mother, friends, and extended family members for Christmas. I stayed with my daughter who lives in the Atlanta area. My mother came from north Georgia to my daughter's house to be a part of the holiday festivities. After visiting several days, my mother prepared for her drive back to north Georgia. After exchanging hugs, saying "I love you," and shedding tears, I watched as my mom backed out of the driveway. I did what I have done a thousand times before: I mentally enveloped my mom and her car in a bubble of white light and silently said a prayer for her safe travel. Much to my surprise, a vision of Mary suddenly appeared, standing on the hood of my mom's car.

She was dressed in soft, flowing garments and wore a drapelike veil on her head that flowed down her shoulders and back. She wore a bodice of soft blue overlaid in sheer white drapes. The veil on her head was white.

Then I heard Mary say to me, "I will go with her."

My eyes instantly teared up; I was deeply touched. I responded mentally, Thank you, Mary. I watched as my mom waved her final good-bye as she moved farther away from the house. It was quite a sight watching the car move down the street in a bubble of white light, with Mary standing on the hood! When Mom arrived home, she telephoned to let us know that she had arrived there safely. Her first words were, "I had the most pleasant drive home!" My mother has always been very special to me and the number-one emotional support in my life. I am very thankful for her. (R.S.#1)[16]

In virtually every instance of Mary's intervention, we can see that she addresses an immediate problem, while leaving the recipients to contemplate the larger implications of her presence in their lives, as well. Mary's words—*"I will go with her"*—not only reassured R.S. in that moment but also conveyed a promise reminiscent of Jesus' own words: "I am with you always, even unto the end of the world" (Matthew: 28:20). As such, Mary's surprising willingness to manifest the specific care and the comfort that we need during a crisis reveals a timeless promise that can, perhaps, sustain us in the absence of further proof.

❈

In summary, Mary has long been associated with the materialization of miraculous phenomena, sacred relics, and healing and

protection in times of need. Such miraculous, phenomenal manifestations are known as "prodigies" in the Catholic tradition,
and they seem to occur around the objects and the places that
Mary has blessed with her presence. In Garabandal, for instance,
Mary kissed innumerable objects submitted by the children—
especially toward the end of her appearances—on behalf of the
faithful onlookers. These personal items, in turn, became a perpetual secondary source of her blessings, even after she ceased to
appear. This dissemination of Mary's essence through kissed
objects assisted the community of believers around Garabandal
in sustaining itself somewhat independently of both the visionaries, who, as we know, went through a period of doubt, and the
local church hierarchy, which rejected the visionaries' claims.
Indeed, the supernatural events and the blessed objects continued to inspire hope and faith in spite of Mary's eventual retreat
and the controversy surrounding the apparitions.[17]

In chapter 3, I told the story of Rachel, who as a sixteen- year-old
had witnessed a statue of Mary coming to life. It had been six
months since I had last seen Rachel. I found myself growing
concerned, for even though she had terminated her counseling
work with me, she had promised to write down her stirring account of encountering Mary and to submit it for inclusion in this
book. Then, just before Christmas, I received a call from her and
she requested an appointment with me.

Three days later, she came into my office dressed in obviously
new, stylish clothes. Good things had happened to her, and she
radiated a joy that I'd never seen coming from her before. She
told me that she'd come to thank me for my help and to tell me

why she had waited to write down her story of encountering Mary.

She shared with me the fact that after remembering the long-forgotten experience, she began to have her doubts. Why would Mary appear to her? Did the statue *really* come to life, or was it only her imagination? Who would believe her? she wondered. The more she thought about it, the more she discounted her own experience. It occurred to her that she had to know if it had really happened; otherwise, she felt she could never share the story with others.

Around Thanksgiving, the opportunity had arisen for her to ask for some proof of her encounter with Mary. She had accompanied her husband to De Paul Hospital—a Catholic facility in Norfolk, Virginia—to have some tests done. While she was waiting, she decided to go into the hospital chapel. From previous experience of Catholic hospitals, she knew there would probably be a statue of Mary in the chapel. She crept across the hallway, entered the chapel, and found herself alone there. A statue of Mary stood off to one side.

Rachel prayed for a while, then got up and walked up to the statue. She said, "I need to know if you really appeared to me. Please show me." As she looked closely at a statue of Mary for the first time in forty years, it suddenly moved. Once again, the face softened and came to life. Mary turned to Rachel and smiled.

As Rachel tearfully finished telling me about her recent encounter, she said that she still wondered how the statue could actually move and take on the appearance of life. Then she said that she knew from studying physics that matter is not the way that we see it at all, but that it is actually in a state of constant movement. She then speculated that there might be a way to alter its state, and its appearance. Searching for something that might account for such a miracle, Rachel finally found the answer that was right for her.

She said, "I believe love can do that."

Many of us would like to think that we are beyond the need for such concrete reassurances of God's love. But if we are honest, most of us retain a childlike fascination with miracles and a yearning for some kind of proof that we are not alone. Smelling invisible roses or seeing a statue come to life can give us just what we need to put our doubts aside and to open ourselves to the divine in that moment, and thereafter.

Surely, just as one's relationship with one's own mother was forged in infancy through a nonverbal, tactile exchange, one's highest spiritual aspirations still rest upon a foundation of early feelings that are awakened and sustained by concrete realities, and not by words alone. As we pass through the most difficult times in our lives, such objects and observable phenomena can serve as anchors in otherwise-unstable circumstances. And as we hold to these things, our feelings can reach out beyond the forms to which we cling and can commune with the being who brought to us these wondrous things.

MEMORARE

Remember, O Most Compassionate Virgin Mary, that never was it known that anyone who fled to your protection, implored your assistance or sought your intercession was left unaided. Inspired with this confidence we fly unto you, O Virgin of virgins, our Mother. To you do we come, before you we kneel, sinful and sorrowful. O Mother of the Word Incarnate, despise not our petitions, but in your clemency hear and answer them. Amen.

6

THE PROBLEM OF SUFFERING

> The purpose of our coming into the world
> is not to eliminate suffering, but to love.
>
> *Mary's words to Mickey Lin*

Early in our relationship, Mickey Lin and I engaged in one of those heated discussions that made both of us feel rather hopeless. I cannot recall what it was about, nor can she; I do remember that I retreated to my office to sleep on the sofa. Mickey, in turn, also tried to get some sleep. After tossing and turning, she went to sleep and had the following experience about the meaningfulness of suffering.

> *Once I finally fell asleep, I felt Mary nudging me to awaken. I felt undeserving of her presence, so I resisted, preferring instead to sink into deeper despair. However, she obviously had other plans for me. She stayed there without saying a word. Finally, I asked her what was the sense of it all if they—Jesus and Mary—could not eliminate suffering? I shared with her my frustrations over the situations in my life that seemed senseless and unnecessary. Mary responded gently by saying, "The purpose of our coming into the world is not to eliminate suffering, but to love." She also said that if I would continue to trust, I*

would eventually see the whole picture and the meaning of the struggle. She insisted that all of the little lessons were valuable and that to remove all of the suffering would hinder our growth.

Like many spiritually sensitive individuals, Mickey struggles with the conflict between preserving personal freedom versus giving without measure in a world full of disappointment and suffering. She is one of the most loving people I know; nonetheless, she is ambivalent about committing herself in a world where she has experienced several traumatic events and near-fatal injuries. Not surprisingly, she was confronted with a choice in a recent dream: An unidentified spiritual presence instructed her to select one of two symbols—a rose or a butterfly—to signify her life path. She knew intuitively that the rose signified a path with a heart, characterized by unswerving commitment and willing sacrifice. In contrast, the butterfly signified unlimited freedom and the power to transcend the circumstances around her. Mickey felt that the correct answer had to be the rose, but she could not bring herself to reject the butterfly entirely. So she answered, "Both!" Once again, she was told to choose one of the symbols, but she adamantly repeated her choice. Instead of failing the test, she suddenly felt that she had chosen correctly, and that she had passed an initiation.

Of all historic religious figures, Mary probably experienced the highest imaginable joy and the most profound, unimaginable grief. With God's blessing, she gave birth to a son who was the living expression of a new covenant between God and man. And then she saw her son misunderstood, degraded, tortured, and killed, while she remained entirely powerless to prevent it. Many have asked, Who suffered the most—Jesus, or the mother who watched him die on the cross?

Given her exposure to the full gamut of human experience, it is understandable that Mary's appearances often parallel significant hardships in the lives of those who witness her presence. It makes sense that *if anyone can understand and comfort the suffering, she can.* In some cases, her manifestations come at the end of a period of difficulty and suffering, but in other cases, her presence foreshadows the onset of a lengthy struggle. The apparition at Knock, Ireland, came at the end of thirty years of famine, but Mary's initial appearance at Medjugorje in 1981 preceded the renewal of racial unrest and civil war in the former Yugoslavia. Regardless of when she appears, Mary typically manifests as an expression of grace and profound love in the midst of struggle— apparently to ameliorate the sense of meaninglessness and victimization that easily insinuates its way into our thinking. Further, her love empowers us to change what we can and then to accept graciously life's inevitable hardships and losses. Mary's statement to Conchita, "You will not be happy in this world, but in heaven," seems less a prediction of Conchita's personal unhappiness than a statement about what we all can expect, as well.

And yet Mary's presence brings profound joy, as well. A compelling apocryphal tradition tells us that the resurrected Jesus went first of all to Mary to reveal himself to her before manifesting to his friends and followers. His adoring words, as found in Coptic apocryphal texts, underscore Mary's gift to him and to the world: "Hail to thee who hast borne the life of the whole world. Hail my Mother, my saintly Ark.... The whole of paradise rejoices because of thee. I tell thee, my Mother, whoever loves thee, loves life."[1] If Jesus went first to Mary—and it is easy to imagine that he would—then the woman who was the "first of the believers of the new covenant," and who presumably suffered the greatest loss of all in the course of its unfoldment, also witnessed the first glorious evidence of its fulfillment. When we examine what Mary means to us beneath the surface of superficial associations, we are bound to find that she is a most complex figure who brings joy and suffering together within herself in a singular experience of love.

Buddha said that life is suffering. This is a hard fact to accept. To those of us who believe we can make a difference, it seems too much like giving up. Indeed, in our search for meaning, many of us initially resist the idea that suffering is unavoidable. We need not regard this as a weakness; theologians and laypersons alike find suffering to be the most difficult fact of life to reconcile with a God who presumably loves us. How can God, we ask, permit the suffering of innocent children, while at the same time allowing cruel and malicious people to escape accountability?

Sometimes we know that our pain and suffering follow as a consequence of our own unwise prior choices. The Eastern concept of karma reflects this sense of personal accountability for our previous actions. Operating from this perspective, we would like to think that we can avoid suffering by paying off our debts and by living a virtuous life thereafter. But it takes a while before the effects from all of our past actions catch up with us—and even if we could weather this process with patience and dignity, we cannot reasonably hope to avoid new mistakes and the consequent costs thereof.

Even if we *could* avoid all further error, a rational assessment informs us that pain and suffering befall even those who lead exemplary lives and deserve the best of everything. Sometimes the capriciousness of nature inflicts suffering through natural disasters, illnesses, and genetic deficiencies. And sometimes our suffering comes not from unwise choices or from nature's random thoughtlessness but from those who hate us without cause. In this case, we experience suffering when our goodness collides with those who are motivated by lesser ideals. Jesus' own plight at the hands of his contemporaries should tell us that we cannot reasonably hope to escape suffering by imitating him. Similarly, the Tibetan guru Milarepa was poisoned by a jealous man, and knew it in time to prevent it from happening. But like Jesus, he saw that good could come from submitting to betrayal and suffering. Milarepa's murderer turned out to be one of his most committed followers once he realized and repented for his grievous error. Each of these spiritual masters saw beyond their immediate pain to the constructive consequences of human tragedy; *they elected to suffer so that good could eventually prevail.*

In meditating on the problem of suffering, I realized that there are two forms of suffering over which we have some degree of control. There is "payback," or "karmic," suffering, which comes when we must account for unfortunate choices or mistakes that we have committed. Payback suffering is hell—figuratively, and perhaps literally, as well. We can learn from this suffering, but there is nothing particularly wonderful about the process. We can choose to accept this ordeal gracefully, or we can disavow any responsibility for it, preferring to complain about life's unfairness. Most of us take the latter approach, demonstrating the truth of Anthony Trollope's contention that a man cherishes, above all else, a good grievance.

Beyond the process of endless accountability, there is redemptive suffering, which comes from doing what is loving and right in a world where the loving thing is not always the safe or popular thing to do. If Jesus' suffering was payback, it was presumably for our sakes rather than for his, for nothing about his life warranted the suffering that he endured. As we contemplate Jesus' passion and enter into his suffering vicariously, we experience *along with him* a less common form of suffering, which comes from a willingness to put love above life itself. Something strange happens when we identify with him through his ordeal: We feel renewed and deepened, not because he suffered but *because he loved through it all.* And, remarkably, we come closer to accepting the previously paralyzing fear of our own pain and mortality. By vicariously entering into the moments of his life when he faced his greatest ordeals, we come to understand how Jesus could tolerate the loneliness of his ordeal and the agony of his death. We may also realize that redemptive suffering contains its own antidote to pain—and that loving *in spite of the consequences* converts our emotional and physical pain into a passion that has healing and redemptive power. Conventional Christianity tells us that Jesus accepted his suffering as a way to atone for our sins. Regardless of whether he accepted it for this reason or because he was making a statement about his uncompromising commitment to loving—or both—it makes sense that this kind of sacrificial loving sends out a beacon that assists others in their spiritual journey.

In several of the accounts of encounters with Mary that I have collected, Mary subtly encouraged the recipient to embrace a willingness to suffer so that good could prevail. She exhibited a tremendous concern for those facing approaching physical or emotional hardship or those already undergoing an ordeal of some kind. But instead of alleviating the conditions under which the recipient labored, she invited that person to surrender a sense of victimization and to embrace love above all else. In these encounters, Mary's presence brought a sense of meaning to situations that might otherwise have provoked a sense of hopelessness or victimization. The recipient, meanwhile, entered a period of testing, in which the newly awakened qualities that Mary represents were challenged and seasoned by real-life circumstances. In these accounts, we can see a mature spirituality emerging— through meaningful suffering—even though the struggles often left the recipients wondering if, by chance, they had taken a wrong turn in life.

Of all possible thankless tasks, parenting an adolescent may take the prize. We may laugh about it before and afterward, but while it's going on, it can be a nightmare. It brings its own form of suffering, for there often seems to be nothing we can do to prevent our relationships with our children from deteriorating into an uneasy silence at best. As tensions escalate, we easily erupt over the smallest infraction because we interpret their thoughtlessness and distractibility as a lack of respect for us. We are often right about this, but no matter how correct we may be, we are sometimes wrong. On occasion, we lash out and accuse them unfairly, thus wounding their emerging pride and losing their respect, deservedly. We drift apart, and yet we desperately yearn for a time when we can fully reaffirm the love that was once so evident between us.

One woman, who was raising her adolescent children alone, felt she was losing all control over them. Without having a clue about what to do, she prayed to Mary instead.

The most profound experience I had with Mary took place near Akron, Ohio, where I lived at the time. About fifteen years ago, my children were in their late teens. Drugs— mostly marijuana—were very common in the schools they were attending. They were getting into heavy metal, and they seemed different to me. It was hard to talk to them and get them to listen to reason. They were at an age when the opinions of their peers were more important than anything I could say to them.

I was very upset and did not know what to do. I was a divorced mother of four and had no support from their father. Also, I really felt alone in my need for some kind of religious influence. Although my children had all gone to church and Sunday school while growing up, they had since drifted away from attending, and they were not even remotely interested in returning to church. One day while I was out driving around the countryside, I decided to visit St. Marys, Ohio, which is about fifteen miles outside of Akron. The whole town is built around a beautiful old country church, and there is a grotto there in a cave that is a replica of Lourdes. In the summertime, all of the services are held outside, where worshipers can sit in a parklike setting.

Even though I'm not a Catholic, St. Marys was always one of my favorite places to go when I was troubled, because the church was always open. So on that day, while the children were all in school, I went there and entered the grotto. Nobody else was in the grotto, even though there were candles burning.

I sat down. Up above the grotto, a ledge supported a statue of Mary. Someone had placed a lei of gladioli around Mary's neck. It was absolutely beautiful. I sat there praying and talking to Mary, asking her what I should do about my children. I said, "You know, you're a mother—you know how these things should go."

All at once, I felt a hand on my shoulder. I'd been

sitting there for a while, and I thought it might be a priest. I turned around and I saw no one. I looked around to see what this could be and I felt this warmth, even though it was a crisp day. I felt a warm glow enveloping me as I continued to feel the hand on my shoulder. I then noticed the birds had stopped singing and everything had become very quiet.

I looked around and couldn't see anyone. Then the warm glow came over me again. It started slowly at the top of my head and worked down—down to the tip of my toes. Then I heard this voice in my ear say, "Don't worry. Everything is going to be all right." The voice, calm and beautiful, said, "Raise your eyes and look at me." So I looked up at the statue and saw a glow coming off of it in pulsating gold rays, like a living energy.

One part of me was in awe, believing; the other, analytical, part of me was asking, How can this be? I realized that the sun was behind the grotto and could not illuminate the enclosure. I kept looking and it kept pulsating and glowing. It moved around. And then I looked at the coral gladioli around her neck. They started glowing, too—but in a more bluish or purplish manner. I heard a commotion, as though people were coming. Then I saw a procession of light beings walking up the path! They were of different sizes, as though they were a family of light beings. They were just moving along toward the statue of Mary, and I wondered what was going to happen when they arrived. Eventually, they reached the front of the grotto, where the candles were. I saw that as they got there, the gold rays emanating from Mary began to extend outward to greet the family. Eventually, the swirls from

Mary absorbed and engulfed the little group. The glow continued and increased until I could see threads of light that were pulsating and waving and suffusing the statue in a golden glow.

While I watched, the sensation of the hand on my shoulder persisted. I wondered what to do, and again I heard the voice say, "Be in peace. Everything is all right." So I bowed my head and prayed to God and Mary. I surrendered my fears about the choices that my children were making.

When I came out of meditation, I became aware that the singing of the birds had resumed. It was no longer so quiet. I raised my eyes and realized that the statue and flowers had lost their glow while I had been praying and meditating. Meanwhile, the feeling of the hand on my shoulder was also gone. Even so, I felt such an overwhelming sense of peace that I knew everything was going to be all right. My obsessive worry gave way to a profound feeling of peace.

When I got back to Akron, I noticed that my children acted more peacefully, probably because they sensed my inner change. It was a turning point for all of us.

I never lost the sense of peace that came upon me that day. Even today—fifteen years later—I remain much more peaceful because of the experience at St. Marys. I was so impressed with this experience that I had a friend, who was a professional photographer, return to the grotto with me and take several pictures of the statue. She mounted one of them for me. Since then, the photo has always occupied a prominent place wherever I have lived. Whenever I see it, I am reminded of the glow that ap-

*peared from nowhere and brought my family a peace that
we had lost.* (P.W.)[2]

In her encounter with a radiant Mary, P.W. witnessed what
was evidently a spiritualized expression of her own family coming under the influence of Mary's grace and healing. P.W. apprehended a view of her family that reminded her that we are
spiritual beings capable at any time of receiving healing and
renewal through our connection with the Holy Spirit. Indeed, the
concept of the Holy Spirit had its origins in the Greek school of
Stoicism. In this tradition, it was believed that a *common spirit*
bound us together into a seamless whole, and this may account
for the emphasis on the Holy Spirit in the New Testament. The
concept of family takes on new meaning when one can experience, as P.W. did, the common spirit that unites us and resolves
our apparently irreconcilable differences.

P.W.'s suffering gave way to a new response to her children
born of the peace that the experience with Mary instilled or
restored in her. Her emotional struggle was alleviated by responding in a new way to a situation that drives innumerable
parents into impotent fits of righteousness—and their children
into full-scale defiance.

As I have already said, we can reasonably assume that Mary's
willingness to serve God's plan brought her the highest joy and
the deepest suffering. Thus it makes sense that her example, if
not her essence, dwells within each of us as a sobering reminder
that the highest spiritual path can be, at times, a path of heartbreaking grief, as well. Given what she has come to mean to us,
Mary's manifestation at a time of personal difficulty can dramat-

ically offset our human tendency to interpret pain as an indication that we have done something wrong. When she comes, we can take heart that our suffering may coincide with an important unfolding process whose overall purpose may remain somewhat obscure to us.

⁂

The encounter with Mary described below took place during childbirth, and it was at once a blessing and an indication of coming trials.

I am most happy to write to you regarding my experience with the Blessed Mother. In fact, I thank you for the privilege and honor to do so. I have never written of this experience before. In fact, it was with great trepidation that I would even speak of it. As you well know, back in 1953, these experiences were regarded as hallucinations rather than as actual encounters.

I was in labor with my firstborn child, J.D., on October 5, 1953. I remembered my dearly departed aunt Lucille advising me to say the rosary during this time. I did so, over and over again.

My child was birthing himself when the nurse stopped him from coming into the world until I could be wheeled into the delivery room. I was given no drugs; it was a natural birth. As I was giving birth, I looked up and saw the Blessed Virgin. She was wearing a pure white mantilla that was flowing down, and a beautiful pale blue dress. She was absolutely beautiful. *I was awestruck. I couldn't tell the nun next to me or anyone in the delivery room that she was there.* I could not speak. *The expla-*

nation for the total beauty, tranquillity, and serene feeling still eludes me. I still cannot describe it. Such peace and such beauty are beyond words. Seeing the Blessed Mother was so awe-inspiring that I cannot to this day express the beauty of such a fantastic sight and feeling.

My son was born with a beautiful halo of golden hair about his head. As you may know, this can mean that the person will face great hardship in life. This has definitely been true for my son, and his ordeal continues to this day. I pray daily for him. May she, in her mercy, shine once more on her anointed one and lead him to the path of righteousness.

I thank you kindly for this opportunity to express my encounter with the mother of Jesus. (P.M.)[3]

P.M. did not realize at the time of her vision that hardship was coming, and she experienced the vision as entirely joyful and ineffably beautiful. In retrospect, however, she saw that Mary had come to awaken a sense of inner strength and spiritual presence that would serve to ease the burden of her grief over her son's troubles.

I asked P.M. what she meant by her son's ordeal. She said that he is a homosexual and that he has expressed many times his loneliness and despair over not being able to have his own children to love and to comfort him. He also struggles with a less ambiguous problem—alcoholism, a disease that runs in his family. It is interesting that P.M. believes that her son elected to enter this life as a homosexual so that he could end the genetic transmission of alcoholism in his family. Whether this is true or not, Mary saw fit to bless mother and son before the onset of a lifelong ordeal that, from a superficial standpoint, might seem tragic and unnecessary. However, if one accepts the near-death vision of Betty Eadie, then P.M.'s assessment makes perfect sense. In Eadie's vision, she understood that souls enter life for a singular purpose: *to help others awaken*. At one point, Eadie even witnessed from her celestial point of view a drunk lying in a gutter.[4] She knew that this soul had elected to experience alcoholism so that he could serve as an awakening influence for another soul who, as a physician, would come to treat his affliction. It seems like an unnecessary and uneconomical sacrifice from one point of view, but from where she stood, however briefly, Eadie knew the eventual awakening of awareness and love was all that really mattered.

When a serious disease strikes a person we love, we yearn for a miracle. Knowing that miracles can happen, we might pray for intervention, realizing that while we may feel unworthy ourselves, our loved ones deserve the very best.

Six years ago I moved to Virginia from New York. I had been in Virginia Beach six months when I received a letter from my younger sister. In the letter, she painfully told me that she believed she had been infected with the AIDS virus and that she was already experiencing some of the symptoms. Needless to say, I was in shock, since my sister had been in a monogamous relationship for eight years. I offered her an airplane ticket to Virginia Beach and said that we would go together for a test.

The test came back positive. The amount of pain that we experienced was unbelievable. My husband and I offered her and her two boys our home. We wanted to approach this situation with alternative medicine and with Edgar Cayce's remedies. This happened in November.

At that time, I was doing some volunteer work with a prayer group and had made a very special friend. I confided my situation to her. She mentioned a promise made by Mary to the three children at Fatima. She promised that if you ask her anything on December eighth at noon, she will grant your wish. So on that day, my sister, my friend, and I went to the meditation room at the Association for Research and Enlightenment in Virginia Beach to pray to Mary for my sister's health. Nothing happened to any of us except that a sense of peace came over me.

That Christmas, we all went to New York to spend the holidays with the rest of the family. My in-laws were living in New Jersey at that time, so my husband and I stayed over at their house. On Christmas Eve, my family and I spent the evening in New York and then we went back to New Jersey late that night. That night, I dreamt Mary came and blessed my sister.

In the dream, my sister and I were inside this building that had arched windows. To our left were many rows of chairs filled with people dressed in white. I believed they were doctors. Then suddenly from one of the windows, light came in and started to approach the doctors. The light turned to us, and as it was getting closer, I saw the Virgin Mary appear in the light. The closer it got, the more clearly I saw her.

She stood in front of us. She smiled at us and touched my sister on the head. Then she turned away from us toward the window and rapidly left the room. As she left the room, I ran behind her and in my dream I asked, "If this is not a dream, please give me a sign." When I looked out the window, the sky had turned to all the variations of mauve, violet, lavender, and blue. Then lights lit up the entire sky as if they were fireworks. The clouds started to take shapes. I saw shapes of angels with trumpets announcing God's presence and I think I saw what I believe was God, my beloved Creator.

I woke up in tears, as I am now writing this to you.

My sister is still alive, battling this disease the best she can. We are grateful that she is still alive and we know that God's presence is within us. I don't know what's going to happen to her, but I know that she will be all right, regardless.

One more thing—when we were children, my sister and I used to sing to Mary on December eighth. On this day in my home country, we celebrate our beloved Mary with singing and sharing of food and sweets. It is a very important celebration for us. When we came to the United States, we lost all that—that is, until we called out to her again that day in the meditation room. (E.K.)[5]

Shocked and overcome with emotional pain, E.K. set about to help her sister open herself to spiritual healing, and her remarkable experience seems to indicate that Mary intervened in the matter. However, it is clear from her account that Mary's apparent intervention did not heal E.K.'s sister once and for all. If she fails to recover, then we are left with the question that Mickey asked Mary in her dream: What's the point? What purpose does the vision serve if not to heal the affliction? We would do well to recall Mary's response to Mickey. She said that *she did not come to eliminate suffering, but to love.* She also indicated that unavoidable suffering can assist us in our spiritual development and that her love can ennoble us to accept the lessons that must come in the inevitable course of living *and* dying.

If we must all suffer as part of being human, then obviously it becomes a matter of how we *live* in the meantime that makes all the difference. *Feeling deeply loved can make all the difference in how we live in the meantime.* Mary's loving presence may not prolong life in every case, but it may effectively forestall the sense of despair and meaninglessness that stalks us during our darkest hours. It is easy to imagine that Jesus felt his mother's love as he prayed alone on that last night.

In our struggle to understand why Mary did not heal E.K.'s sister outright—or at least grant her a reprieve—we might consider other factors that could determine whether her intervention promotes healing of the body along with the undeniable impact on the soul. In several instances of healing in the New Testament, the afflicted persons had to do something in order to complete the process initiated by Jesus. On one occasion, Jesus told the lepers to go tell the priests that they'd been healed; only as they did so did they realize that they had been healed (Luke 17:11–19). In another instance, Jesus told a man who had been blind from birth that he had to go and wash the mud from his eyes before his vision could be restored: "When he had thus spoken, he spat on the ground, and made clay of the spittle, and he anointed the eyes of the blind man with the clay./And said unto him, Go, wash in the pool of Siloam" (John 9:6–7).

Only after complying with the Master's command did the blind man discover that he could see. So one question we might ask following an intervention from Mary or Jesus is: What am I called to do to continue the process that they have begun?

Another reason that the outcome of a Marian encounter may

remain indeterminant has to do with the limitations of her mediational role, at least as it is defined by centuries of Catholic theology and mystical speculation: The church regards her as the *mediator* of grace, not its source. She is our advocate to Christ, who then may *or may not* "consent to be moved" by his mother's request.

The tradition that Mary advocates for our needs when Christ might otherwise refuse "to be moved" has its roots in the account of the wedding at Cana. It was there that Mary asked Jesus to supply wine for the wedding feast.

> And when they wanted wine, the mother of Jesus saith unto him, They have no wine.
>
> Jesus saith unto her, Woman, what have I to do with thee? Mine hour is not yet come.
>
> His mother saith unto the servants, Whatsoever he saith unto you, do *it*. (John 2:3–5)

His resistance and her quiet persistence give us an intimate view of their relationship and how it may have worked to balance Jesus' vision of his future role with Mary's here-and-now human concerns. Her focus was on the immediate needs of those around her, while his was on the purpose of his life and the appropriate timing for revealing this purpose to others.

This dynamic interplay between a spiritual master and the woman who softens his strength for the benefit of others who may suffer for the lack of mercy or love can be found in other traditions. It is probably true that history often overlooks the crucial role that women have played in midwifing a spiritual vision that might have otherwise assumed harsher and less outwardly loving forms.

At a crucial time in the founding of the Tibetan Buddhist

tradition, for instance, the wife of Marpa the translator ensured the transmission of his teachings to his successor, the great guru Milarepa. Without her help, Milarepa would have probably killed himself, or at least abandoned his quest.[6]

When Milarepa came under Marpa's teaching, he had already committed a fatal error for an aspiring devotee: He had used black magic to kill his evil relatives. Knowing this, Marpa assumed an especially harsh attitude toward his student, whom he secretly loved above all the others. He gave Milarepa instructions to build several buildings, and as soon as Milarepa would finish one, Marpa would angrily insist on him tearing it down, saying that Milarepa had not listened to him. To compound the difficulty for his student, Marpa refused to allow Milarepa to attend the ceremonies that would have allowed Milarepa to receive his master's formal initiations. Time after time, Marpa scolded and beat him in front of his peers, and he threw him out of the temple. Later, in private, Marpa would weep because of the stance he knew he had to take.

Throughout this time, Marpa's wife consoled Milarepa and advocated for him. Marpa became outwardly angry at all of this, but his wife's efforts gave Milarepa hope at a time when he was depressed and suicidal. Without her efforts to cushion Marpa's wrath, neither man could have done what he was called to do: Marpa to remain uncompromising in his efforts to ferret out Milarepa's vestiges of personal pride and lust for power, and Milarepa to remain steadfast in his desire to acquire his master's great teachings.

And so we see that Mary and Marpa's wife intervened at crucial times in the unfoldment of two great nascent spiritual movements, thereby assisting the founders in humanizing their work with those who needed their clemency as much as their wisdom.

In some of the well-known apparitions, Mary's communications support this traditional view of her circumscribed but nonetheless essential role in bringing Christ's healing power into the lives of those who suffer. For instance, in the famous apparition at Pellevoisin, France, in 1876, Mary actually admitted not knowing whether the visionary Estelle Faguette would survive her illness. As Estelle lay dying of tuberculosis of the lung and bone, Mary appeared at the foot of her bed and told Estelle that she wanted her to spread her glory abroad *if* she lived through five more days of suffering. Estelle heard her say, "Fear nothing! You know very well that you are my daughter. Courage! Be patient. My Son consents to be moved. You will suffer another five days in honor of the five wounds of my Son. On Saturday, you will be either dead or cured. If my Son gives you back life, I want you to spread abroad my glory."[7]

As we are accustomed to thinking of such beings as all-knowing, we might puzzle at the fact that Mary could assure Estelle only of the *possibility* of her recovery. We are left to believe that the process hinged entirely on Jesus' will, which Mary could not command. Through Estelle's vision, we experience Mary as the mediator, much as she was at the wedding at Cana.

It is clear in these accounts that Mary knows Jesus but does not command him. In such stories, neither Jesus nor Mary emerges as a mere extension of the other; by implication, the unity between them is constantly reaffirmed by consent. Of course, this is how ordinary human relationships function well: They preserve each person's freedom to choose. If Mary and Jesus appeared to us as one being with a single voice, then there would be no relationship between them that could inform us about the virtues of cooperation, love, and sacrifice that we extol so highly in our relationships.

※

We have seen how Mary's love can give us the strength to face difficulties we may be unaware of at the time of her appearance. Unaware that her mother would soon become seriously ill, a woman experienced a vision of Mary in an orb of light.

If I may be allowed, I would like to share an experience I had. Although it occurred almost twenty years ago, it has remained as powerful and influential an experience as if it was happening now.

I was on the edge of a cornfield just at the entrance to a forest. I loved that hidden corner, and I went there often to sit on the earth, surrender my cares, and melt into all being, so to speak. This particular time, I felt a presence just above me, so I raised my eyes. As I did so, it seemed as if my whole consciousness—indeed, my whole being— was raised to a higher level, as if vibrations became conscious, or I of them. There was an incredible buzzing sound, and I was intensely aware of the rapid vibrations of absolutely everything. It was as if everything was vibrating at a very high speed.

On a tree branch just above me, I saw a circle of light begin to form. The light concentrated more and more while at the same time radiating outward. Then in the center of that light I saw Mary. She was small and she moved along the branch toward me. The power and intensity of the apparition were phenomenal, so much so that my mind and being could not contain the experience. Mary hovered on or just above the branch for a few seconds and

*then either she disappeared or my mind snapped out of a
level of being able to attune to her. Seconds later, a deer
came out of the woods (I had never seen a deer there) and
came very close to me before darting away.*

*I was left limp, yet totally awed by the majesty and
power of this visitation, which I knew in the core of my
being was directly from the higher realms. My body shook
with amazement, fear, and ecstasy. I was afraid—not of
Mary, who was so unconditionally loving while being om-
niscient—but of the* power *of the energy. I knew if I were
not insulated by my openness to her, so to speak, I would
have burnt up right then and there.*

*A few months later, my mother was diagnosed as being
in the very advanced stages of cancer, and my family was
plunged into the agony of her suffering and of having to
shift our entire worldview. It was then I knew why Mary
had come to me. She had come to protect me, to be a
comfort and reassuring essence, to pour love into me as I
went through a terribly, terribly shattering phase of my
life.*

*Since that experience, Mary has come to me often. She
has never returned as an outer vision; rather, she appears
to me in times of meditation or visualization. Anytime I
need a nurturing, loving, completely understanding presence, she is there for me. I trust she is here always and will
be my guide and companion whenever I am desperate,
confused, or terribly unsure. I feel absolutely sure that
everyone is under the wings of her love and protection, and
I feel very blessed to know this consciously. (A.T.#2)*

A.T.'s experience with Mary suggests that while her presence
instills a lasting sense of peace, the gift is often commensurate

with the challenges ahead. Just as so many people report receiving a financial windfall just prior to unanticipated losses, it is as if Mary comes to prepare us and insulate us against the loss of hope that could easily befall us at times of crisis and despair.

A.T.'s encounter with Mary parallels the reports of many of the well-known apparition visionaries, who typically describe an electrified atmosphere and a radical shift in awareness just prior to Mary's actual appearances. The children at Fatima heard a clap of thunder before they saw her approach in a cloud of light and settle upon the branch of a tree. And former priest and healer Ron Roth was literally knocked off his knees by Mary's presence during his first visit to Medjugorje (see page xiii). The power of her presence is a well-recognized feature of Marian encounters.

My own limited experience bears this out. For instance, just the other night I dreamt I was with Mickey Lin and our friend M. B.[8] We realized that Mary was about to appear. As we watched a particular place where we believed she would manifest, I felt my mind suddenly open up to her. The atmosphere around us became electrified, and the influx of her love and power was nearly overwhelming. As she began to appear to us, I cried out in joy, "Mary!" And then I awakened, knowing once again that I probably would have seen her if I'd remained silent! Nevertheless, I experienced communion with her for a moment, and such moments I shall always treasure.

People who are unfulfilled in their marriages may eventually consider the question of whether to stay and make the best of it or to end the relationship. With few legal and societal obstacles to divorce, many opt to follow the dream of a better life on their own or with someone new. As a therapist, I have come to believe that each situation is different; although people may judge a person's choices, each person's requirements for growth may differ from the needs of the people who wish to guide him. Ultimately, ending a marriage can be a very lonely and difficult decision. The contributor of the following account knew this all too well.

The last line of the song "My Rosary" reads "to strive at last to learn to kiss the cross." That line captures an almost fatalistic willingness to accept the will of God. In 1956, I had an experience that gave me an opportunity to do so.

It was March, and a stormy March at that, when my wife and I began having sexual problems due to her illness. We were on the verge of breaking up when I was practically forced to accept an out-of-town job.

One stormy night, I had gone to bed in the hotel where I was staying, when an area-wide power failure occurred. Not knowing this, I awoke, to find my room flooded with light. I looked around and I saw our Blessed Mother half-seated on the low dresser beside my bed. She was dangling a long rosary from her right hand, with the crucifix lying on the backs of her fingers.

Not really believing my eyes, I propped myself up on one elbow, but the vision was still there. She never spoke a word. She merely extended her hand. I was somehow directed to kiss the cross, and I did. Then she smiled—a benediction—and disappeared. The light was gone, too. Needless to say, I found it very difficult to sleep. I lay and thought and tossed.

I would have dismissed the whole thing as a dream,

except for one thing. The next morning, the owner of the hotel stopped me as I came down the stairs and asked me about the brilliant light in my room. Doubly shaken, I told him it had to be my lantern, and he was satisfied with that. He had been on the street, asking a utility crew how long the blackout would last, and he had seen my room ablaze with light.

It happened that the job finished in a few days, so I returned home—without any notion of separating from my wife. For almost thirty years, I nursed my wife, but at last she died.

That event changed my whole life. From that night, I have remained a dedicated servant of those who need help. I do not do this in an organized fashion; I simply serve those whom I encounter in my everyday life. To these people, I have dedicated my whole being. I give without thought of recompense. I just give. (C.H.)[9]

C.H.'s response to Mary's offer of the cross was twofold: to accept the hardship of his relationship *and* to experience the joy of surrendering to a path of service. Consequently, he apparently remained free of the regret and resentment that often accompany a decision to remain in a difficult relationship.

We might conclude that Mary appeared to C.H. to encourage him to remain in his marriage. Perhaps so. However, his willingness to kiss the cross might signify a more important and fundamental commitment. His act of submission may have cemented a relationship *with Christ through Mary*, which, from that moment, superseded any other relationship, including his marriage. From this point of view, his compliance with Mary's invitation bound him to Christ but freed him to choose his course in life without risking the loss of his relationship with God. By the same token, it empowered him to undertake willingly a difficult course of action that might have seemed excessively self-sacrificing from a less spiritually committed point of view.

In Catholic theology, Mary always points to Christ, and she stands just below him in the heavenly hierarchy as our advocate before him. But on another level, she gives us something from herself, as well—her own unique *experience*, which can inspire us and console us as we experience the heights and depths of earthly life. From the following account of a Marian encounter, we can see how Mary's *empathy*, born of her own experience, can foster healing during times of greatest loss.

> *I lost my father one year and one day ago. Since then, I have prayed the rosary more devoutly, but I recited it weekly with a group prior to my loss. As part of my Catholicism, it is customary to offer up one's Holy Communion to a departed loved one, or to those souls in purgatory. So, on one occasion, I was in line to receive Communion. I was third in line, and a statue of Mary stood off to my left. As I silently offered to my father the Communion I was about to receive, I heard very clearly an aged woman's voice say, "I lost someone, too. I lost my son."*
>
> *At that very moment, it was my turn to receive Communion, and my eyes looked upon Jesus on the cross. I knew then who had spoken to me.*
>
> *Several days later, as I prayed the rosary over my daddy's grave, I saw tears falling on the grave marker— and they were not mine.* (K.C.)[10]

As Mary comes to us—in our own experiences or through the heart-opening accounts of others—it may seem surprising that she holds out a cross for us to kiss, or a grief to be remembered. But through her presence, we learn that suffering has a place in our development, just as it had a place in her life as the mother of Jesus. We, too, apparently must learn that there is always something to take up, and always something to give up, before we can fully accept the greater destiny that awaits us.

The other night at our rosary group, we considered the Sorrowful Mysteries—those events leading up to and including the Cruci- fixion—as we prayed the rosary. Many of us were moved to tears as we contemplated Jesus' last hours and his mother's vigil at the foot of the cross. One woman, A.G., who has encountered Mary on several occasions, had a vision of Mary coming into the room in a bright white mist. She was dressed in gray and was visibly sad, but she went around the circle, blessing each of us before she disappeared in the bright mist. Another woman, M.B., saw nothing, but she experienced Mary's presence nonetheless. She sat alone after the meditation was over. I went over to her and asked her how she was doing. She could hardly speak. She was in a state of profound gratitude, but she was deeply saddened, as well.

"She was here tonight, and I can still feel her presence," she said with barely controlled emotion. "She came to say good-bye to her son.

"I don't know how she did it," she said.

And I said, "Neither do I."

Consecration Prayer to the Immaculate Heart of Mary

Oh, Most Pure Heart of Mary, full of goodness, show your Love towards us. Let the flame of your heart, Oh, Mary, descend on all people. We love you immensely; impress on our hearts true love so that we long for you. Oh, Mary, gentle and humble of heart, remember us when we sin. You know that all people sin. Grant that through your most pure and motherly heart we may be healed from every spiritual sickness. Grant that we may always experience the goodness of your motherly heart and that through the flame of your heart we may be converted.

The Way of Surrender

Those who go on are the great and strong
spirits, who do not seek to *know*, but are
driven to *be*.

Evelyn Underhill

In addition to physical and emotional suffering, another kind of ordeal awaits many people who follow a spiritual path. This form of suffering afflicts us most intensely when, after having chosen to give ourselves more fully to God, we are made aware of old attitudes and behaviors that compromise our capacity to serve. While various character weaknesses may have posed no particular impediment to us in the past, they now threaten to undermine the more exacting commitment that we have made. In response to our need to become aware of and resolve these disabling attitudes and behaviors, Jesus and Mary may come to us as loving but stern taskmasters who challenge us to let go of much of what we once considered acceptable.

Mickey's son, Jeff, was only fourteen at the time of his three visions, but he had already evidenced a level of spiritual commitment unusual for a teenager. He had served as an altar boy in the Catholic church and had begun meditating on his own. He was known among his friends as someone who would give the shirt off his back to help them. As a consequence, perhaps, he "qualified" for the kind of wake-up call usually reserved for those of us who have had more time to erect barriers to our relationship with God.

As Mickey and I sat down for supper with our two boys almost two years ago, the subject of spiritual experiences came up. Ryan had told us several months previously that he had dreamed of encountering Jesus in the hallway outside his bedroom. This time, however, it was Jeff's turn. He nervously told us about his first vision. He said he had been awakened in the middle of the night by a radiant presence at the foot of his bed. He was scared and tried to hide under the covers. But the being, who appeared to him as an angel with wings and all, told him not to be afraid of her. She went on to encourage him to face up to his fears, and to be careful.

A few weeks after sharing his first experience with us, Jeff encountered another presence at the foot of his bed. He and his girlfriend had argued the night before, and he had gone to bed upset. As soon as he fell asleep, he became aware of a dim light in the room, so he opened his eyes and saw a light at the foot of his bed. This time, a male voice told him, once again, to face his fears, and to be ready for someone to come into his life.

Jeff wondered if the voice meant another girlfriend! But then, two months later, he realized that the angel had been referring to someone else.

We had driven up to our log cabin in the Blue Ridge Mountains—a place where I have often experienced deep, spiritual dreams. As Jeff fell asleep, he was again awakened by a light that he said shone as brightly as five halogen lamps. A figure began to emerge from within the light. As the figure got closer, Jeff saw that the person was a woman, and she looked just like the ceramic statue of Mary that Mickey had recently made. She looked very alive and real to Jeff. She was wearing a baby blue cape with a hood, and she had sandy blond hair down to the middle of her back. Underneath her cape, she wore a gown with a rainbowlike glitter to it. When she spoke, she told Jeff that he had to face up to his fears. He still did not know what that meant. Then she told him that he always needed to take care of himself and that he should never be afraid of her. She said that Jeff should be returning to church and continuing his faith, which he has done. Then she told him that he had to be ready. He wondered for what. Then he heard "The end." The light then went away and Mary slowly disappeared.

Jeff will doubtless review these encounters as he grows up. If Mary never again appears to him, he will nonetheless reflect on whether he is fulfilling Mary's simple request. The question, Am I ready? will surely come to mind as he faces the various endings and new beginnings throughout his life.

�֍֎

Not long ago, Mickey Lin received a similarly unforgettable calling to remedy a problem in her spiritual life. She awakened in the middle of the night to the sight of a "shield of moving energy" at the doorway to the bedroom. Then she heard a strong voice say, *"Rise, for he comes!"* In her own words, this is what happened next.

> *I felt my astral body rise up in response to the command, even as my physical body continued to sleep. Then I saw the Master on the other side of the doorway, with a very sad expression. I asked him to enter, but he would not come in.*

He said, "My heart aches, for you are swaying from taking the thorns from my heart. Your thoughts dissuade you from my devotion." I felt great shame and sorrow, because I knew exactly what he was talking about.

Immediately, I crossed the room to kneel at his feet for forgiveness. He bent down, raised me to my feet, and embraced me. Then he said, "I love you most for your childlike heart—for loving without condition." This was all I heard in terms of an actual voice, but I understood him to be saying, Your desire for vengeance shows a lack of trust and faith in me. But your continuous desire to love with a wounded heart is a great honor and devotion to my heart.

Up until just before this vision, Mickey had managed to refrain from worrying about other peoples' judgments. She found it possible to do what she believed was right without defending herself from criticism. When criticized, she just let people believe what they wanted to believe about her. At the time of this vision, however, she had begun feeling victimized by people lashing out from their own emotional woundedness. In reaction, she found herself wanting to get back at them. By indulging these fantasies, however, she knew that she had temporarily lost the sense of spiritual freedom and unattachment that had once prevailed. The experience with Christ challenged her to relinquish her need to get back at those who wanted to do her harm. By reaffirming those qualities within her that we associate with Mary, Jesus reminded Mickey of the kind of cocreative relationship that she could have with him—if she could surrender the natural urge to seek revenge.

When we are called by the Holy Spirit to do more with our

lives, it seems that a host of messengers confronts us with the ways that we have compromised our highest ideals. Virtually everyone seems intent on "weighing us in the balance and finding us wanting." This seemingly endless wake-up call can feel like punishment, but the painful process brings blessings in disguise. For the confrontational process helps us to face and resolve the issues—like Mickey's need to get back at her detractors—that stand squarely between us and a more complete acceptance of our spiritual calling. Presumably, some rare individuals are ready to give up everything in their quest for spiritual communion and wholeness. Consequently, they face very little of the struggle that faces those of us who hold on to our old ways. But most of us do not go gently into that process of spiritual surrender. As C. S. Lewis said, we hold back and relate to our spiritual calling like a good man who pays his taxes. "He pays them all right, but he does hope there will be enough left over for him to live on." Lewis points out that the spiritual life is much harder and much easier than that: "Christ says, 'Give me all.' "[1]

The life of the great thirteenth-century German Dominican mystic Henry Suso provides us with a wonderful example of how the Holy Spirit will work with us to illumine any remaining obstacles to our communion with the divine.

Suso was a renowned ascetic visionary—as virtuous as one could hope to be. He frequently experienced ecstatic visions, demonstrated fervent outpourings of devotion, and spent long hours in communion with what he referred to as the "Eternal Wisdom." Evelyn Underhill, author of the classic treatise on Christian mysticism, *Mysticism*, says Suso was "at once artist and recluse, utterly impractical, he had all the dreamer's dream of the world of men."[2]

One day while praying, he felt himself leaving his body, and he encountered a young man. The man told Henry that he had done such a fine job in the "lower school" that he was being admitted into the "highest school." Suso was delighted, even though he did not know what this opportunity would mean. The young man then ushered Suso into the presence of the master, who proceeded to give him a knight's armor and spurs. Being a humble man, Suso objected, saying he had not earned the spurs in battle. The master smiled and said, "Have no fear. Thou shalt have battles enough!" Then the master told Suso to cease performing all of the strenuous disciplines that he had practiced up to that point. From now on, the master said, *he* would administer the tests.

Suso followed these instructions and waited, wondering what lessons the "highest school" would bring him. A few weeks later, the ordeal began. A woman who was pregnant out of wedlock accused Suso of being the father of her unborn child. Suso's previous harmonious existence, free from the burdens of everyday life, was summarily shattered by this accusation. He could not fathom why the woman would accuse him of such a grievous sin, and he struggled with a deep sense of victimization. His passage through this ordeal was ensured, however, by two acts of profound courage. When another woman in the community came to him in secret, offering to kill the child for Suso's sake, he asked the woman to bring the bastard to him, for his curiosity and compassion compelled him to see the source of all his troubles. Thinking that he wished to destroy the child, the devious woman complied. As Suso held the baby, he felt such love that he decided to claim the child as his own and to support him thereafter! Needless to say, this generosity served only to confirm the rumors of his patrimony. Years of turmoil followed, until Suso finally gave up all concern about his welfare. Surrendering all pretense of control over his life, he essentially said—as Mary had said—Let it be done unto me according to your word. Thereafter, his situation speedily improved. Suso's humanity had been awakened and conjoined—through the fires of his ordeal—with his formerly untested saintliness.

Whether we profess to be Christian, Jewish, or Buddhist, it is hard to avoid the fact that giving all is at the heart of every great spiritual tradition. And while the thought of making a complete commitment awakens more than a bit of anxiety in most of us, it may also stir within us a sense of deep relief. Most of us, I believe, can sometimes feel what it would be like to let go completely and follow the promptings of a higher calling. This distant music calls sweetly to us, but reason balks at the idea of this level of commitment and throws up frightening scenarios of poverty, mental instability, social alienation, and emotional deprivation. It doesn't take long before most of us are back to affirming the status quo and giving away only as much of ourselves as it takes to secure a modest sense of virtue.

Eventually, many of us discover that we cannot hide from this calling forever. Just as Henry Suso discovered, the Holy Spirit eventually ferrets out those things to which we cling—those fears, grievances, and self-limiting beliefs that, however trivial they may seem to us, stand in the way of a full embrace of life and communion with the divine. If we are so fortunate, we learn about these barriers in time to do something about them—before we encounter the Master and find, as Mickey did, that we have more work to do before the Christ spirit can enter our lives completely.

In many of the accounts of encounters with Mary that I have obtained in my research, the recipients describe not only encountering Mary "out there" but entering a process of imitating, internalizing, and incorporating her being within themselves. As they move toward a full identification with her, they also must face and resolve the barriers to this transformation, usually in the form of unacknowledged, self-limiting beliefs and fears. In the encounters described in this chapter and the next, we will vicariously experience what it is like to be asked by Mary *to suffer to become more like her* by facing and surrendering these limitations. We will see this process continue in the next chapter to the point where the recipients can reasonably say that Mary now lives within them, through them—and even *as* them.

Mickey Lin's sobering encounter with Jesus pointed out to her the ways that she had failed him by reacting vengefully toward those who had presumably hurt her. But in the dream vision described here, Mary confronted other limitations in Mickey's thinking in a more gentle, even playful spirit.

The financial and emotional stresses of blending two very different families brought us a lot of uncertainties and insecurities. I found myself doubting myself as never before. It is my belief that this is why Mary appeared with a comforting message.

In my slumber, I entered a black swirling motion. In the midst of this darkness, a globe appeared. It looked to me like the view of the earth from outer space. I was mesmerized by the deep blue and green. Focusing on the center, I began to realize that there were two angels kneeling, facing each other. I thought they were praying, and I wondered what they were praying for. Then the most ra-

diant bluish white light appeared between the two angels.
It turned into a fair-skinned woman wearing a white
habit with a blue sash.

This woman smiled at me in a most accepting and
loving way. From this orb of elegance and beauty, she
extended her hand to me and said, "Take this and pray
with me." She handed me her rosary, which was made
entirely of elongated white river pearls. I felt so over-
whelmed by such a beautiful gift. As I marveled at the
gift, I became aware of a troubling thought: I thought
there was supposed to be only one *pearl. I silently told*
myself that all these pearls must be a mistake. That's
when I heard her say chidingly, "Dear child, you are not
one of limitations!"

In a subtle way, Mary conveyed to Mickey a sense of abundance at a time when she was feeling anxious about her capacity
to earn a living. But significantly, Mary did not hand her money.
Instead, she gave her a rosary in which each "rosebud" represents a Hail Mary—a prayer for the abundant grace and protection available to us through Mary. Thus Mary's gift conferred
upon Mickey an abundance of *grace*, from which everything else
presumably would flow. This all hinged, apparently, on Mickey's
response—that is, whether Mickey would join Mary in prayer
and accept the gift.

The pearls may also represent the spirit with which one prays
the rosary. Everyone knows that the mind tends to wander when
praying repetitious prayers. But it is also true that when such
repetitive praying is paired with focused feeling, it can deepen
one's experience of divine presence as perhaps nothing else can.
In the light of Mary's historical emphasis on the rosary in general,

along with her recent messages to pray with much more feeling, her gift to Mickey makes perfect sense: Every pearlescent bead reveals a kind of lustrous beauty obtainable only by applying layer after lustrous layer around a central grain of sand—the same movement that one makes in circling the rosary. In praying the rosary, repetition and concentration combine to make our highest dreams coalesce into observable beauty: The bit of sand that we represent in the greater scheme of things takes on a new identity over time.

When Jesus called the disciples, he presumably did so with a full knowledge of their weaknesses and faults. Still, he chose to teach them and, eventually, to commission them to do his work. When we consider how he chose these men *in spite* of their faults, we have to wonder what it was about them that informed Jesus they could serve him anyway. For that matter, what informed Christ that Paul could become the disciple that he did? We might also ask if something within ourselves overshadows the limitations that otherwise stand in the way of serving him. Are we, like Mickey, possessed of a childlike heart that can redeem our weaknesses in his sight? Or are there other virtues that coexist alongside our weakness of character and will?

A man who had been unfaithful to his wife throughout his twenty years of marriage—and who had rejected God throughout—turned to Mary and the rosary out of sheer desperation. After he prayed the rosary daily for three weeks, Christ came to him in spite of all that he had done to deny Jesus.

I was raised in a very religious Roman Catholic home where devotion to the Blessed Mother was taught. As young children, we would gather together at night to say the rosary with our mother.

At the age of nine, I became an altar boy and eventually entered the seminary to study for the priesthood. Approximately a year prior to entering the seminary, my brother, who was fifteen years old at the time, died of leukemia after a three-week stay in a hospital. His death devastated me. There was no one closer to me, and to this day I still feel the pain of seeing him die in that hospital room. The following September, I began my studies for the priesthood, only to become more acutely depressed. As time went on, I eventually left the seminary. With each day, I became further depressed, with the contemplation of suicide becoming more and more prevalent.

A year after leaving the seminary, I entered undergraduate studies. Along with my depression came anger. I became more and more hostile toward God. I eventually abandoned the church and Mass and began to study Buddhism. My study and practice of Buddhism lasted over fifteen years. Meditation became a way of dealing with the overwhelming pain that existed within me. It was not God-centered, but purely utilitarian.

During these years of consciously trying to eliminate God from my life, my saintly mother continued to poke and prod me into returning to church. On one such day, the fear of God was enough to cause me to return to praying the rosary. My praying continued for three weeks, at which point my life changed.

On this particular day, I was walking through my home, which was empty except for me. As I walked through the dining room, I was suddenly thrown to the floor, and

I began to cry with an intensity beyond my understanding. I then heard a voice within me repeat very distinctly three times, "You can live your life any way you want, but you can no longer deny me." I had the undeniable sense that I was hearing Jesus' voice. This shook me to my very core.

I can't say exactly how long I remained on that floor or continued to cry, but the experience has remained the most profound and transforming incident of my life.

Needless to say, I was not leading an exemplary life by any means. The only part of my life that had changed was the fact that I was saying the rosary.

Today, I am eternally grateful to the Blessed Mother for her intercession before Jesus, where she pleaded for my soul. I live with the truth that the mother of Jesus and her son love each and every one of us beyond our earthly understanding. I have no doubt that anyone who approaches Mary approaches God as well.

I hope that my experience may help others realize that there is truly a loving mother available to us in Mary, who carries us in her arms before Christ, her son. (B.F.)[3]

B.F.'s encounter with Christ took him completely by surprise and left him with a clear mandate to change his life. However, the overwhelming authority of Christ remains softened by his acceptance of B.F.'s freedom of choice; indeed, he leaves B.F. free to do anything *except to deny him*. Perhaps Jesus recognized in B.F.—as he apparently did in Paul—a capacity to serve him in spite of the conscious choices he had made up to that point. Whether this capacity takes the form of a childlike heart or a penchant for radical honesty, it is likely that even the worst of us possess a redeeming quality that the Christ spirit can use in the furthering of love.

⚘

In an earlier chapter, R.S. saw Mary appear over her mother's car and assure her that she would protect her mother on her journey home. This remarkable intervention comforted R.S., but it also cemented a relationship with Mary that perhaps accounted for her subsequent face-to-face encounter with another divine messenger. This time, Jesus appeared to let her know that she was "not where he wanted her to be."

> *It was the early 1980s and my life was in turmoil. I had two healthy children, a nice home, and a husband whom I loved but who was a tormented Vietnam veteran who had turned to alcohol to deal with the war's insanity. He refused to admit that he was alcoholic and would not seek treatment. I was very unhappy, but I lived with the hope that my husband would come to his senses. My needs were not being met; I was an emotional wreck.*
>
> *In the context of my misery, a man from my church approached me to have an affair. He stated that he had been attracted to me for some time, that he had an unhappy marriage, and that he felt that I was unhappy, too. He was charming and made me laugh. I told him that I would think about the situation and let him know of my decision in a few days.*
>
> *The next morning, I was at home alone, as my children were in school and my husband was working. I was in the kitchen, washing my hair at the sink; my head was under the running water. Suddenly, I knew that someone was*

in the kitchen with me. I came up from under the faucet, which was still on. Water from my hair was running down my clothes and onto the kitchen floor.

I turned around, and there, standing in my kitchen, was Jesus! Precious Jesus! I immediately fell to my knees and started crying uncontrollably. I said his name over and over—"Jesus, Jesus"—with my head bowed. His power raised my head up and I saw his two outstretched hands. He said to me, "You are not where I want you to be."

I have never felt such love. I felt so unworthy to be experiencing this visit. His love was so divine that I cannot find words to describe it. I felt his touch in my body, mind, and spirit; it was wonderful! I asked him to help me and to forgive me. Then I became aware that he was fading—that he was moving away from me. I cried, "Please don't go; I can do anything if you are here with me. Please don't go!"

I do not know how long the water had been pouring from the faucet or how much time had passed. I do know that the sound of the running water brought me back to the present. Water was all over the floor and my clothes were soaked. I felt exhausted, and I was in awe of what I had experienced. I also felt sad that he had gone.

At that time, I interpreted Jesus' words to be a message not to engage in the affair, and so I did not. I came to learn, however, that his words had an even deeper meaning. I began to face the reality that I could not live with the alcoholism anymore. I began counseling with my minister and started attending Al-Anon, a twelve-step self-help program for families of alcoholics. I got the courage to divorce my husband and got my kids and myself into counseling with a great therapist who was just the person we needed. Several years later, I reentered college after a twenty-year absence. I started acknowledging the psychic gifts that I had been aware of even as a child. I majored in psychology and planned to work in mental health.

But God had another plan. Today, I am a program director in an outpatient program for substance abuse! I encounter many Vietnam veterans. I have just returned to college again to pursue either a special study in substance abuse or a master's degree; the spirit hasn't presented a clear decision yet.

I know without a doubt that Jesus' words totally changed my life, and are still changing my life. They gave me the courage to change my direction. *And his visit was so precious that I still find it difficult to describe. I repeat, I have never experienced such love. Unworthy as I feel, I know that God has a mission for me, that he saw something in me that I couldn't see in myself, and that he honored me with a visit from his son.*

In so many ways, I feel that I have only just begun. (R.S.#2)

R.S. took a variety of steps on the basis of her visitation from Jesus. Out of a willingness to change the direction of her life, she activated a fuller capacity to serve others. Once again, it is interesting to note that Jesus did not specify what changes needed to take place. He essentially entrusted her with the task of setting her own course. But his dramatic interventions left no doubt that urgent changes were necessary.

Of all the challenges that must have faced Mary in her lifetime, grief must rank near the top. Some people believe Mary knew so completely Jesus would rise from the dead that her suffering was minimal. Most of us, however, probably find it hard to imagine her experiencing anything other than the most severe, wrenching pain as she saw him die. In Catherine Emmerich's visions of the life of Mary, she observed Mary experiencing anguish for the rest of her life because she longed so much for reunion with him.[4]

Knowing that Mary probably suffered immensely, she comes to mind as someone whose encouragement *to cease* grieving would carry tremendous weight. For what better source of guidance can there be than one who has borne a similar ordeal with grace?

The woman who experienced the encounter with Mary described below had become attached to a man who personified for her many of the attributes of Christ, and upon whom she became dependent as she poured out her pain and hopes in letters to him.

I had been corresponding with M for many months. Without realizing it, two things occurred within me that set me up for the rug getting pulled out from under me. I had developed a strong tendency to transfer my needs to him. Also, confused with all I was experiencing, I was turning to him for help and guidance when I should have been turning to Jesus. It was really very selfish and a terrible thing to do to M, and I am very sorry for it. In all fairness and with great respect, he was always gracious, generous, and patient with me.

The thing is, I am a very expressive individual. The Lord has given me many beautiful, expressive gifts. But I have been like a caged and muted canary—always stifled and afraid to sing. But with M's gentleness and kindness—as well as the inspiration of his excellent writings—I felt safe and understood. I believed he was listening and that he cared. But with more than a thousand miles between us, as well as taking into consideration the unbalanced and confused state I was in, I was very out of touch with the reality of his situation or of the nature of our friendship. Eventually, he did the wise thing of saying, "Enough is enough," and he terminated our correspondence. I was very hurt and couldn't seem to stop crying.

So there I was, weeping and weeping. It became chronic. The more I cried, the more it upset the balance of my already-delicate state. I felt paper-thin and oddly disconnected from my body. I felt all control slipping away.

But then one morning in the wee hours, I felt myself waking up. I was very lucid—that is, aware of the bed and the covers. But I was also aware that I was in an altered state of consciousness: There was a sweet, velvety feeling all through and around me. I found myself whispering aloud in a low tone, "Mary! Beautiful Mary!"

Then in my mind, I saw my typewriter. Then I saw the cover being placed over it and it being turned around backward. Next, I heard Mary say, "That's what women are made of—strength and fortitude." It seemed that the experience was now over, and I lay quietly, trying to comprehend what she had meant. But apparently, I didn't understand adequately, because I heard another voice say, "She came to tell you to refrain from pining."

In looking up the meaning of pining, I came to realize

*that it referred to my continual weeping and lamenting,
but it also referred to a habitual way of relating to life. I
often expect myself and my relationships to be perfect here
and now, and when I or the relationship falls short, I
agonize over it. I have found guidance in her message to
me—both for the immediate situation regarding M and in
regard to a long-standing need to address this tendency to
feel victimized.* (K.F.)[5]

Living in the world means eventually losing everything to
which we cling. We like to avoid this sober realization as much as
we can, but if we are honest with ourselves, it lurks behind every
thought and feeling. In recognition of this heartbreaking truth,
Mary has said to several visionaries that they will experience
happiness in heaven but not on earth. With this succinct sum-
mation, Mary conveys what seems like a rather pessimistic, even
fatalistic, view of earthly life from someone who might be in a
position to make a difference. But if we accept that Mary and
Jesus sacrificed much of what the world would consider desirable, even necessary, so that love could prevail, then why would
they expect less of us? Of course, religion that is based on salvation through faith, or vicarious atonement, is based on the idea
that Christ's sacrifice frees us from having to atone for our own
sins. But perhaps salvation *also frees us to do more* in difficult,
challenging situations. Perhaps salvation also means choosing a
meaningful—and perhaps difficult—life as fully as Jesus and
Mary once did.

※※

In the following account of a near-death encounter with Mary, a
woman describes facing a choice between freedom and the task

of taking care of those she loves. Like Mary, she made the decision on her own, and with her heart.

I was lying in my hospital bed—in extreme pain from an allergic reaction to a drug—when Mary appeared to me and motioned for me to follow her. She spoke to me without moving her lips—it was as if I could read her thoughts. I went to her—I was above the head of my hospital bed. I was out of my body, as I could see myself in the bed. I do not remember leaving the bed. At one moment, I was in the bed, and the next moment, I was floating above it. I could also see my husband sitting in a chair to the right of my bed. I had no emotional feeling toward myself in the bed, nor toward my distraught husband in the chair.

I could also see all the rooms above the floor where I was located. I could see down the hallway and into the nursery, where my infant son slept. The view of the hospital floor was much like one sees when playing with a dollhouse: I saw no roof, only several rooms separated by walls. I noticed the room across the hall from mine. It was a waiting room that contained a statue of Mary.

The minute I floated to Mary, I was no longer in pain. I felt nothing. Mary prompted me to follow her up a corridor that was filled with brilliant light and the most beautiful music. I felt completely at peace within myself and total love and unconditional acceptance from her.

The first thing I said to Mary was how very beautiful she was. She had the appearance of a young girl. She was dressed in a full-length gown, with a blue piece that draped her head and fell to her feet. Her feet were bare except for golden sandals.

As we continued up the corridor, I felt that we were going to see God. The corridor made a sharp turn to the left. From this angle, I could see that the light was even more brilliant, and the love that flowed down was stronger than any I have ever encountered. Just before we reached the angle, I told Mary, "No, wait. I can't go with you. I have two kids to care for."

Mary stopped, turned to me, and said, "It won't be easy."

I said, "I know, but I must go back." At that very instant, I was back in my body, again racked with the terrible pain.

That night, a young student nurse came to visit me and brought a tray of things to clean my skin. (In those days, trays with the necessary instruments and medications were wrapped in material much like that of today's Ace bandage.)

We talked at length. She was homesick, having to stay at the hospital and miss the Christmas holidays with her family in Georgia. She especially missed her younger brother. She used forceps to apply medicine to the burned areas of my skin.

The next day, I asked several people about the student nurse, but all assured me that no such person worked in the hospital. *(At the time, I remembered her name, but I have since forgotten it.)*

When I insisted that she was indeed real and had treated me the night before, I was told that no tray had been ordered for me that night. I looked around the room and spotted the tray sitting on the dresser, complete with forceps and gauze pads!

Not only was the used tray in my room but my burns had imprints of the gauze pads! I later learned that the student nurse had been killed in an auto accident years before my arrival at the hospital. After the visit by the student nurse (angel?), my condition gradually improved, and I was released from the hospital about six days later. During my convalescence, I couldn't wait to get better so that I could inspect the room across from mine. A credit to my sanity followed when I viewed the room and it was exactly as I had seen it while floating above the hospital floor.

Mary was indeed right: My life was not easy for many years. I experienced recurring nightmares about the medical experience and replayed the near-death encounter. I carried extreme guilt around with me because I had not been concerned about leaving my husband to go with Mary, as I had been about leaving my two kids.

For years, I was afraid to share my encounter with anyone lest they consider me crazy. I agonized over being "special," as only very special people in the Catholic church's history had been blessed by encounters with Mary. I became aware much later that we are all special. But I couldn't understand at first why I had had the encounter.

I later understood that the encounter was meant to bring me comfort at a very stressful time in my life and that I could/would relay that same comfort to others by sharing my encounter. I stopped worrying about getting out there to share with others, but I have since realized

> *that God will send others to me throughout my walk*
> *through life.* (T.A.)[6]

On the surface, it seems that Mary was dispassionate, almost insensitive to T.A.'s struggle about whether to leave her children behind. Her apparent aloofness appears strange. But then when T.A. decided to return to earth and heard Mary say, "It won't be easy," we hear words that spring from Mary's own experience, which was, we can presume, not easy. In not taking a position, Mary communicated to T.A. that returning to earth was a decision that could be made *only* by her. Given the fact that T.A. heeded her own calling—to take responsibility for those who loved and needed her—it is easy to see the whole experience as an initiation; that is, perfectly suited to elicit a response that would carry her back into life with much more to give. It is a response that affirms life, with full recognition of the price that one must pay in loving.

When I first encountered Jesus in an out-of-body experience, I sensed an overwhelming love emanating from him. And yet he asked me in an almost dispassionate way, "Are you ready to leave the earth yet?" I said no, and it was probably the best response, but I believe that either answer would have been acceptable to him. He did not judge me, but he wanted me to make a firmer decision on the matter—to get off the fence in regard to living fully. When he then said, "Then go out and do what you know to do," he left so much up to me. Once again, he did not seem concerned with anything but the resolution of my ambivalence about being in the world.

When T.A. made a heartfelt decision to return to her life in spite of the difficulties that awaited her there, she imitated Mary, who, likewise, consented to let it be done unto her according to

God's will. She was ennobled by a decision that placed her love for others above her own immediate and complete fulfillment in spirit.

In the following account, another woman, A.T., tells of making a similar decision to live through an ordeal, without distancing herself from the feelings that engulfed her at the time.

> *When my niece died unexpectedly at age ten, my family fell apart. It was a very upsetting time for us, and everyone seemed to react by trying to deny their grief, to block it out and to "soldier ahead." I was simply too overwhelmed by grief to shut out my feelings, so what happened was that I was carrying the grief for the entire family. I was quite unstable, as my family found it necessary to attack me to keep their own feelings locked up. I remember feeling so terribly vulnerable and wobbly then, yet from somewhere an incredible feminine energy came to me and kept reassuring me. I was told by this presence to stay in my body, to stay with my feelings, and to keep grounded. I knew I had to do my grieving in a "feminine" way—that is, by walking through the awful ordeal and embracing the earthiness of it versus cutting it off and "soldiering ahead," the masculine way. This reassuring voice and energy kept coming to me, telling me that it was okay and that someday I would get through the pain and move on, as I have. (A.T.#3)*

By shouldering this burden fully, A.T. brought grace into an otherwise-unbearable experience of loss. In this way, she imitated Mary, whose whole life we associate with a willingness to bring the divine into the human heart under the most heartbreaking conditions imaginable.

From Mickey's encounter with Jesus' wounded heart to A.T.'s willingness to bear the grief of her niece's death, we learn that we are called upon to put aside our fears and resistances and to give more of ourselves than ever before. Jesus and Mary invite us not so much to *transcend* our limiting circumstances as to *enter into life more completely* with a depth of openness and love that, paradoxically, frees us from the pain and constraints that we would ordinarily seek to avoid.

Indeed, this form of suffering contains within it its own antidote: a recognition of the meaningfulness of our ordeal and an unfolding relationship with two beings who embraced the heights *and* depths of human experience as an acceptable and necessary part of loving.

HAIL HOLY QUEEN

Hail Holy Queen, Mother of Mercy, our life, our sweetness and our hope! To thee do we cry, poor banished children of Eve; to thee do we send up our sighs, mourning and weeping in this valley of tears! Turn then, most gracious Advocate, thine eyes of mercy towards us, and after this, our exile, show unto us the blessed fruit of thy womb, Jesus. O clement, O loving, O sweet Virgin Mary! Pray for us, O holy Mother of God, that we may be made worthy of the promises of Christ.

IMITATING MARY

Mary's life is a rule of life for all.

St. Ambrose

The practice of imitating others begins early in life. It is common for some girls to dress up like their mothers and make a mess of things just to feel what it's like to be a grown-up. Little boys pin their fathers' war medals on their chests so they can feel powerful in a world where they are still small and vulnerable. Through this imaginative play, children do more than simply pretend; they gradually become what they imitate.

Just because we grow up does not mean that the urge to imitate others diminishes or becomes less important in our development. As C. S. Lewis points out, these childlike impulses assist us in growing up spiritually, as well.

> Very often the only way to get a quality in reality is to start behaving as if you had it already. That is why children's games are so important. They are always pretending to be grownups—playing soldiers, playing shop. But all the time, they are hardening their muscles and sharpening their wits, so that the pretense of being grown-up helps them to grow up in earnest.[1]

In many of the historic apparitions and personal encounters with Mary, she essentially invites us to imitate her. She urges us to love and to forgive others, to practice prayer and fasting, and to remain in constant adoration of Christ. Indeed, everything that she has given to us—through the biblical record, the well-known apparitions, and the personal visions we have considered herein—comprises, in essence, *a method of imitating her.* Some individuals in particular have embraced these methods and have embarked on an ambitious spiritual quest to imitate her and to serve the one she serves. My friend M.B. is one such person.

When I ran into her for the first time in over fifteen years, I told her about my research into Marian visions and dreams. As we parted, she quietly said that she would be willing to share some of her own experiences of Mary with me. Needless to say, I was eager to meet with her to hear her story. A few weeks later, we met in a café overlooking the Atlantic Ocean and talked about her experiences of encountering Mary on several separate occasions. As she finished talking, she said, "I feel Mary inside of me now. She is always with me."

As we have seen in the previous chapter, individuals who wish to enter into a mystical, cocreative relationship with Christ by imitating Mary must first face and resolve their resistances to a fuller relationship with the divine. We will now consider a few individuals who, like M.B., may already have resolved the significant impediments to their internalization of and identification with the Holy Mother. Consequently, they have entered into a relationship with Mary in which she has become, as St. Teresa of the Child Jesus once said, "more mother than queen"—and perhaps for some, even more friend than mother. Engaged in ongoing communion and identification with the divine feminine, they feel that *Mary now lives in them and through them as their own higher natures.* By becoming one with her, these individuals become wedded to the Christ spirit within themselves, and instruments of blessings in a variety of ways.

Of course, it is a daunting challenge to present their stories succinctly, for their entire lives—not just a single dream or vision—reflect their commitment to a cocreative relationship with God. And that richly moving story is not a simple thing to tell. Nevertheless, what follows are highlights from the lives of such individuals.

⁂

Among the rich dreams and prayer experiences that M.B. shared with me, she revealed a startling memory that she had disclosed to only a few close friends. She knew it was the kind of thing that most people would find hard to accept. But if her recollection seems grandiose from one point of view, it is devastating from another. In essence, she recalled that *God had passed her over in favor of Mary.* Here is her story in her own words.

> *I was raised a Catholic; and at a very young age I felt an intense—even extraordinary—devotion to Mary. I participated in all of the church rituals related to Mary, and I regularly prayed the rosary. Even in later years—before I came to my present understanding and when I was no longer involved with the Catholic church—I still carried the rosary. Occasionally, I would even recite it.*
>
> *When I was exposed to the Edgar Cayce material on the Essenes and Mary's alleged place among them, she became the pattern I chose for my life. I began to regard her as the example for all of us who wish to conceive and*

give birth to the Christ spirit in our lives. This idea took on new meaning when I actually experienced having been associated with Mary in what seemed to be a past lifetime.

I remembered this experience for the first time during a baptismal service a few years ago. Although I had been baptized as a child, I felt that it was an appropriate thing to do it again—especially since it would be a full immersion.

The minister described the full immersion as an act of surrender. He advised me to lie down in the water and to surrender to the realization of my true spiritual identity.

When I entered the baptismal chamber, there were steps going down into a large pool area. When I saw those steps, something happened to me. I went into an altered state of consciousness—there is no doubt about that. And I suddenly found myself with other young Essene women on a flight of stairs—a place where I knew the Holy Spirit first designated Mary to be the channel of the Christ Child. Needless to say, that memory has since become very, very important to me.

Subsequently, I underwent a hypnotic regression, during which I remembered more about the experience. As I returned to the experience of being with Mary as she was chosen, I also recalled something else—my anger at God for not choosing me. *I wasn't mad at Mary, for she and I were friends.* I was mad at God. *I was angry because I couldn't see that Mary was any better than I was.* And then I realized I had fallen into the error of making comparisons between Mary and myself. *I realized, too, that as long as I was preoccupied with making such comparisons, I was not ready to become a channel for the divine.*

Then, about five years ago, I saw a woman in meditation whom, at first, I thought was Mary. She was dressed in robes, with a cloak covering her head. The lower part of the cloak was covered with feathers. It took me quite a few weeks to figure out that the woman was an image of my own higher self—a sort of a Marian image with an American Indian influence. This synthesis of the two traditions was not surprising, since I lived with Native Americans when I was a young woman.

Since then, meditation has brought Mary even closer to me. She has approached me many times in meditation. Sometimes she'll just appear and silently hand me a rose of one color or another. I know the particular colors have meaning, but I don't always know what to make of it.

As I was going into meditation one day, I asked of her, "How can I help to prepare the way for the return of Christ?" A little while later, she appeared to me in a vision and I saw her roll up her sleeves. It reminded me a little of what the nuns who taught me in grade school used to do—they would often fiddle with their robes when they were trying to get all that fabric out of the way. As Mary rolled up her sleeves, she took me by the hand and led me to a sink where we proceeded to wash dishes together. In that moment, we were just two women doing what needed to be done. *Interestingly, I have an expression that I have used before and since this encounter: "Talking doesn't do it; reading doesn't do it;* living is what does it." *And I always say that if you can't wash dishes with me, you haven't got it.*

Not long ago, I asked of Mary, "How can I be of greater use?" In apparent response to this question, she appeared to me in a clear vision. Instead of answering my question, she asked me, "Are you sure?" It was as though she was asking if I really wanted to know the answer. Because she seemed so serious, I hesitated and did not give an immediate answer. So she repeated, "Are you sure?" And then I said, "Yes," because I knew that I wanted to play a part.

I don't know exactly what Mary was referring to— probably many things—but shortly thereafter, I had a brainstorm and asked author Annie Kirkwood if she would like to come to the East Coast to do some lectures on Mary. We had previously struck up a friendship by phone. Well, Annie said yes, and we ended up doing two tours together on the East Coast. Before we were finished, we had covered eighteen cities. I've never done anything like that, and it came together just perfectly. (M.B.)[2]

One might ask—assuming for the moment that M.B.'s past-life recollection is true—what would have happened if she had been entirely open to the opportunity to bear the Christ Child? Would *she* have been the one who was chosen? Common sense dictates that the process of serving God has nothing to do with a contest. If each of us has the capacity to enter into a state of profound spiritual responsiveness, then any one of us can serve God—if not as completely as Mary did,[3] then surely in ways that spring from our own unique strengths. Of course, there are countless ways that the spirit can use us in furthering the influence of love in this world.

Mary's question, "Are you sure?" reminds us that commitment itself may be more important than the particular direction we choose to take. She seems to say that there is no point in providing answers to our questions unless we are sure that we intend to follow through.

M.B.'s recollection that Mary was an Essene maiden concurs with suggestions made by other sources. The nineteenth-century visionary nun Catherine Emmerich described in great detail Mary's relationship to the Essenes through her grandparents and her more distant forebears.[4] And the most famous psychic of the twentieth century, Edgar Cayce, went so far as to say that Mary was an Essene. While one might dispute these psychically derived claims, Emmerich's visions have received the church's approval; and Cayce's psychically derived insights into presumed past lives have, according to R. H. Drummond, "become part of the most significant data of the phenomenology of religion in the twentieth century."[5]

Mary's involvement with the Essenes would seem to fit with what historians now believe about this sect of Judaism. Conventional historians now agree that the members of the Essenes practiced extreme asceticism and ritual purification in order to prepare for the coming of a great teacher of righteousness. While they were once considered extremists by historians, we now know that their ideas were more mainstream than previously believed. "Scholars originally thought that the Dead Sea Scrolls, with their tantalizing references to the coming of a Messiah, represented the quirky tenets of a fringe sect of Jewish ascetics known as the Essenes. But experts now believe that the texts . . . reflect beliefs widely held in 1st century Judaism."[6]

Regardless of the ultimate truth of Mary's affiliation with the Essenes, M.B. recalled a scenario similar to that described by

Cayce—that several Essene maidens, including herself and Mary, had offered themselves as channels for the coming of the Savior. Obviously, only one woman eventually fulfilled the role of mother of Christ. As M.B.'s distant memory resurfaced, she recalled the anguish that befell her when she first realized that Mary had been chosen. She believes that ever since that time, her soul has brought forward a sense of inferiority buried deep within her unconscious memory. By remembering the experience, she has finally been able to give voice to the question that was previously only a pervasive sense of self-doubt and sadness: Why not *me*?

Ultimately, we must decide for ourselves whether reincarnation is a fact, an erroneous and dangerous belief, or a meaningful myth. Regardless of our position on this matter, M.B.'s anguished recollection captures the psychological dilemma of virtually anyone who draws close to the Holy Family through the imaginary reliving of their experiences. Without sanctioning a belief in past lives, the Catholic church has long supported such vicarious reenactments of the biblical drama—most notably through the Spiritual Exercises of St. Ignatius of Loyola and through the fifteen mysteries of the rosary (see Appendix A). These exercises involve visualizing and reliving the most significant moments in the unfoldment of Mary's and Jesus' lives.

What happens to us when we are willing to enter into these intense experiences? Whether we have lived before or not, we begin to feel what they must have felt and to consider the ultimate questions that they once faced. Indeed, the more we vicariously retrace their steps, the more their willing sacrifices, in particular, bring into question our own capacity to do what they did and to become what they became. How many of us have asked ourselves, for instance, Would I have consented to "let it be done unto me" knowing the disbelief that a virginal conception would have stirred? Or, Could I, like Jesus, have shown such immense compassion in the face of the world's harsh treatment? Or, Could I have witnessed my own son's crucifixion? It is only natural that we ask such ultimate questions of ourselves, for Jesus and Mary were humans, too, regardless of the lofty positions they have come to occupy in our Christian tradition.

The urge to join them—to become handmaidens to the incarnating spirit—may run deep within us all. For instance, another woman shared with me a dream vision that resembled in many ways M.B.'s memory of having prepared for Christ's coming. C.R.'s dream captures the sense of deep inadequacy that may creep in as we consider becoming willing channels of the divine spirit. But it also reveals the culmination of persevering through the gauntlet of doubt and fear—a relationship with Christ himself.

I came across a pyramid-shaped mound that had a smooth, rounded top. It stood in the middle of a vast flat plain. At the base of the mound were many women in long dresses, circling the mound as if in prayer. I noticed that each woman wore a tie, as if the tie had to be worn in order to qualify for membership in the group. One woman stood out, as her tie was different from the rest. It was hand-sewn, whereas the others looked mass-produced. I thought to myself that she probably fashioned her own tie in order to join the procession.

I joined the people circling the base of the mound. They were praying, and I realized that we were circling a sacred mound. It had spiritual significance.

I remember praying the Hail Mary, and it occurred to

me that the Mother of God must have appeared atop this mound. That was why the women were praying around it.

As I walked around, I had a feeling that the Mother of God would soon appear. I was afraid. Then the women circling the mound started to leave. I looked at the top of the mound. I was alone, and I think there was a statue of Mary at the top with figures surrounding her. I grew fearful again thinking she might appear. Once everyone had gone, three joyful women came down from the mound. They actually floated from the top of the mound and knelt beside me. We prayed the Hail Mary. A face that I thought might be Mary's appeared, but it was only a face without a body. It was of a tired woman—not old, but worn by life.

I thought this must be the Mother of God. I wasn't as frightened as before, but I still had a feeling of unworthiness. After all, why should she come to see me?

Then I realized there was more to come. I looked to the sky and saw a figure coming from way off in the distance. It grew larger. Much to my amazement and shock, I saw that it was Jesus Christ. He appeared as a handsome young man wearing a long white gown with a flowing red cape. He had long hair and a beard, as depicted in popular pictures.

This was a jovial, playful Jesus Christ. He danced as he flew through the sky. I was overwhelmed by the fact that Jesus Christ was appearing before me, for me; it was so overwhelming, I woke myself up.

I don't know what this means; perhaps the dream was pointing out an obstacle that I put in my way. Fear, perhaps? (C.R.)[7]

It is not surprising that most of us find it difficult, as did C.R., to believe in our capacity to be like Mary and to welcome fully the coming of the Christ spirit. Whether we feel that we have been passed over, as did M.B., or feel unworthy and afraid, as did C.R., most of us remain convinced that ultimately we are different from and inferior to Mary and Jesus.

Of course, we have had help in developing this pervasive and largely unexamined sense of inferiority. Before the time of Christ, God was considered separate and far off from us. He resided on the mountaintop or in the temple, but not as a presence within us. Through Jesus, God presumably reached out and became one of us. But can we, in turn, build the bridge from our side of the great divide and become as he is? Jesus seemed to say that we could and would—especially when he asserted that *we* were gods in the making, that *our* bodies were the temples of the living God, and that *we* would do greater things than even he had done.

This view, which had the potential of endowing all of humanity with unprecedented promise, was opposed by a majority of the church fathers during the first few centuries of Christianity. Why? Because in elevating man, this vision also emphasized Christ's humanity—a fact so disturbing in its fuller implications that it was easier to avoid it altogether. Indeed, as I have mentioned already, most of the so-called heresies that were propounded after the time of Christ merely underscored our kinship with Jesus—through spiritualizing us, or humanizing Christ, or by declaring that we are essentially the same as he is.

For example, the church excommunicated the fifth-century English monk Pelagius (A.D. 360–417) for suggesting that "grace is given to all to enable them to know and choose the good."[8] Today, many Christians would agree that one can freely choose to be good. St. Augustine and his orthodox colleagues, however, found this notion of our intrinsic goodness contrary to the conventional view that we receive grace *only after* acknowledging our sinfulness and our need for redemption. The controversy rose to a fever pitch when a king asked Pelagius to bless his daughter prior to her marriage with some words of wisdom that would assist her throughout her life. Pelagius replied, in essence, that if the woman would look within herself, she would find the goodness that she needed to make wise choices. St. Augustine was so incensed by this presumptuousness that he urged Pope Innocent I to declare Pelagius a heretic. Later, a friend of Augustine's bribed the emperor Honorius with a gift of eighty fine horses to persuade him to send Pelagius into exile.

In stark contrast to the orthodox Christian view that we possess insufficient goodness to lead us to the light, Buddhists and Hindus believe that separation from God is a problem of *perception*, not of fact. The Hindu mantra *Tat Tvam Asi* means "I am that Thou art." The good news is that we are already godlike and complete. The bad news is that we just don't know it. In the same spirit, the Tibetan great mantra, *Om Mani Padme Hum*, essentially describes in a few pregnant syllables the process of the divine incarnating fully in the body and through the human heart[9]—a pinnacle achievement available to us all, according to that tradition. In light of this, Eastern spiritual practices are designed to overcome the *illusion* of separation from that which we seek. But most of us in the West have been steeped in a tradition in which God stands forever apart from his inferior creations. Thus, we are challenged with finding a way of crossing over into the Promised Land, when our traditional beliefs in a distant God and our own unworthiness have a way of barring us from full admission.

One time-honored tradition has been to imitate Jesus. However, because orthodox church fathers like St. Augustine have perennially emphasized Jesus' equivalence with God—and our comparative decadence—Jesus looms much too large for most of us to consider imitating. Indeed, after the church got through elevating Christ to his historic position in the Trinity, the bridge that Jesus had established between humanity and God was seriously undermined.

Because of this, imitating Mary as a way to experience a cocreative relationship with God has become an obvious substitute for the imitation of Christ. After all, she was one of us before and after she gave birth to Christ. It is easier to imagine becoming what she was, for *she assented to her calling from within the context of her humanness.* But alas, Mary has drifted away from us, as well. As the church fathers asserted Jesus' prior and eternal oneness with God, Mary's humanness was similarly diminished, leaving her uniquely imbued with a kind of divinity by association. In declaring Mary free from original sin, the dogma of the Immaculate Conception virtually removed her from our ranks. As Marina Warner points out, Mary's elevation to near-equal status with Christ has definitely had its downside.

> Soaring above the men and women who pray to her,
> the Virgin conceived without sin underscores rather
> than alleviates pain and anxiety and accentuates the
> feeling of sinfulness. . . . Any symbol that exacerbates
> the pain runs counter to the central Christian doctrine
> that mankind was made and redeemed by God, and,
> more important, is a continuing enemy of hope and
> happiness.[10]

Two thousand years of theological speculation about Mary's greatness has ultimately rendered her much too far off and too fine to provide a ready example of how we might resolve our sense of separation from God. But as one Catholic priest recently remarked to a friend of mine, "People don't want theology; they want love." So perhaps it is not surprising that many of us still venture to enter into an intimate, imitative relationship with this being in spite of the distance that organized religion has erected—however unintentionally—between us and her. Indeed, in our private moments, when our prayers are driven more by yearning than theological correctness, we may turn to Mary as an example of one of us who entered into a complete relationship with the divine. In those moments, we may find that we, too, harbor the ageless dream of our own suitability as a partner to God. In knowing and imitating Mary, we may find the best evidence that our dream can come true.

❈

Most of the recipients of the major historic apparitions were shocked when Mary first appeared to them. Even though Lucia of Fatima, for instance, experienced earlier visions, which in retrospect can be seen as preparations for the eventual apparitions, most of the visionaries had no foreknowledge that such blessings would ever come their way. In the following account, Dorothy Cox recounts her experiences of Mary's growing presence in her life. Like those individuals whom we have come to associate with Mary's major manifestations in our time, Dorothy simply did not see it coming.

I had a difficult time growing up. When my father came back from the war, he became an alcoholic, so there were a lot of problems at home. Such experiences certainly send a person on a quest for meaning in life. At fifteen, I was propelled forward to find God, so I decided then that I wanted to become a minister, but my father wouldn't let me. My religious background was Anglican, but now I am open to all religions.

When I was about twenty-one, and after our first son was born, I developed multiple sclerosis. For years, I felt that I would never get well. Late in my thirties, I went to a naturopathic doctor and improved somewhat. But in my forties, I became very ill again—to the point where I felt I would never recover enough to carry on.

When I weighed about eighty-nine pounds and was depleted and weak, I began desperately looking for healing in other ways. It was the beginning of a turnaround.

I had always been quite religious, but I hadn't visited psychics or spiritual healers. But during this time of desperation, I went to a woman who was a massage therapist and worked with healing prayer. After I asked her to intercede for me, she received a message about a Marie who would facilitate my healing and the healing of others, as well. I was puzzled by the message and at first I couldn't see how it related to my healing in any way.

Around 1989, I became very interested in facilitating the healing of others, even though I wasn't completely well myself. I became involved in various healing groups and began to pray for the intervention of the Holy Spirit. I still wasn't making any sense of the reference to a Marie.

About this time, we asked a Catholic priest—Father Cox—to baptize my granddaughter. Thereafter, we went to him for counseling because we were having family problems. At times, he and I talked alone about healing. When I was with him on one occasion, I began to see a flashing blue light filling the room. When I asked him if he was aware of it, he said, "Yes, and there seems to be more here today than usual."

As I knelt for him to bless my work with healing, I felt the energy cover my head. He said, "Of course, you know whose light this is, Dorothy." I said, "No, I'm not quite sure." He said, "It's Mother Mary." I then thought, Marie! Mary! It's another name for Mother Mary!

Since then, several of the people for whom I have prayed have experienced some tremendous changes. One woman, who had been praying every day for a month or more, asked me to assist her in the healing process. As I worked with her, she said she felt as though a curtain parted and a tremendous blue light came through to her. The energy was so powerful that she felt she was on fire. Somehow it brought healing to her. After the session was over, she said, "I'm just burning up." Since we had both prayed to Mary, we attributed the healing energy to her.

Father Cox, who died recently, was very devoted to Mother Mary. One day, I visited him, and again the room filled with such beautiful energy, I thought I would levitate to the ceiling. I told him what was happening, and as he blessed me, I felt a beautiful energy come over me. There was a storm that day, and as I walked home from church, I thought, How would we know for sure if we had been healed? I asked this of the Holy Spirit.

That night, I had the most remarkable dream. I was a child looking for the God of my childhood. As I walked up and down the streets looking for the Anglican sanctuary where I had worshiped with my grandparents as a child, I came to a church that I recognized as the one I was looking for. I went in and entered the inner sanctum, which was filled with icons of Christ. Father Cox then came forward dressed in white.

Then the door of the room opened and a voice said, "I am the open door. No man cometh to me except through Christ." Then Father Cox lifted me up, and the voice said, "Thou art healed."

That summer, my friend Helen told me about the events at nearby Marmora—a farm between Peterborough and Ottawa, Ontario, where Mary has appeared to thousands of visitors. Located in a tiny village and owned by a family who has made many pilgrimages to Medjugorje, Marmora has a grotto and a healing spring. She told me that the Venezuelan visionary Maria Esperanza de Biancini[11] was coming to the farm and would talk about Mother Mary.

A few days later, four of us drove to Marmora for the first time to hear Maria Esperanza. I was quite moved by all the singing and the energy there. When I prayed, I didn't see the deep blue light that I usually see. Instead, I saw a rosy pink light everywhere.

The next day, I was filled with energy, and I felt I had to write. I recognized that it was coming from Mary, so I prayed until the Holy Spirit was with me. I felt that she had a message for me because of my being in Marmora. I wrote down the first message, grateful that she was speaking to me. I wondered, Will there be any more messages? I received a yes for my answer.

About every second day, I felt a surge of energy around my head, and then I resumed writing. When I asked how long it would last, I was told that there would be a total of twenty messages. I prayed every night. Whenever I felt the energy around me, I knew that it was time to write again.

We went back to Marmora on September eighth— Mary's traditional birthday. It rained; then the sun came out. Sue and I knelt in the field and prayed. At one point, Sue nudged me and said, "Look up at the sun!" I thought, Good heavens. I'm going to be blinded if I look at the sun. I tried to look up and I saw it pulsing, but I couldn't keep looking, so I closed my eyes and put my head down. Then I saw a rosy light, and out of this rosy light came Mary. She was dressed all in white, with a blue mantle over her head. Out of her heart came a flashing white light. Sue also saw her in the sun. We were ecstatic on the way home.

A few nights later in a dream, I saw Mary as a white statue. I stood in front of her, naked. I believe it meant that I could hide nothing from her. She knows our hearts and souls more than we do.

When I had the courage to put these messages into a booklet, I thought at first that they were meant just for me. But I was told, "What would be for you would be for others, too."

Even though the messages seem simple, Mary says that she will give us more only once we have done the things that have already been given. In the messages, she tells us to go within to find our inner God-knowing. She urges us to live with our families in love each day, to say the rosary, and to have devotion to her, to Christ, and to God. Further, she wants us to thank God every day for the simple things.

The messages she has given me—such as the one that

follows—are not so much prophetic messages as simple messages about living our lives each day in communion with God.

"Here I do come at this time to prepare the way for the coming of my son, Jesus. Just as John the Baptist foretold his coming to me, I come now to prepare you for him. I call to the lost sheep to come again into the fold of my mantle—to return to him through me. I call to you in love. At times, I weep for the plight of my children and the many difficulties they are experiencing at this time. Here, now, is a time of purification, fasting, and reconciliation to my son through my immaculate heart. I call to all of my children to come to the remembrance of your oneness. For as I look upon your faces, you are all mine." (D.C.)[12]

One might think that the experience of Mary as an internalized presence comes only as a result of a long process of venerating and imitating her. While this may be true in most cases, it may not take very long for some individuals. In the following account, for example, L.N. describes the experience of Mary coming to her for the first time to establish herself as an abiding presence in L.N.'s inner life. In a single encounter that took place after several months of inner preparation, L.N. apparently received Mary once and for all.

My first encounter with Mary came as a complete surprise. During the six months before she came to me, I underwent an isolated period of contemplation and spiritual study. In retrospect, I realize that I was being prepared for significant changes. With more help than I could have ever imagined receiving, dense layers of negativity were lifted, I now realize, by grace and love under the direction of our Lady. With a love that even now I can just barely allow myself to feel, she patiently showered her grace upon me.

I had gone to a meeting with a new friend for the second time. Everyone seemed so advanced and secure in their spiritual paths. We were all instructed to assist one another with healing in whatever way we could. I felt totally out of place, and I was convinced that I had nothing to offer. I sat there in my neck brace and arm brace, and with only partial use of and feeling in my other hand. Even so, I tried to bring in the love and light to help the first two people who asked for help.

When it came time for a third person to receive assistance, I volunteered. I lay down on the floor and tried to relax. The other two people had quickly been able to understand where their problems were coming from and what they needed to do to achieve release. However, I wasn't too sure I could even lie still and breathe, much less know or feel anything except the pain running through my body from the surgery and physical therapy sessions. I called on all of the angels I had sensed hovering around me earlier that day as I tried to paint.

I had never undergone a healing session, so I was calling on anyone I could think of to help me. I took a few deep, relaxing breaths and suddenly remembered how sorry for myself I had felt the day before when I didn't have enough money or any transportation to go to Conyers, Georgia, where Mary was then appearing to the visionary Nancy Fowler.

I then remembered that it was important to ask for

*what we wanted. So I asked to be allowed to go to Con-
yers, and then I let go of the request. I really couldn't
understand why that concern had drifted in to interfere while I was supposed to be calling on my helpers for
healing.*

*I finally wriggled into a more comfortable position on
the floor and began to let go. I started to sense something
totally new and different—yet somehow familiar in a
strange way. I heard the leader announce to those in the
group that they should prepare themselves for a presence
unlike anything they had ever experienced before. She advised them that they should welcome the visitor with open
hearts.*

*I started to get up, thinking that my turn must be over
or that we were doing something new. I was curious as to
who would assist in bringing in this new spirit of love. Just
then, the leader asked me to relax and focus my attention
on my heart. She asked me to feel what might be there
for me.*

*At first, all I could feel was a scared little girl crying
and wanting to hide. The leader encouraged me to love her
and then to release her, which I did. The leader asked if
anyone else was there in my heart.*

*Suddenly, I felt a small, warm, glowing presence inside
of me gently becoming more prominent and apparent. I
focused more and more inwardly to experience this beautiful sensation that was so strange and exciting at the
same time. I felt an inner smile coming up from deep
within my being—a smile I had never felt inside before.
The feeling became clearer and much more intense the
more I asked for it to reveal itself to me. The feeling of pure*

and compassionate love spread all through and around me. My entire being wanted to giggle with joy. I felt the presence of a pure love come up and around me, showering every atom of my body with the most incredibly beautiful silver-blue and golden light I had ever seen. I felt a mother's loving arms holding me tenderly and sending healing into every part of my being.

The intensity and love of this presence continued to flow through and around me, as if I were one with it—or a part of it. I felt deeply cherished for the first time in my life. *Tears of joy streamed down my face.*

I lay there cradled in my true mother's arms, bathed in infinite love and ecstasy, with my eyes still closed. Then I saw our Lady gently overshadow my body. The giggle started to come up from inside me again. I heard her whisper to me, asking if she might speak through me to the group. She told me that she had come to me more clearly in response to my request to be with her in Conyers but that she had always been with me, waiting for my willingness to allow her to be with me. She also said that she had a message to share with the group.

I silently agreed with every part of my being to help her in any way. My silent yes filled me with a wave of gratitude for being alive. The group leader asked for her to tell the group who she was. I noticed that my mouth started moving and the words were being spoken by our Lady.

Then she spoke a greeting to them, telling them that she was our Lady, Mary, the mother of Jesus. She told them that she had come to share the love and light of the Creator with each of them and to encourage them to continue showering their healing and love, as well. She told them how deeply loved and cherished each one was. She told them how special they were and how they could share the gifts the Father had so freely given to them. She told everyone that they all possessed gifts of healing that could be used for the benefit of their brothers and sisters and of the planet. She asked them to follow the Holy Spirit like little children, trusting the guidance within their hearts. She asked them to love themselves as they were loved. She told them that she was always with them and she encouraged them to ask for her help in everything that they did. She then thanked them for allowing her to be with them.

I felt a deepening sense of love and peace cover me in a veil of protection. I felt a deep relaxation and ease in my body. Mary then held me to her breasts. She gently started to leave, letting me know that she was always with me.

As I sat up gradually, I could feel a change within me. My body felt lighter and as if there was a shift in the flow inside of me. The essence of my beingness was not the same. I stood up and noticed a shaking in my knees. Several members of the group confirmed my experience of the words I had heard her speak.

Later that night when I was home alone with my dog, Scarlet, a sense of awe and wonder filled my thoughts. I began to question why Mary would have chosen someone like me to come to and share with others. I lay in bed tormenting myself by recollecting all of the terrible things I had done. I tried to explain to our Lady what a mistake she had made in choosing me. Tears of anguish flowed from my heart as I bared my soul to her. I turned to cuddle Scarlet, fully expecting that the only love I would ever feel or deserve to feel was the love of my furry com-

panion. However, our Lady came to me again and filled me with her love and compassion. I felt her hold me in her arms and gently rock me in the cradle of divine love. She whispered to me that I was truly loved and cherished. She said that she would always be with me and available to me at my asking.

Indeed, she is now always with me—always. *And I know that she is always available to each one of us. You have only to ask her to be with you.* Call to her. Allow her love to open your heart. (L.N.)[13]

L.N.'s experience of Mary's motherly embrace—her unconditional and complete acceptance—resembles the relationship that the visionaries at Garabandal, for instance, enjoyed with Mary over the course of two thousand apparitions. For some of us, this kind of caring may compensate for the deficiencies of nurturance in our lives; for others, Mary's love builds upon the foundation laid by caring parents.

As we have seen, Mary rarely exhibits in these personal encounters the kind of sternness for which she has also become known. She is much more likely to comfort than to challenge, to confirm rather than to criticize. There are several ways to explain this difference. The explanation that makes sense to me is simple: Each of the recipients of the encounters we have examined *were open to her.* They were not closed off and in denial about their relationship with God; they were seeking and open to what they needed to do.

In contrast, when Mary speaks to the world as a whole through intermediaries, she speaks to a very mixed audience, some of whom are open to her and ready to do her bidding and some who are not. Thus we see that she balances her loving messages with stern warnings about what will happen if we fail to mend our ways. However, no matter what we have done before, when we open our hearts to her, we are pleasing to her. As we know, even the prodigal son enjoyed his father's special graces after doing everything wrong; of course, he could receive this affection only after returning home. Similarly, Mary's affection for those individuals who open their hearts to her shows the pleasure that one might feel when a lost child has finally come home.

If we seek to imitate Mary and to incorporate her qualities of tenderness and responsiveness into our lives, we may eventually enter into a profoundly personal relationship with Christ himself. Whether male or female, we will doubtless come to serve the Master as a partner and companion, mystically wedded to his being. C. S. Lewis captures this idea by saying that "what is above and beyond all things is so masculine that we are all feminine in relation to it."[14]

In the final analysis, we are called upon to cast aside our own agendas, to become receptive, and to submit to the Master's purpose and to his supremely affirming love. In the following two accounts, S.E.—whose encounter with Mary is described on page 248—tells about how she encountered God the Father and then Jesus and communed with them in the light.

The reader should keep in mind that these two experiences actually represent the culmination of years of meditation and prayer work through which S.E. incrementally approached this fulfillment. For the purposes of this book, I have left out much of what might be termed the *process* of S.E.'s journey and focused instead on the culmination of her arrival. Of course, such an approach always runs the risk of overlooking the meaningful struggle that typically precedes—and often follows—such life-reorienting experiences.

*E*arly in 1989, I was meditating one day using what I call the "light prayer," and I found myself in a great hallway. It was ornately decorated and elegant as a castle. I was flying or floating down the hallway, passing pairs of angels posted on each side. They were very friendly and encouraged me onward. At the end of the hallway, I saw a double door, separated by a solid piece of wood. The angels opened the door on the right, and I entered.

I found myself in a great hall. It was empty except for three thrones, with three steps leading up to the thrones. Then I started flying from the doorway to the base of the three steps. I was surprised to see three persons seated: God the Father on my right, God the Son in the middle, and my mother Mary on the left.

I was surprised to see what I considered to be a naïve representation of God the Father. From my previous experience, I knew God as the absolute, the infinite, the eternal, the omnipresent source of all of creation. I had lots of direct experience of the magnificent, transcendent God. So to have God sitting there in human form seemed quaint, even naïve, to me. But I had no control over this, and the vision continued.

I presented myself at the base of the steps and knelt. I referred to him as my liege lord, and I was dressed as a knight but without any armor. I swore my faithfulness and promised to do his will at all times.

The Father never looked directly at me. He wore jewel-encrusted slippers and pants and robes made from heavily brocaded fabrics. His clothing was covered with gold, copper, and burnished colors. He wore a headdress that covered his head and blocked a view of his face.

I prostrated myself at his feet in adoration of him, but he reached down and lifted me and had me sit on his lap. I found great joy in discovering his fatherly affection toward me, but I wondered why I could not see his face. Then, as he held me, he turned toward me and I could see him.

His face was pure light—*beautiful golden-white light. He leaned in and kissed me with this light. I was absorbed into the light.*

At that time, I don't think I was aware that the Bible says that you can't see the face of God and live. If I'd read that, it wouldn't have mattered, because in my experience, a direct experience of God supersedes all jurisdictions. Perhaps you would die if you saw his face with earthly eyes, but not, I believe, with eyes of the spirit.

This experience recurred many times in meditation. Then one day, he stood up, dropped his garment, and appeared before me as a shapeless figure of light. Then my garment dropped away as well, and I was pure light, too. I moved toward him and merged with the light. I was still myself, but I was equally dispersed in his light.

Then Jesus and Mary stood up, shed their outer forms, and came into the light, as well. The four of us were as one. They showed me that this was our true nature, that all of mankind is this light, and that all of sin can be erased by instantaneous forgiveness.

This was the most transforming experience I've had, and it served as the basis for all that God has planned for me. This experience of my true nature comes back to me each day as I go through everyday circumstances.

⚜

A few months later, in August of 1989, I returned to the throne room for a slightly different experience. This time, I encountered Jesus face-to-face.

I was in deep meditation and found myself in the same great hall. Again, the room was empty except for the three thrones and the steps leading up to them. I was wearing the same gown I always do, except in my first visit to the throne room I was dressed differently. I was in a floor-length indigo velvet dress. I was barefoot, and my hair was long and loose (whereas in waking life, I have medium-length hair).

I flew to the thrones without hesitating. On the right, I saw the Father; in the middle, Jesus; and to my left, Mary. Jesus stood up and walked down the three steps. He was very handsome. He had long medium-light brown hair and wore a white long-sleeved tunic. It reached his feet, which were bare.

I prostrated myself before him, but Jesus raised me up and escorted me a few steps forward. No words were spoken. Then he turned to face me. He embraced me and leaned forward to kiss me. Just as our lips would have touched, everything abruptly changed. Instead of feeling his lips on mine, my consciousness expanded like a bomb exploding: Everything turned to light. It was wonderful. In that moment, I knew that he had married me and that our marriage would last forever.

After meditation, and for the next few days, approximately every twenty minutes I would feel intoxicated with the Holy Spirit. But it did not interfere with my daily chores. (S.E.#1)[15]

S.E.'s experiences of spiritual union may represent the pinnacle experience of all of us who walk the spiritual path, yearning above all else for reunion with God. Through her experience, she has come to enjoy an extraordinary intimacy with the personhood of God. Some of us might find this uncomfortable. Thinking that God is somehow more austere and impersonal than our best friend, or a lover, we might balk at the idea of embracing and kissing the Lord. Yet the history of Christian mysticism reveals that communion with the divine builds upon, rather than departs from, what we already know about love: It both resembles *and* overshadows our experience of human love. Indeed, even sexual feelings may enter into the encounter with the divine.

I am reminded, for instance, of a Christ encounter in which a woman who was experiencing sexual frigidity in her marriage awoke, to see Christ hovering over her bed, facing downward, with his arms outstretched. She felt deeply loved *and* sexually aroused, much to her later embarrassment. But the experience apparently healed her frigidity![16]

The level of personal intimacy in the encounter with the divine probably has to do with how we normally relate to others—or at least would like to relate to others—and the wounds that we bear from the past. Some people have been so deprived of affection from lovers and caregivers that they carry an unrequited yearning that wells up in any meaningful relationship. For them, the highest spiritual experiences give them a chance to express and to experience love—and thus to heal the wounds of the past—in a way that satisfies their unique unfulfilled needs. Others of us may express this level of affection in all of our close relationships. Whether such expressions of intimacy spring from unfulfilled need or from a characteristic spontaneous openness is hard to determine without probing into personal areas that lie beyond the scope of this book.

In the end, S.E. exhibits a down-to-earth quality that rounds out her spiritual initiations: *Her chores still matter to her.* Like M.B., who learns from Mary that washing dishes serves God's unfolding purpose in this world, S.E. demonstrates an interest in what matters *here and now.* Like all genuine mystics, S.E. returns from the mountaintop, rolls up her sleeves, and embraces the work that lies before her. For her, that has meant supporting a Bosnian orphan, home-schooling two teenage daughters, and working in her own quiet way toward the unification of all Christian denominations.

Imitating Mary means becoming active in the world in a way that uplifts and heals others. Each of the recipients discussed heretofore has turned to some form of a healing ministry as a way of expressing his or her commitment to Mary and to God. It is clear from their accounts that our efforts are crucial in bringing about constructive change in the world and that we must not simply await the spirit's intervention in our lives. In essence, we can see that when we accept the invitation to imitate Mary, *we become that force of change that the world desperately needs.*

The following two accounts reveal the impact we can have on situations that are constantly unfolding in our lives. Both recipients have had multiple experiences with Mary and Jesus and now serve them whenever called to do so.

I awakened in the middle of the night on Christmas Day in 1977 and felt guided to go to my altar and pray to Mary. I remained there for about a half an hour in prayer, when the phone rang at around 1:00 A.M. A friend was calling to ask me to pray for his wife, who was in advanced labor. They were having a home birth and the midwife couldn't get there in time to deliver the baby, so the husband had to do the job. I went back to the altar to pray. White light filled the whole room and the presence of the Mother filled me with waves of powerfully intense but very serene energy as I focused prayers on the birth process. The energy waves subsided gradually as the experience came to a close. Then the phone rang and my friend elatedly announced the birth of his second daughter; the mother and child were both in good health. (C.N.#2)

My favorite place on earth to go when the burdens of the world become too much is the Grotto of Lourdes in Emmitsburg. Here I've had several occasions to hear Mary's voice.

Three years ago, I went to the grotto to thank Mary for a healing. While in prayer, I saw the silhouette of a full-term pregnant woman. I asked Mary, "Who is it?" She said, "Your daughter." I asked, "Is she pregnant now or will she be?" Mary answered, "Pray for the unborn child." Two months later, my daughter announced she was pregnant. I continued to pray every morning and night. The baby was born nine weeks early. He could breathe on his own but had an immature digestive system. Today, he is a healthy, happy, loving child. I feel Mary's vision and words to encourage me to pray saved his life. I have always had a great devotion to Mary and feel she guides my steps. (C.L.)[17]

I consider myself truly fortunate to have met so many people who share a mystical relationship with Mary and Jesus and whose whole lives now revolve around serving them in their individual ways.

These days, Mickey still tells me about her Marian encounters, but I know she finds it hard to describe their richness and subtlety. At this point, I hesitate to ask, for fear of intruding into the most sacred of relationships. Also, I find I have less of a need to know, for a sense of Mary's presence envelops me more and more now—a reassuring embrace that silently informs me of what Mickey would tell me anyway—about the Holy Mother's love for her, for me, and for all of us.

Around the winter solstice, Mary appeared to Mickey again, dressed magnificently in red and gold. Mickey then felt Mary approach her and take her into the comforting folds of her mantle. The next day, Mickey told a friend about the experience, and this friend shared something that we did not know: Mary appears every Christmas dressed in red and gold to the visionaries at Medjugorje.

Someday I would like to see Mary as easily as Mickey and others do, but if we feel the Holy Mother as an abiding inner presence—and if we sense our own unfolding responsiveness to serve as channels of the spirit—then we will doubtless come to know the feminine face of God just as surely as those who see the colors of Mary's mantle and hear her quiet words quell the noise of the mind's incessant chatter.

Imitating her and *becoming* more like her may be all that really matters after all.

ROSARY PRAYER

Oh God, Whose only begotten Son, by his life, death, and resurrection, has purchased for us the rewards of eternal life, grant we beseech Thee, that meditating on these mysteries in the most holy Rosary of the Blessed Virgin Mary, we may imitate what they contain, and obtain what they promise, through the same Christ our Lord. Amen.

9

RESPONDING TO MARY'S REQUEST

Whatsoever he saith unto you, do it.

Mary's words at the wedding at Cana (John 2:3–5)

As we open our minds and hearts to Mary, we begin to realize that she comes to convey a simple request. Whether she remains silent and invites the recipient to *feel* what she wishes or conveys her message in simple terms for a visionary to share with others, her intention never wavers: *She wants us to submit fully to a relationship with God*—to unleash our fullest capacity to love and respond to the spirit's call. Indeed, when Lucia, the principal visionary at Fatima, was asked to summarize Mary's most important message at Fatima, she said, "The main request of our Lady is that we offer up each day whatever God requests of us."[1]

Who among us can say that he has met this challenge? If we could fulfill this singular request, then we would be living fully in service to our highest spiritual calling: *We would be free.* But such complete spiritual surrender remains out of reach for most of us—unless, perhaps, we can approach that state of complete responsiveness through a process of gradual change. Mary's own life demonstrates this process better than anyone else's in our Christian tradition. For if Jesus represents the culmination of the process of God's becoming incarnate, then Mary surely represents the consenting partner who sees the process through to completion.

Not surprisingly, Mary's manifestations to individuals reveal various steps that we might take toward embracing her spirit of willingness and offering up whatever God asks of us. Indeed, if one is ever to meet this challenge, one must embody an array of qualities that when taken together make an assent possible. As a final stage in our examination of Mary's manifestations, I have summarized some of the steps that we can take toward becoming more like Mary and enjoying a relationship with spirit very much like hers.

We Can Commune with Her

Mickey heard Mary say that I had to come to know Mary *through my own experience.* Indeed, Mary has made it clear that we should *all* take these words to heart. She calls upon each of us to accept the *direct* experience of her presence as a first step toward responding to our spiritual calling more fully than ever before. She does not expect any of us to remain on the outside looking in. She invites us to "come under her mantle" and to find a relationship with her that is deeply fulfilling and secure. In traditional Catholic terms, the wearing of the scapular—which represents a piece of her mantle—announces our willingness to consecrate ourselves to her heart and to come under the protection of her love once and for always. Whether we are Catholic or not, the scapular symbolizes something precious that most of us can relate to—*a loving relationship that will never fail us.* But to enjoy this sense of perpetual communion and protection, we must be willing to submit to an intensely personal, feeling-based experience with her. To put it simply, *we must become like her children.* This is where many of us part company with Mary and

Jesus and the personhood of God. For such an apparent blind leap of faith often bears an uncomfortable resemblance to earlier experiences in which other protectors failed us and when our trust gave way to disillusionment.

❧

The other day, I had an unforgettable experience that raised questions in my mind about the relationship between the divine feminine and our biological mothers.

I had taken some time off to meditate at my office. I was not feeling at my best, and I hoped that meditation might restore my lagging sense of well-being. I turned off the lights and sat on my old sofa, knowing that my next client would arrive in about an hour.

Before long, I found myself becoming drowsy, so I fully expected to get nowhere in my search for that clarity that characterizes my deepest meditations. But after about thirty minutes, something unexpected happened to me.

I found myself in a brightly lit place that, for some reason, I immediately recognized from long, long ago—from before the beginning of our time on the earth. Meanwhile, I experienced the purest, most exquisite joy I've ever known. There was a total absence of fear, and I possessed a complete awareness of our origin and our destiny as souls. I knew that I was part of the consciousness that had foreseen everything from the beginning of time and had prepared the way of return to our oneness with God. And, for the span of only a few moments, I seemed to commune with one being in particular—a feminine presence who seemed to be the principle source of my joy.

As I departed from that place, the only image that remained in memory was that of a woman's breast. *And then, I was back on my office sofa, but the experience was not over. A wave of love gently washed through me, and I could feel it working to heal and restore me. Then the experience was over.*

A skeptic might argue that I had recalled nothing more than an early experience of nursing at my mother's breast. However, such images play an important role in spiritual experiences: They evoke powerful emotional memories that can serve to amplify and deepen our experience of spiritual realities. During the Middle Ages, the faithful thought nothing of speaking of Mary's milk as a symbol of God's grace. Indeed, church-sanctioned paintings often portrayed Mary issuing milk from an exposed breast.

While we might cringe at such graphic images today, our experience of our biological mothers represents our first encounter with an all-powerful other who can either take us under her mantle or cast us out. As we pass through this early emotional exchange with our mothers, we emerge from infancy somewhere between two extremes: believing, on one hand, that those we love will always stand beside us, and convinced, on the other, that betrayal awaits us at every turn.

Ultimately, perhaps we all bear some wounds from childhood that keep us from receiving God's love without recoiling out of fear or a sense of unworthiness. Marion Woodman has said that the inner child is, and will always be, an orphan. If, as this suggests, we all carry some degree of perpetual insecurity, then how can we hope to submit to the Holy Mother's embrace?

With this in mind, I have often puzzled at others' capacity to open themselves to Mary when their relationship with their own mothers has not been secure or happy. If we are deprived of early nurturing experiences, then where can we find the trust that we need to have a relationship with Mary or Jesus—or anyone for that matter whose power over us might awaken old fears of desertion or betrayal? Obviously, many of us manage quite well in spite of the lack of early nurturance from our parents. In such cases, it could be that others have provided the love that we needed along the way. Even in the absence of such parental surrogates, the emotional problems that remain between ourselves and our parents can, in many cases, be resolved through a combination of prayer work, therapeutic exploration, and healthy interpersonal discussions.

Not surprisingly, our first attempts to commune with Mary can bring us face-to-face with this unfinished business with our parents. *We may not be able fully to receive the Holy Mother into our life until we can face and resolve our unfulfilled feelings toward our human parents.*

A story concerning the great Tibetan yogi Milarepa provides us with a poignant example of how our unresolved issues with our parents may fiercely assert themselves just as we are making our greatest progress on the spiritual path.[2] Milarepa had been a devotee of his teacher Marpa for several years, whereupon he entered a period of seclusion for his advanced yogic practice. Marpa had taught Milarepa everything that he himself had mastered, but it was time for Milarepa to take the next step on his own. In accordance with the tradition at the time, Milarepa allowed himself to be sealed in a cave, and he received his food and water through a small opening in the temporary wall. One night, however, the memory of his mother came flooding back to him. Having heard nothing from her in years, Milarepa suddenly had to see her. Without further hesitation, he broke down the wall of his cell and went to plead with Marpa to allow him to go back home. Marpa granted Milarepa his freedom, knowing that he would never see his successor again. Marpa and his wife spent their last night with Milarepa crying and holding one another until the sun rose on their last day together.

When Milarepa arrived at his childhood home, it lay in shambles. He found the remains of his mother—a mere pile of bones—stacked on the floor of the once-grand manor house. The villagers had been so afraid of Milarepa's reputed psychic powers that no one would enter the house to dispose of his mother's remains properly. Crushed by his grief, Milarepa slept on the floor beside his mother's bones.

This heartbreaking experience deepened Milarepa's commitment to the path of unattachment to the world, and for years he lived as Buddha had once lived—deprived of all comforts and worldly possessions, eating only wild nettles and an occasional gift of food from hunters. In time, however, he left such extremes behind and reentered the world as a powerful teacher who had known both the heights and depths of human experience, and whose memory of his mother's loss doubtless impacted his spiritual unfoldment just as profoundly as Marpa's teachings had.

As we face the challenge of healing our memories from childhood, we might ask ourselves, *How do my relationships with my parents and other caregivers affect my ability to accept a relationship with Mary? What do I need to do to resolve any problems that could spill over into my relationship with the divine?*

We Can Engage in Regular Spiritual Practice

My friend and spiritual mentor, Hugh Lynn Cayce, used to say that we really have only one choice in life—to pray and meditate or not to pray and meditate. Referring to prayer as *the practice of talking to God* and to meditation as *the practice of listening to God,* he considered everything else to be, by comparison, an unfree choice. He was also fond of saying that we already knew too much and that it was high time for all of us to engage more diligently in spiritual practice. Transpersonal theorist Ken Wilber concurs with this idea when he says, "Practice is everything."

In every major apparition, Mary has urged us to engage in daily spiritual practice. Above all, she recommends the recitation of the rosary, a practice that is still foreign to most non-Catholics. In several of the apparitions, the visionaries have observed Mary wearing the rosary beads on her wrist. Beginning with Bernadette's encounter with Mary at Lourdes, many visionaries have even recited the rosary along with Mary during the apparition. And in many of the personal visions that we have considered, Mary wears the rosary, or offers it to the recipient to be used in that person's spiritual practice. As the reader may recall, Mary offered her rosary to C.H. to be kissed at a time in his life when his commitment was wavering (see page 171). Of all the features associated with Mary's appearances, the rosary is the most prominent symbol of the *spiritual practice* she wants us to engage in.

Of course, the rosary is a rather pure devotional practice, not an intellectual exercise. As such, many people have associated it with a kind of unthinking faith. There is a true story about a young man who boarded a train near Paris one day and sat beside an older man who was quietly praying the rosary. After some time, the young man pompously addressed the older man and told him that this was the age of science and that great changes were afoot. Consequently, he said, such practices as reciting the rosary were no longer relevant. The older man listened respectfully without objecting to the younger man's opinions. As they parted, the younger man introduced himself, only to find that the "backward" gentleman was none other than the great scientist Louis Pasteur.

Indeed, the rosary has been associated with many of the intellectual and spiritual giants of the church. According to legend, Mary appeared to the founder of the Dominicans, St. Dominic, in the early 1200s and gave him the first rosary, saying, "This is the precious gift that I leave to you."[3] Because Dominic spent so much of his life teaching the virtues of the rosary, it is understandable that legend credits him as the person to whom Mary first gave the rosary. Actually, however, the rosary evolved into its present form over the course of many centuries. Well before the rosary as we know it fully emerged in the 1500s, ninth-century Irish shepherds used to carry rocks in their pockets and would toss one of the rocks away as they counted off their prayers. Further, as early as A.D. 500, St. Brigid of Kildare was known to pray using a string of little wooden or stone beads.

(For the benefit of readers who are unfamiliar with the rosary, I have outlined the standard approach to reciting the rosary in Appendix A. I have also included the traditional prayers that are most commonly used and have suggested ways of altering the recitation of the rosary to conform with your own needs.)

While the *content* of the various traditional rosary prayers may provide unique time-proven benefits, the *disciplined practice* of reciting the rosary—at least in some individually tailored form—may constitute an equally important addition to one's spiritual life.

Indeed, Conchita said at Garabandal that Mary never cited the advantages of particular prayers when she spoke of the importance of reciting the rosary; it was the practice itself that was most important. Father Pelletier believes that when Mary emphasized the *practice* over the selection of the prayers, she was "attempting to reach the broadest possible number of souls and therefore did not want to propose a form of prayer that would definitely go beyond the reach of some and that could easily discourage many others."[4]

Beyond advocating the disciplined recitation of the rosary, Mary also emphasized *how* one should recite the rosary—that is, with deep feeling and careful concentration. To this end, she recommended praying *slowly*, with emphasis on each word, and pausing between phrases. Onlookers who succeeded in overhearing Conchita and the other three girls praying the rosary along with the apparition were impressed with their slow, careful enunciation of each word. By having them pray in this way, Mary assisted the girls in recapturing the meaning of the prayers, for such meaning is so easily lost in the hasty repetition of familiar words.

From a different tradition, but addressing the same issue, Tibetan Buddhist Lama Govinda asserts that the key to a rich meditation and prayer life depends on rediscovering the power of words to evoke ineffable experiences. Govinda points out that the word "in the hour of its birth was a center of force and reality, and only habit has stereotyped it into a mere conventional medium of expression."[5] By focusing on *how* we recite the words, says Govinda, we can tap the deeper meaning behind familiar prayers and sacred passages—and make old forms come alive again.

We might ask ourselves, *What form of spiritual practice am I called upon to do? Do I need to adopt Mary's precious gift of the rosary, or breathe new life into my own familiar practice by going about it in a more deliberate, conscientious manner?*

We Can Take Bold Steps to Change Our Lives and to Make a Difference in the World

From the evidence that these accounts provide, it should be clear to us by now that Mary sometimes intervenes to steer us in bold new directions. She comes not only to invite us into her protective embrace and to engage us in spiritual practice but also to illumine our individual and collective denial of what we are doing that can, in time, precipitate disastrous consequences.

In many of the major apparitions, Mary indicates that we must work diligently to atone for our collective choices if we wish to avert an eventual worldwide chastisement. Fortunately, Mary brings us the good news, as well: that individual prayer and meditation, and other "microcosmic" gestures of love, can exert a powerful impact on our collective fate. A few of us can apparently make all the difference in the world.

As a psychotherapist working on the level of the individual psyche, I have also come to realize that we each face our own individual chastisements, if you will, if we remain in denial about the need to make significant changes in our current relationships, careers, and personal behaviors. Of the many personal encounters with Jesus and Mary that I have studied, *not one* of them addresses the possibility of a worldwide catastrophe. But many of them—especially those encounters with Jesus—mention, or at least bring to mind, unresolved *personal* issues that stand in the way of a closer relationship with the divine and our fellow human beings. A few of them even call for immediate action in order to avert tragic personal consequences. Like the Holy Family, which was warned by the angel to flee Herod's soldiers, we, too, may need to take firm and dramatic steps to protect what is most precious to us from the consequences of our own choices—or from the destructive intentions of others. As sobering as these encounters may seem at first, they may wake us up before it is too late.

The reader may recall that one recipient, R.S., saw Jesus appear to her in her kitchen and he said, "You are not where I want you to be" (see page 189). Like so many of the brief messages uttered by Mary and Jesus in other encounters, we can apply these words to ourselves. For how many of us can say that we are where they want us to be, or doing what we need to do? In the following story, one man tells how he finally found the courage to act decisively after Mary appeared to him in the midst of a crisis.

*M*ary *came to me during a time of crisis for me.*

A couple moved into apartment next door to us in June of 1995. On June nineteenth, it became evident that the woman was being physically abused. It happened on that night, and once again in July. Then it began to increase in frequency, until it was happening two to three times a week in September. Every noise coming from the apartment would send me into a panic. I would just freeze and not be able to move, and I would shake with fear. Even though I heard horrible screaming, I could not move to call 911. Each time after the screaming stopped, I would lie awake—sometimes for hours—hearing the woman screaming inside my head.

I got to the point of not wanting to go home at the end of the day. I didn't want to sleep. I was a bundle of nerves at home, irritable because of lack of sleep. Looking back, I can see that my wife and I were like the couple in the commercial for ending domestic violence who would turn out their light instead of calling the police to intervene next door. I began to pray and meditate, with the intent of finding an answer. But for months, my wife and I remained in denial of our need to do something.

Through my prayers to God and Mary, the beginning of an answer came to me. One night in September of that year, I had a dream that I woke up very suddenly. Mary was hovering at the foot of my bed. She appeared to be sitting Indian-style, dressed in light blue and surrounded by white light that filled the entire room. She said nothing, but she put her hands together as if in prayer and told me telepathically to pray for the world and for the current crisis in which I found myself. She said that an answer to the problem would be given to me.

The abuse happened again, and again I did nothing. I continued to pray and meditate and received the same message inwardly. Then the abuse happened again. Without even thinking, I ran to the phone and called 911. Then I called our apartment manager and urged him to take action to stop the violence.

I knew then that the answer for me was to take action—to do what I could to end the suffering. Mary moved me to take control of my life to end my own pain. I could only do that by asserting myself to stop the abuse. Yet throughout, I knew that it was also important to have compassion for my neighbors, who were in crisis. (D.S.)[6]

As we enter into a closer relationship with Mary, we may find that we, too, are called to *act decisively and boldly to make a difference in this world.* In anticipation of such a calling, we might ask ourselves, *How am I not where I need to be? What bold changes must I make to unleash my greater capacity to serve my spiritual calling?*

We Can Remove the Barriers to Responding to Our Calling

As the reader may recall, M.B. felt angry that God had passed her over in favor of Mary (see page 202). In her alleged past-life memory, she felt ready to bear the Christ Child, and yet she engaged in a kind of jealous comparison making that hindered her responsiveness to the spirit's call. If we honestly scrutinize our own attitudes, we might find that we, too, labor under real or imagined errors in thinking that impede our openness to the spirit. Fortunately, most of us are not world-class sinners. We are not like the great Tibetan guru Milarepa, who began his adult life using his prodigious psychic powers to kill his evil relatives, then spent half a lifetime making up for it.[7] No, when the call comes for us to give more of ourselves to God, we are likely to face less grievous sins standing in the way. Indeed, for many, if not most, of us, *self-limiting beliefs, grievances, and fears* pose as much a barrier to our capacity to serve God as any other form of real or imagined sinfulness. Ferreting out these internal constraints requires the utmost in honest self-scrutiny, and it may even require some form of therapeutic process in order to get around our penchant for hiding the sobering truth from ourselves.

Last year, for instance, I had to face the fact that I was carrying a great deal of resentment for persons who I believed had judged me unfairly. I was refusing to "take the thorns" from the Master's heart, and my spiritual life was suffering. So I began praying for purity of heart to assist me in letting go of old grievances. Fortunately, I believe that Mary intervened to help me let go of this unnecessary preoccupation. I found out about this, once again, from a friend who witnessed Mary coming to me during our rosary group. Significantly, she knew nothing about my struggle to purify my heart.

During the meditation, I saw a bright light enter the room. As it cascaded down ever so softly, I saw the Holy Mother appear in the center of the light, wearing a gray dress and soft white veil that cascaded down over her body. She was so lovely. Her feet were bare and never touched the ground. A great sense of peace came over me, and tears flowed down my cheeks.

She held a red rose and smiled as she walked around the group, touching the top of each person's head in some form of blessing. As she seemed to levitate around the group, she suddenly stopped in front of Scott. Her rose turned pure white as she touched his heart three times. I could see her mouth the words, Purity, purity, purity. *Then her rose turned red, and she resumed touching the rest of the group. Then she returned to the center of the room, smiled, and just faded away in the light.* (A.G.)[8]

I have found that no matter how much spiritual assistance we receive, we still have to do our part. It is an ongoing, daily process. Today, Mary has become a source of love and reassurance to me. I can almost always feel her near to me, and sometimes I think I may eventually see her appear. But I must still *choose* this gift of her loving presence rather than giving in to the obsessions and worries that rise up to claim me.

We might ask ourselves, *What limiting attitudes and beliefs prevent me from opening up to her presence right now?*

We Can Accept That We Are Worthy

Many of us often fall prey to one erroneous belief in particular that effectively prevents us from receiving the full measure of God's grace: the conviction of our own unworthiness. I have found in my work with dreams and mystical experiences that many of us reach the threshold of an ecstatic experience of the divine in deep dreams and visions, only to stop short of accepting the light fully. Why? Because in the critical moment when we are called upon to receive the ultimate gift, the conviction of our unworthiness asserts itself. One woman, for instance, dreamed that Jesus came knocking on her door. Believing that her house was too messy, she refused to open the door. Like this woman, most of us prevent such life-changing experiences from happening by thinking, Who am *I* to deserve this gift?

It may be true that *the greatest barrier to our readiness for full communion with the divine is the belief that we are not worthy.* Given our penchant for self-doubt and self-loathing, it is not surprising that most encounters with Mary and Jesus leave recipients convinced, above all else, that they *are* loved and that they *are* worthy. The reader may recall that one woman heard Mary say, "I choose you," and another heard her say, "I'm just like you." In a moving Christ encounter, only one woman could see Jesus at a prayer meeting. Like many of us would have done, she asked, "Why me?" He answered, "Why not you?" These firmly affectionate, inclusive messages are by no means extraordinary. Indeed, most of the spoken messages in the accounts of the visions that have been included in the previous chapters reiterate this basic assurance that Mary loves us without condition and wants us to think of ourselves as lovingly as she does.

If we are committed to a path of imitating Mary and conceiving the Christ spirit in our own lives, then obviously we must hold fast to the conviction that we are worthy of the task. We might then ask, *How do I disqualify myself from feeling worthy? How can I join those who feel "qualified" on the basis of simply being loved?*

We Can Accept the Price of Being in the World

No matter how much we are blessed with experiences of divine presence—whether it comes in the form or Mary, Jesus, an angel, or a less personified presence—the stress of life can erode our sense of meaning and undermine our commitment to the spiritual path. Our infrequent moments of spiritual communion can seem irrelevant, at best, when compared to the real-life pressures that bear down upon us. In the following encounter with Mary, the recipient, S.E., receives a simple but profound teaching applicable to us all.

I was in my bedroom, making the bed. I stopped abruptly because I instantly knew, with great excitement, that Mary was coming that night. That's all I knew, and I continued making the bed. After a full day of normal activity, I went to bed without thinking about the "announcement" I had felt earlier in the day.

Later, while asleep, I became lucid—that is, aware that I was dreaming. I was being escorted down a hallway of an elegant building by two men in suits. They walked beside me, each of them holding my arm, guiding me along.

We passed by an open door on my left. It was a small, cluttered room. I glanced in and I saw a statue about two and a half feet tall of the Blessed Mother. It was made of gray stone. The statue was tilted, carelessly laid among the stuff. As soon as I saw the statue, I lost all my composure and screamed in desperation, "Mother! Please come to me." I surprised myself with the intensity of my need for her.

At that moment, the two men held me more firmly and led me past the door to an elegant bench that was set against the wall of the hallway. They left me there. As I sat waiting, I looked toward the doorway to the room.

All of a sudden, a bare foot stepped through the door-way, followed by a glowing pink skirt. It was her! She walked out of the room, looking tall, strong, and very real. She was truly glowing. Every inch of her was glorified. She was wearing a pink dress, topped with a baby blue cape with a hood.

She walked over to the bench and sat down beside me. I was stunned, and I said to myself, "This is an apparition." I relaxed and opened myself to absorb her presence. She sat close to me and leaned in to speak to me. I looked into her eyes and found I couldn't look anywhere else. There was a magnetic force, a force that held my eyes. I thought, This is why people say she is so beautiful—it's the magnetism.

She was beautiful, but she did not look like the statue. I can only say that her eyes were all black. She talked and she talked. I never said one word. She told me many things, but I was able to remember only one message. She told me that when bad things happen—when there are evil intrusions into my life—there is something that I can do. At this point, even though I looked into her eyes, I had a vision of the little statue in the room. As I saw it from a close-up position, I noticed little dust balls hanging from her chin. The statue was dusty all over.

She said, "The dust that was thrown on my life was from the devil." (I understood the dust to mean the distractions, inconveniences, and malicious behaviors.)

She then said, "Wipe the dust away and I am there."

When I woke up the next morning, I felt great. In the days that followed, whenever I felt stress, I would remember her words and feel her knees and see her leaning in,

> *speaking so intimately to me. She has* always *been there.*
> (S.E.#2)

It is significant to note that the above experience took place *after* S.E.'s "transfiguration" experience with the Father and her "mystical marriage" with Jesus (see page 225). Fully empowered by those ecstatic experiences, she apparently still needed one thing that we all need once we've glimpsed our true spiritual destiny: the patience and willingness to look beyond the world of dusty illusions and to hold fast to the truth. In a similar spirit, but in another spiritual tradition, Lama Govinda had a vision at the beginning of his journey into Tibet; in the vision, he saw the Tibetan version of the divine feminine, White Tara, "the Savioress." In his ecstasy, he prayed in words that affirmed his willingness to help others to see beyond the veil that clouds our perception of our ultimate spiritual natures.

> I, therefore, pray to thee, O mother of suffering beings
> and to all the Buddhas here present, to have mercy
> upon humans whose eyes are covered with only a little
> dust, and who would see and understand if only we
> would linger a little in these our dream-forms until our
> message has reached them or has been handed on to
> those who are able to spread it for the benefit of all
> living beings.[9]

Just as Jesus surprised me by pointing to Mary as the next stage in my spiritual development, Mary—with her willingness to wear the dust of ordinary life—seemed to represent the next step for S.E., as well. This may seem confusing, for we are told that we come to Christ *through Mary*. How is it, then, that some of us discover Mary *after* coming to know Christ? Think of it this way: In our search for spiritual communion, we may meet the feminine face of the divine on the journey up the mountain. In the form of a virgin or a maiden, she can teach us the importance of surrendering to the divine and conceiving a new life in the spirit. Then as we bring this new life back into the world, we encounter the divine as the mother. Then she invites us to come under her mantle *as her children*, as well as to accept the hardships as *"mothers"* that inevitably accompany a "path with a heart."

S.E.'s encounter reminds each of us that we face a simple choice in every moment: whether to succumb to the temptation of hopelessness or to make the effort to find God's abiding presence beneath the dust that so often shrouds our lives. The message assures us of the spirit's immanence, but it also reminds us of the work we must do to claim what is available to us.

We might then ask, *How can I brush the dust from my life and find the loving presence that's always there?* Or, in practical terms: *What do I need to do right now to discover the immanence of God's love that is temporarily hidden from my view?*

We Can Restore a Sense of Harmony in a Fragmented World

We live in a time of psychological, social, and biological disintegration—when the structures that once held us together have weakened under the influence of cynicism and selfishness and mutating organisms. This erosion of integrity is evident on all levels, and we desperately need something that will reestablish our sense of organization and security.

When my mother was diagnosed with pancreatic cancer and given a few months to live, I felt the tremors of emotional and familial disintegration. I turned to prayer as a way to help her and myself at the same time. Before I got down to concerted prayer, I spent several days painting a mandala—a healing ritual I discovered by accident when I was an adolescent and have repeated periodically ever since. *Mandala* means "magic circle" in Sanskrit, and it defines any circular, square, or otherwise radially symmetrical design. Mandalas have traditionally been associated with God, wholeness, and the Holy Mother. Buddhists and Hindus use them in meditation, but mandala forms can be found in all sacred traditions, including Christianity.

I often painted mandalas during times of change and upheaval in my twenties. On the following nights, I would often dream vividly of my mother, or other mother figures. This was not surprising, for the mandala—like a good mother—encircles and contains us during times of crisis. In the Hindu tradition, this image of healing and restoration is referred to as a "divine incorporation" because it reflects in visual form the process of the spirit incarnating in the world and bringing order to it.[10] So as the consuming force of cancer threatened my mother's health—and, in turn, my own emotional equilibrium—I used the mandala to draw upon an ever-available motherly force of spiritual protection and containment for both of us.

After completing the mandala, I meditated on the image and prayed for her healing. In that moment, I experienced a rare degree of faith: I knew that my mother would recover. Of course, I cannot say for sure if my prayers had anything to do with her recovery, and frankly, I cannot fully comprehend the level of conviction I felt at that time. But she went into remission for almost three years before she died abruptly. I have been told that only about one person in a hundred lives that long with pancreatic cancer. My stepbrother, who is a physician, said to my brother and me after she died, "It does *not* happen that way with that kind of cancer. Her recovery had little to do with the chemotherapy. Something miraculous kept the cancer at bay, and that 'something' ceased to function all at once, right before she died." Whatever we call it—whether Christ, Holy Mother, or Holy Spirit—it encircled the disease within my mother's body and restored her health for a season.

My own experience brings to mind the reason that so many of us are drawn to the Holy Mother at this time. Previously, the binding influences in society, in the church, in our families, and within our own bodies seemed adequate to counteract the influences that normally threaten those things of greatest value to us. But things have changed. In the words of W. B. Yeats, "things fall apart; the center cannot hold and everywhere the ceremony of innocence is drowned." Most of us can *feel* the sobering truth of these words. It is not the first time that the world has faced such an absence of protective structures, but one can reasonably argue that we are more exposed at this time to psychological, social, and biological disintegration than since the late Middle Ages, when superstition, rampant viciousness, and plague ravaged Europe's body and soul. In her book *A Distant Mirror: The Calamitous 14th Century*, Barbara Tuchman presents the compelling hypothesis that our own pervasive malaise mirrors the decay of the late Middle Ages and may again precede the dawn of a new age.

In these times, we all need something strong enough to organize and counteract the influences that threaten to undermine what is good and healthy. Death, of course, is inevitable, but something less noble is afoot: The containment that we need for our health and development is seriously threatened. The AIDS epidemic is one concrete example of our collective inability *on all levels* to withstand the forces of disintegration in the world. Some people advocate a return to family values as a way to reclaim the stability that we desperately need. Others extol the virtues of holistic treatment in boosting the immune system's response to new and more virile strains of disease. But it is likely that the solutions go beyond anything that we can orchestrate on our own. We must commit ourselves, yes, but we also need help—not from ordinary sources but from *within and beyond ourselves*—to restore our sense of integrity. In this context, Mary offers us a way of containing the forces that would otherwise divide us. How? By asking us to commit ourselves to various forms of self-sacrifice—such as prayer, fasting, and repentance. *It may seem ironic, but the divine feminine offers us containment and spiritual protection at the price of letting go of ourselves and doing what God asks of us.*

No wonder Mary comes to us now, when we are most in need of a sacred enclosure to encircle the fragments of our former selves and to forge them into a new being conceived in love. Perhaps our desperate need will motivate us to do what we've been loath to do before—to surrender fully to God's will. The force of love that she brings to us, the tangible gifts that she bestows on us, and the acts of sacrifice that she requires of us may work together to restore our capacity to contain and nurture the good within us and in the world.

We Can Serve the One She Serves

When Jesus was dying, he addressed his mother and his disciple John, who were keeping vigil beneath the cross. He said something that people have wondered about since the beginning of Christianity. He referred to John as Mary's son, and to Mary as John's mother: "When Jesus therefore saw his mother, and the disciple standing by, whom he loved, he saith unto his mother,

Woman, behold thy son! Then saith he to the disciple, Behold thy mother! And from that hour that disciple took her into his own home" (John 19:26–27).

On the surface, Jesus was saying, Take care of each other now that I am leaving you. But one can interpret his words more globally as a final directive meant for us all. From this perspective, Jesus gave us to his mother and gave his mother to us. After surrounding himself with twelve men during his brief ministry— several of whom misunderstood him regularly, and one of whom betrayed him fatally—he turns to his mother at the very end. Such a gesture raises a question that he himself never answered: Where *does* the feminine fit in our spiritual lives?

In the Middle Ages, a powerful new myth arose that offered us a solution to this question.

The story concerned the search for the Holy Grail—the chalice from which Jesus served his disciples at the Last Supper. Many storytellers contributed to its emergence, tracing the bold design of an evolving new vision of wholeness from pieces of earlier myths and stories. Like all great myths and spiritual truths, we can comprehend it best by allowing ourselves to suspend our analysis and to *feel* its meaning.

Obsessed with the idea that the lost Grail could be recovered if one was pure enough in heart, the legendary Grail knights went off in search of the Grail in the forests and in the castles of Britain and Europe. While the story revolves primarily around the search for the Grail, the culmination of the myth goes beyond its mere discovery. It concerns the resolution of a long-standing problem: the wound of the Fisher King.

Amfortas, or the Fisher King, was the keeper of the Grail, but ironically, he could not heal himself with it. Further, as a reflection of his own woundedness, the land around him lay in waste.

Years earlier, he made the mistake of impulsively provoking a pagan knight. In the skirmish, Amfortas managed to kill the knight but was wounded grievously. He languished thereafter in the Grail Castle.

With his impulsive aggression, the young Amfortas bears a resemblance to the disciple who cut off the Roman soldier's ear when Jesus was arrested, and to Judas, who may have betrayed Jesus to get him to demonstrate his messianic power. Indeed, Amfortas symbolizes that part of our nature whose unexamined thirst for power blinds us to Christ's charity toward all, including the pagan knight that dwells within us and in our enemies. The redemption of humanity's greatest evil—its malicious aggression—is the underlying need that gave rise to this compelling story. It is no wonder that when Jesus was dying upon the cross, he pointed us to the feminine spirit as a way to heal the animosity that ultimately sabotages our chances for spiritual fulfillment.

We are told that in his youth, Percival somehow found his way into the Grail Castle and encountered the ultimate test of the Grail knight: In witnessing the Grail, would he think to ask the question, Whom does the Grail serve? Percival was totally unprepared for this test. As the Grail appeared to him from behind curtains and floated past him, he sat speechless, overcome by its radiant beauty. Unfortunately, Percival's mother had advised him years before not to ask questions; and in this crucial moment, he complied, to his own detriment. In failing to ask the question, Percival was summarily dismissed from the castle, unable to comprehend what he had done wrong.

Little did Percival know that *experiencing* the Grail was not the end point of his search. He had to *respond* in a way that expressed the Grail's essence. He had to rouse himself from his mother's silence, but he had to avoid the zeal that had blinded Amfortas in his ill-fated battle. He had to redeem the aggression in himself and in the Fisher King. Like Mary, *he could do this only by offering himself in service.*

Years later, after many hard lessons, Percival found his way back to the castle. As a mature and seasoned knight, he again beheld the beauty of the Grail. This time, however, his voice served him well. Stirring himself out of the ecstasy of merely *receiving* the grace of the Grail, he asked, *"Whom does the Grail serve?"* With this question, Percival implicitly offered *himself* in service to the Fisher King, whose festering wound could be healed only by a knight's willingness to ask a question that no one had previously thought to ask. In asking this crucial question, Percival ceased to be the passive witness *or* the combative warrior: *He became a vessel.* Like Mary, he exhibited a responsive spirit that healed the Fisher King's wound and released the waters to flow again on the wasteland.

✼✼✼

When I recall Percival's quest for the Holy Grail, I am reminded of our own spiritual journey. When the spirit first dawns in our lives, it can awaken a love that is so intense, we cannot bear it. Yet, like Percival, we may zealously seek it again and again, mistakenly thinking that the experience of light and ecstasy will fulfill our spiritual calling. We may not see at first into the heart of the truth—that we are called to give love, not only to experience it. Like Percival, we may remain unresponsive and in a state of self-satisfied bliss. No amount of spiritual experience may be able to rouse us to respond to the spirit's call *without hesitation* and to accept the sacrifices required of us *without regret.* That is why, I believe, Jesus points us to Mary—to the Ark of the Covenant and to the Grail. He knows that we can quickly reach the limits of our own development. Without understanding and *feeling* Mary's complete responsiveness to *her* call, we cannot begin to answer *our own*.

For most of us, our responsiveness to the spirit's call will remain forever incomplete. But each day, strive to understand and to embrace your calling more completely than ever before. Thank Mary for the example she provides and for the deeply felt love that she brings to you. And thank Jesus for asking you to behold his mother as your own.

In whatever form we can know her best, and through whatever spiritual tradition answers to our needs, the Holy Mother wants us to do a great work together—to become like her and to offer up what God requests of us without quibbling over the fine points of religious beliefs. Like Jesus' two radically simple commandments, Mary's singular appeal to us leaves little room for analysis and argument. It all comes down to one question: *Will you do what the Spirit asks of you?*

It is my hope that you and I can say, as Mary once did, *Let it be done unto me according to your word*—and that we can offer ourselves to the one she serves and fearlessly do whatever the Spirit requests of us.

In this way, I believe, we will finally find the freedom to become what we are destined to be.

MAGNIFICAT

My soul magnifies the Lord, and my spirit rejoices in God, my Savior. For he has regarded the low estate of his handmaiden. For behold, henceforth all generations will call me blessed; for he who is mighty has done great things for me, and holy is his name. And his mercy is on those from generation to generation. He has shown strength with his arm, he has scattered the proud in the imagination of their hearts, he has put down the mighty from their thrones, and exalted those of low degree; he has filled the hungry with good things, and the rich he has sent empty away. He has helped his servant Israel, in remembrance of his mercy, as he spoke to our fathers, to Abraham and to his posterity forever. (Luke 1:46–55)

Appendix A

How to Recite the Rosary

The recitation of the rosary has evolved over a period of at least fifteen hundred years. For instance, the prayer that is repeated most frequently in the recitation of the rosary, the Hail Mary, is a synthesis of three sentences that came to be used together over the course of many centuries. The first two statements are taken from two New Testament passages—the angel Gabriel's salutation to Mary (Luke 1:28) and Elizabeth's greeting to Mary (Luke 1:42). This part of the Hail Mary was used as early as the fourth century. The last sentence, "prompted by a need to join petition with praise,"[1] was introduced in the seventh century. The name Jesus was added in the 1300s. Finally, the current version was formally adopted in the sixteenth century. It is: "Hail Mary, full of grace, the Lord is with thee. Blessed art thou amongst women, and blessed is the fruit of thy womb, Jesus. Holy Mary, Mother of God, pray for us sinners now and at the hour of our death. Amen."

Obviously, the recitation of the rosary represents a continually evolving form of spiritual practice. Knowing this, some people feel constrained by the rosary's currently well-defined structure and wish to move on and explore alternative approaches. Before you embark on your own experimentation, however, I would suggest that you thoroughly learn the approach that Catholics currently use. Personally, I have found that if you are willing to stick with it, the traditional approach to the rosary may surprise you with its beauty and its potential for deepening your prayer and meditation periods. If you apply yourself to the standard approach, you will eventually feel more comfortable with it, if not deeply rewarded. It is easy to forget that "creativity moves well in harness"—that the fruits of spiritual practice are usually found by going *through*, not around, a disciplined approach of some kind.

Reciting the Traditional Rosary

Even though you can pray the rosary by counting off the prayers on your fingers, most people find that the beads are a convenient way to keep track of the process. If you do not have a rosary, you can easily obtain one for a few dollars at any religious-supply store. Also, many Catholic churches sell them in their bookstores on the church premises. Of course, you can also make your own rosary out of a wide variety of wooden, glass, or semiprecious gemstone beads. If you make your own, be sure to use *strong* string, because a weak string will easily break under regular use. Also, be sure that the rosary you select clearly indicates by *feel alone* where you are in the process. Some rosaries may leave you confused if the beads are not spaced out sufficiently or are too small for your fingers.

The complete rosary involves, first of all, reciting a series of introductory prayers; reciting fifteen decades (ten recitations) of Hail Mary along with accompanying prayers; and contemplating each of fifteen mysteries between each decade. By so doing, one completes three trips around the circular array of beads. Most people, however, recite only five decades in one sitting, thus making only one complete circuit around the rosary beads. As for the time required, you can complete five decades in thirty minutes to one hour, depending on how quickly you repeat the prayers and how long you contemplate each of the mysteries. The following pages include: a list of the fifteen mysteries, a drawing of a rosary, which depicts the placement of the traditional prayers, that will guide you around the rosary, and the prayers that are currently used in the process.

Assuming that you wish to make only one circuit of the rosary beads, select the set of five mysteries that you feel inspired to consider during your prayer period. Then consult the drawing (see page 269), which lays out the sequence of prayers along the string of beads. When the instructions call for a prayer that is unfamiliar to you, simply read the prayer off the sheet of prayers until it becomes familiar to you.

It is very important to recite the rosary *slowly*, pausing in between each prayerful phrase and going deeply into the contemplation of the mysteries. Many authorities, including St. Simon de Montfort, author of the classic treatise on praying the rosary,[2] assert that praying only a portion of the rosary *with careful concentration* and deep feeling is far better than racing through the whole fifteen decades.

Exploring Your Own Path

After having become familiar with the foundation that the Catholic church has laid for us in reciting the rosary, you may wish to experiment with your own prayers and mysteries.

First of all, remember that the rosary is a mandalalike structure that evokes an awareness of what Jung called the archetype of wholeness—or the pattern of God—that resides within each of us. From a Judeo-Christian standpoint, since we were created in the image of God, this archetype might be considered the imprint, or characteristic signature, of our own Creator. Whenever we contemplate or execute this shape—whether it takes the form of a circular drawing, a three-dimensional structure such as a Buddhist stupa, or a ritualized circular movement such as those practiced by the whirling dervishes—we inevitably stir deep feelings of wholeness and harmony that spring from the deepest source of our beings. So whatever changes you make to the prayers, you may wish to preserve the structure and the circular movement of the rosary.

Also, realize that the traditional approach represents a movement back and forth between what might be called "nesting" prayers and the contents of that "nest"—that is, the mysteries. The Lord's Prayer and the Hail Mary in particular affirm an *incarnational thrust* that brings the spirit down into the heart and body. Of course, these prayers first take us beyond ourselves by invoking the names of God and Mary. At first we say, "Our Father, Who art in heaven" and "Hail Mary, full of grace." But then, these prayers *affirm the movement of the spirit into our lives.* Indeed, they translate the *sublime into substance* through these affirmative statements: "Thy kingdom come; thy will be done, on earth" and "Blessed is the fruit of thy womb, Jesus."

In a vision of Mary last year, Mickey received a revised form of the Hail Mary that further emphasizes the incarnation of the divine by affirming our capacity to *blend* with Mary's essence: "Hail Mary, full of grace! The Lord is with thee; blessed art thou amongst women, and blessed is the fruit of thy womb, Jesus. Holy Mary, Mother of the world, pray for and blend with us, your children—now and through the days of our lives."

I have met several people who use alternative forms of the Hail Mary; a few individuals, like Mickey, have reported receiving these modifications from Mary herself. Rather than deviating from tradition, these modifications actually reflect the evolving, flexible devotional form that the rosary has come to represent.

As we recite the incarnational prayers leading up to the contemplation of the mysteries, we can more easily feel spirit moving into our hearts and extending into the furthest reaches of our human needs and concerns. Then, imbued with this feeling, we can more meaningfully appreciate those mysteries that comprise the founding or defining events of our spiritual lives.

And so, as you preserve the *framework* of the rosary, you may also wish to emulate in the formulation of your own prayers the *incarnational thrust* of the traditional prayers, so that the process will exert maximum impact on your life right here and right now. There are innumerable prayers that can affirm this process of the spirit taking on a practical and observable form. For instance, by adopting a prayer such as "Let me be an instrument of thy peace" as a substitute for one or more of the Hail Marys, you will be affirming a *specific* way in which the spirit can incarnate, or express itself, in your life. You will be defining the shape of things to come by choosing from among the many "names of God," or ways that the spirit can manifest in human activity.

As for the mysteries that you choose to contemplate, they are, in essence, *those events that represent for you the highest expressions of spirit in action.* If you are Christian, you may wish to stay with the fifteen traditional mysteries, or perhaps substitute other New Testament accounts for the traditional mysteries. Former Catholic priest and spiritual healer Ron Roth recommends for those of us in need of healing that we substitute the contemplation of several of the healing miracles performed by Jesus for the traditional mysteries.[3] Or you may wish to imagine what *might* have taken place at various crucial moments in the unfoldment of the Old Testament or New Testament stories. For instance, I often imagine what it could have been like when, according to an apocryphal tradition, Jesus appeared first to his mother on Easter morning. I imagine Mary lying alone in the twilight, mourning her son's death, when he enters her room from behind her and calls her by name. This "mystery" has represented a remarkable discovery for me—one that never ceases to move and to inspire me. Let your imagination serve you in your search for such treasures.

Some people who are less conventionally religious in their spirituality may find that the best "mysteries" for them to contemplate are the most uplifting moments of their own lives. They may choose to recall their most moving dreams, their intellectual and emotional breakthroughs, or their experiences of profound love. While such recollections are ostensibly secular in content, these treasured moments can serve to remind us that the spirit has manifested in the course of our lives—and will doubtless arise again and again through our own experiences.

Whatever you choose, remember that *practice is everything,* and that the particular content of our practice is probably far less important than *just doing it* with an open mind and a responsive heart.

Appendix B

The Fifteen Mysteries of the Rosary

The Five Joyful Mysteries

1. The Annunciation—The Angel Gabriel announces to the Virgin Mary that God wishes her to become the mother of his son. Mary obeys with humility. *Pray for a profound humility.**

2. The Visitation—Mary visits St. Elizabeth, who is to be mother of St. John the Baptist. She assists Elizabeth for three months. *Pray for charity towards our neighbor.**[1]

3. The Birth of Christ—Jesus Christ, the Son of God, is born in a stable. His mother places him in a manger. Shepherds and wise men visit him. *Pray for detachment from things of the world, contempt of riches, and love of poverty.**

4. The Presentation—Mary and Joseph take the Child Jesus to the Temple at Jerusalem to present him to his heavenly father. *Pray for purity of body and soul.**

5. The Finding of the Child Jesus in the Temple—Having lost Jesus, Mary and Joseph seek him. After three days they find him in the Temple. *Pray for the gift of true wisdom.**

The Five Sorrowful Mysteries

1. The Agony in the Garden—Jesus prays in the Garden of Olives. The thought of his coming sufferings and of our sins causes him to sweat blood. *Pray for contrition for our sins.**

2. The Scourging at the Pillar—Jesus is stripped, bound to a pillar, and scourged until his body is covered with wounds and blood. *Pray for mortification of our senses.**

3. The Crowning with Thorns—A crown of thorns is pressed into the

* *Petitions recommended by St. Louis de Montfort.*

head of Jesus. His eyes fill with tears and blood. He is mocked and spat upon. *Pray for contempt of the world.**

4.   The Carrying of the Cross—Jesus carries his heavy cross to Calvary. Mary makes the stations of the cross with her suffering son. *Pray for patience in bearing our crosses.**

5.   The Crucifixion—Nailed to the cross, Jesus, after three hours of agony, dies in the presence of his mother. *Pray for the conversion of sinners, the perseverance of the just, and the relief of the souls in purgatory.**

The Five Glorious Mysteries

1.   The Resurrection—Victorious over death, Jesus rises from the grave, glorious and immortal, on Easter Sunday. He reopens the gates of heaven. *Pray for the love of God and fervor in his service.**

2.   The Ascension—Forty days after his resurrection, Jesus ascends, in the presence of his mother and his disciples, into heaven. *Pray for an ardent desire for heaven.**

3.   The Descent of the Holy Spirit—Ten days after the ascension, the Holy Spirit descends in tongues of fire upon Mary and the disciples. *Pray for the coming of the Holy Ghost into our souls.**

4.   The Assumption of Mary into Heaven—Mary, Mother of God, was taken body and soul into heavenly glory after the course of her earthly life. *Pray for a tender devotion to Mary.**

5.   The Crowning of Mary as Queen of Heaven—The Mother of God, to the joy of all the angels and saints, is crowned Queen of Heaven by her son. *Pray for perseverance in grace and a crown of glory.**

Meditation on the mysteries is the most important part of the rosary. Put yourself in the presence of Jesus and Mary and live the mysteries with them.

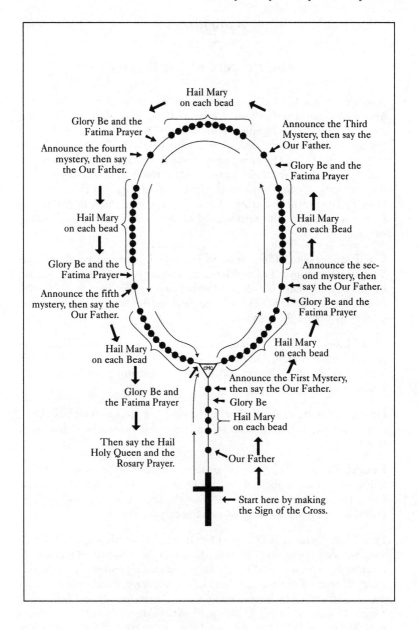

Appendix C

The Prayers of the Rosary

Apostles' Creed. I believe in God, the Father Almighty, Creator of heaven and earth; and in Jesus Christ, His only Son, our Lord; Who was conceived by the Holy Spirit, born of the Virgin Mary, suffered under Pontius Pilate, was crucified, died, and was buried. He descended into hell; the third day He arose again from the dead; He ascended into heaven, sitteth at the right hand of God, the Father Almighty; from thence He shall come to judge the living and the dead. I believe in the Holy Spirit, the holy Catholic Church, the communion of saints, the forgiveness of sins, the resurrection of the body, and life everlasting. Amen.

Our Father. Our Father, Who art in heaven, hallowed be Thy name; Thy kingdom come; Thy will be done, on earth as it is in heaven. Give us this day our daily bread; and forgive us our trespasses as we forgive those who trespass against us; and lead us not into temptation; but deliver us from evil. Amen.

Hail Mary. Hail Mary, full of grace, the Lord is with thee. Blessed art thou amongst women, and blessed is the fruit of thy womb, Jesus. Holy Mary, Mother of God, pray for us sinners now and at the hour of our death. Amen.

Gloria. Glory be to the Father, and to the Son, and to the Holy Spirit, as it was in the beginning, is now, and ever shall be, world without end. Amen.

Fatima Prayer. After each decade or mystery of the rosary say the following prayer requested by the Blessed Virgin at Fatima: "O my Jesus, forgive us our sins, save us from the fires of hell, lead all souls to Heaven, especially those most in need of your mercy."

Hail Holy Queen. Hail Holy Queen, Mother of Mercy, our life, our sweetness and our hope! To thee do we cry, poor banished children of Eve; to thee do we send up our sighs, mourning and weeping in this valley of tears! Turn then, most gracious Advocate, thine eyes of mercy towards us, and after this, our exile, show unto us the blessed fruit of thy womb, Jesus. O clement, O loving, O sweet Virgin Mary! Pray for us, O holy Mother of God, that we may be made worthy of the promises of Christ.

Rosary Prayer. O God, Whose only begotten Son, by His life, death, and resurrection, has purchased for us the rewards of eternal life, grant we beseech Thee, that meditating upon these mysteries in the most holy Rosary of the Blessed Virgin Mary, we may imitate what they contain, and obtain what they promise, through the same Christ our Lord. Amen.

Notes

Introduction

1. J. T. Connell, *Meetings with Mary: Visions of the Blessed Mother* (New York: Ballantine, 1995), p. 1.

2. A. Govinda, *The Way of the White Clouds: A Buddhist Pilgrim in Tibet* (London: Hutchinson and Co., 1966), p. 50.

3. In regard to the identities of the contributors, I have used only their initials at the end of their accounts. If I included more than one account from the same person, I then numbered the accounts by the order of their appearance—e.g., "M.L. #2." Since most of the recipients have unique initials, and since most of them contributed only a single account, most of the accounts are identified by the contributors' initials alone.

4. C.N. is a married forty-year-old mother of two who works as a nurse. She spent several years in a monastic Christian order, known as the Holy Order of Mans, at which time she practiced intense meditation, prayer, and service work. She was raised as a Protestant and is a modern Christian mystic with a special closeness to Mary.

5. Louis-Marie Grignion de Montfort, *True Devotion to Mary*, eds. Fathers of the Company of Mary; trans. F. W. Faber (Rockford, Illinois: Tan Books, 1985), p. 18.

6. See A. Kirkwood, *Mary's Messages to the World* (New York: Putnam, 1995).

7. See J. A. Pelletier, *Our Lady Comes to Garabandal* (Worcester, Massachusetts: Assumption, 1971).

8. J. Campbell, *The Masks of God: Creative Mythology* (New York: Viking, 1970), p. 65.

9. H. Weiner, lecture at the Association for Research and Enlightenment, Virginia Beach, Virginia, 1985.

10. See A. Harvey, *Hidden Journey: A Spiritual Awakening* (New York: Henry Holt, 1991).

11. A. Harvey, presentation to the Easter conference at the Association for Research and Enlightenment, Virginia Beach, Virginia, 1996.

12. R. Grant, "The Author Who Saw Jesus," *Venture Inward,* March 1995.

13. G. S. Sparrow, *I Am with You Always: True Stories of Encounters with Jesus* (New York: Bantam, 1995).

14. C. G. Jung, *Psychology and Religion: West and East,* vol. 11 of the *Collected Works of Carl G. Jung* (Princeton, New Jersey: Princeton University Press, 1969).

15. G. S. Sparrow, *Lucid Dreaming—Dawning of the Clear Light* (Virginia Beach, Virginia: A.R.E. Press, 1976); *I Am with You Always.*

16. E. Shillebeeckx and C. Halkes, *Mary: Yesterday, Today, Tomorrow* (New York: Crossroads, 1993), p. 51.

17. See R. Faricy and L. Rooney, *Our Lady Comes to Scottsdale* (Medford, Ohio: Riehle Foundation, 1991).

18. R. Faricy, foreword to Connell, *Meetings with Mary.*

19. J. A. Pelletier, *Mary Our Mother—Notes on Garabandal* (Worcester, Massachusetts: Assumption, 1972), pp. 37–38.

20. C. S. Lewis, *Letters to Malcolm: Chiefly on Prayer* (New York: Harcourt, Brace and World, Inc., 1963), p. 22.

1. My Coming to Know Mary

1. C. G. Jung, Psychological Commentary, in R. Wilhelm, *The Secret of the Golden Flower: A Chinese Book of Life* (San Diego: Harcourt, Brace and World, Inc., 1964), p. 104.

2. D. T. Suzuki, *The Essence of Buddhism* (London: The Buddhist Society, 1947), p. 41.

2. Mary's Manifestations and Her Secrets

1. See T. Kuhn, *The Structure of Scientific Revolutions* (Chicago: University of Chicago Press, 1962).

2. J. Ashton, *Mother of All Nations* (San Francisco: Harper & Row, 1989), p. 188.

3. M. O'Carroll, *Theotokos: A Theological Encyclopedia of the Blessed Virgin Mary* (Wilmington, Delaware: Michael Glazier, Inc., 1982), p. 164.

4. Scapulars were originally made for the laity who wished to associate with a religious order. A scapular bears the picture of Mary or of the saint in whose honor it is worn, or of the object of devotion it signifies. The Catholic church has always maintained that wearing a scapular without respect for the interior disposition it represents will not benefit the wearer.

5. D. Blackbourn, *Marpingen: Apparitions of the Virgin Mary in Nineteenth-Century Germany* (New York: Alfred A. Knopf, 1993), p. 4.

6. Ibid., p. 4.

7. Ibid., p. 8.

8. S. L. Zimdars-Swartz, *Encountering Mary* (New York: Avon, 1991), p. 26.

9. D. Blackbourn, *Marpingen*, p. 5.

10. J. Beevers, *The Sun Her Mantle* (Westminster, Maryland: Newman Press, 1954), p. 142.

11. Zimdars-Swartz, *Encountering Mary*, p. 165.

12. J. A. Pelletier, *Our Lady Comes to Garabandal* (Worcester, Massachusetts: Assumption, 1971), p. 207.

13. Matthew 1:19–25.

14. Zimdars-Swartz, *Encountering Mary*, p. 38.

15. E. Shillebeeckx and C. Halkes, *Mary: Yesterday, Today, Tomorrow* (New York: Crossroads, 1993), p. 68.

16. Ibid., p. 12.

17. C. Dixon, "Mariology: A Protestant Reconsideration," *American Ecclesiastical Review*, May 1974, pp. 306–307.

18. A. Kirkwood, *Mary's Messages to the World* (New York: Putnam, 1995), p. ix.

19. Zimdars-Swartz, *Encountering Mary*, p. 88.

20. J. A. Pelletier, *Our Lady Comes to Garabandal*, p. 120.

21. D. Blackbourn, *Marpingen*, p. 6.

3. Awakening to Mary's Presence

1. A. C. Emmerich, *The Life of the Blessed Virgin Mary—From the Visions of Anne Catherine Emmerich* (Rockford, Illinois: Tan Books, 1970), p. 15.

2. Rachel is a pseudonym for a sixty-year-old massage therapist and mother of four. She has a special love for the mountains and is currently realizing her dream—building her own cabin on a piece of property in West Virginia. Raised as a Baptist, she does not attend church today, but she is a mystic and worships God in people and in nature.

3. R. Bucke, *Cosmic Consciousness* (New York: E. P. Dutton & Co., 1969), p. 150.

4. S.O. is a fifty-year-old divorced mother of two; she works as a substance abuse counselor. Raised a Catholic, she maintains her affiliation with the church and is a lector, or spiritual reader, during the Mass. She meditates regularly, works with HIV-positive patients on a voluntary basis, and teaches courses and lectures on HIV/AIDS education.

5. R. Wilhelm, *The Secret of the Golden Flower: A Chinese Book of Life* (San Diego: Harcourt, Brace and World, Inc., 1964), p. 36.

6. A. Saint-Exupéry, *The Little Prince* (New York: Harcourt, Brace and World, Inc., 1943), p. 67.

7. J.A. is a fifty-four-year-old single teacher who specializes in reading and learning disabilities. She has been a Catholic all her life, and she feels that Mary has always been there for her.

8. M.F. is a forty-four-year-old divorced mother of two; she works as a nurse. Raised a Catholic, she calls herself an "angelist" and seeks the "ever-present awareness of God." She meditates and works with her dreams on a regular basis.

9. R. Laurentin, *Our Lord and Our Lady in Scottsdale* (Milford, Ohio: Faith Publishing, 1992), p. 25.

10. L.D. is a fifty-one-year-old married mother of two; she works in word processing. She plays the accordion and likes camping. Raised a Catholic and then a Lutheran, she has no denominational preference today.

11. J.C. is a fifty-six-year-old married mother of one; she is a secretary. She is drawn to the arts and works in stained glass. Raised as a Catholic, she remains an active member of the church. She engages in regular prayer and often analyzes her dreams. She has had encounters with Jesus and angels, as well as with Mary. She has experienced numerous miracles, which she attributes to "keeping the faith."

12. See G. S. Sparrow, *I Am with You Always: True Stories of Encounters with Jesus* (New York: Bantam, 1995), p. 202.

4. The Lessons of Mary's Silence

1. L. Johnsen, *Yoga Journal*, July–August 1993, p. 63.

2. T.P. is a sixty-five-year-old widowed mother of three; she works as a nanny. She has meditated for over twenty-five years, up to several hours a day. She was raised a Catholic, considers herself a "universal student" today, and is a follower of Yogananda. She has had numerous encounters with Jesus, Mary, and angels.

3. M.O. is a sixty-six-year-old married mother of two; she works as a commercial artist. She was raised a Catholic and remains an active member of the church. She has practiced meditation and prayer for thirty years, and she involves herself in various volunteer service organizations.

4. M.J. is a fifty-two-year-old married mother of four; she works as a paralegal. She is also an artist by training and worships in the Native American tradition. The Virgin Mary, she says, is the "last 'religious'

person" she ever expected to encounter. She has become psychically gifted, even though she finds it hard to acknowledge. She works regularly with her dreams, has meditated for thirty years, and has had encounters with Christ and "the Creator" as well as with Mary.

5. W. Starcke, *This Double Spiral* (New York: Harper & Row, 1967); *The Ultimate Revolution* (New York: Harper & Row, 1969); *The Gospel According to Relativity* (New York: Harper & Row, 1973); and *Homesick for Heaven—You Don't Have to Wait* (Boerne, Texas: Guadalupe Press, 1988).

6. M.W. is a thirty-eight-year-old divorced woman who works in a metaphysical education and research organization. She has studied the Course in Miracles extensively, is a regular meditator, and works with her dreams as part of her spiritual path.

7. M.F. is a fifty-one-year-old father who is separated from his wife. He is an actor and writer, and he is deeply devoted to Jesus and Mary. He was born in Ireland and immigrated to Canada. Raised a Christian, he is particularly involved today in studying and presenting in dramatic form the spiritual philosophy of Edgar Cayce and the story of the early church.

8. G. S. Sparrow, *I Am with You Always: True Stories of Encounters with Jesus* (New York: Bantam, 1995), p. 196.

9. M.H. is a seventy-five-year-old mother of one child and is separated from her husband. Formerly, she worked as a social worker. She is totally disabled but publishes a monthly newsletter dedicated to uplifting others. Raised as a Baptist, she worships today as a soldier in the Salvation Army.

10. A.T. is a forty-seven-year-old single teacher who lives in Japan. In addition to teaching English as a second language, she also teaches tai chi, writing, drawing, and painting. Raised as an Episcopalian, she currently has no religious preference. Deeply spiritual, she has had numerous experiences of the holy light and many encounters with divine beings.

11. J. A. Pelletier, *Mary Our Mother: Reflections on the Message of Garabandal* (Worcester, Massachusetts: Assumption, 1972), p. 10.

5. Mary's Tangible Gifts

1. See A. Govinda, *Foundations of Tibetan Mysticism* (New York: Weiser, 1960), p. 59.

2. A. M. Hancock, *Wake Up America* (Norfolk, Virginia: Hampton Roads, 1993).

3. Padre Pio was a Capuchin priest who lived at the San Giovanni Rotondo friary in Italy for most of his life. He was the first priest to develop the stigmata—the visible bleeding wounds that Christ suffered when he was crucified—and was blessed with many supernatural gifts, including prophecy, healing, and bilocation. When he died, new skin grew over his wounds, and not a drop of blood was found in his body. A movement is under way to have Padre Pio canonized.

4. *Richmond Times Dispatch*, April 17, 1992.

5. G.W. is a sixty-eight-year-old married mother of four; she is a retired bookkeeper, writer, and reporter. She composes songs and sings as a hobby. Raised a Lutheran, she converted to Catholicism but is not an active member of the church today. She meditates every night, works regularly with her dreams, and says that she feels her soul is her church.

6. C. G. Jung, *Psychology and Religion: West and East*, vol. 11 of the *Collected Works of Carl G. Jung* (Princeton, New Jersey: Princeton University Press, 1969), pp. 48–49.

7. K.P. is a thirty-year-old married mother of three; she is an astrologer and a housewife. She was raised a Catholic but does not currently worship in the church. She experienced psychic visions in childhood, then resumed having these experiences two years ago, when her problems with chronic pain began. While various phenomena associated with Mary occurred around K.P., she has never encountered Mary herself. Her husband, T.P., who experienced Mary's presence as he massaged his wife, was also raised a Catholic. He is an engineer.

8. F.L. is a forty-year-old married mother of two; she currently works as a massage therapist. Her hobbies are walking and dancing, and she is trained in movement therapy, Reiki, and polarity therapy. Raised as a Catholic, she considers herself today a Christian with a New Age emphasis. She meditates for an hour about five times a week.

9. A novena is a prayer dedicated to Mary or a particular saint that is done on a regular basis in order to obtain some healing or blessing.

10. E.M. is a fifty-two-year-old divorced woman who is trained in the teaching, computer, and marketing fields but is currently in a career

transition. She enjoys writing as a hobby. Raised as a Catholic, she currently worships in the Unity Church. As a result of her encounter with Mary, she now feels deeply called to serve others and to motivate them to "be the best they can be."

11. L. Carroll, *Alice's Adventures in Wonderland*, ed. Donald Gray (New York: Norton, 1992), p. 52.

12. C. S. Lewis, *Letters to Malcolm: Chiefly on Prayer* (New York: Harcourt, Brace and World, 1963), p. 21.

13. A rosary ring is an abbreviated form of the complete rosary that one can wear. The ring has ten raised knobs, or "rosebuds," and one small cross on its outside surface, assisting the wearer in counting off ten Hail Marys before contemplating one of the Mysteries of the Rosary. (See Appendix A.)

14. L.H. is a thirty-five-year-old single woman who is a professional photographer and outdoor enthusiast. Raised as a Catholic, she continues to worship in the Catholic church. Prior to her encounters with Mary, L.H. considered herself inactive in serving God, but since her encounters, she has begun to assist others "in bringing the Blessed Mother's message to everyone."

15. See J. Annerino, "Sacred Stones: Mexico's Hidden Miracle," *Arizona Republic*, April 16, 1995.

16. R.S. is a fifty-year-old divorced mother of two; she works as a substance abuse counselor. Her hobbies are dancing, rock hunting, drumming, and music. Raised as a Southern Baptist, she has no denominational preference today. She has meditated since she was a small child, and she regularly works with her dreams. She is blessed by the presence of many spiritual guides and has had many experiences of the divine light.

17. See Pelletier, *Our Lady Comes to Garabandal*.

6. The Problem of Suffering

1. E. W. Budge, *Coptic Apocrypha in the Dialect of Upper Egypt* (London, 1913), p. 190.

2. P.W. is a sixty-one-year-old divorced mother of four, and she has a vast array of interests and skills. She is an ordained minister, a Reiki practitioner, and a psychic. She plays chess and spends a great deal of time working on her computer and with on-line services. Raised as a Methodist, she worships today in the Unity School of Christianity.

3. P.M. is a sixty-five-year-old divorced mother of three; she works as a secretary. She has prayed daily all her life, and often she feels the presence of angels. Raised as a Catholic, she remains an active member of the church today.

4. B. J. Eadie and C. Taylor, *Embraced by the Light* (Placerville, California: Gold Leaf Press, 1992).

5. E.K. is a thirty-seven-year-old married mother of three; she works as an executive secretary. Her hobbies are music, dance, and reading. Raised as a Catholic, she is a member of a nondenominational church today. She has on occasion experienced the holy light in her dreams.

6. W. Y. Evans-Wentz, *Tibet's Great Yogi Milarepa* (London: Oxford University Press, 1951).

7. J. Beevers, *The Sun Her Mantle* (Westminster, Maryland: Newman Press, 1954), p. 131.

8. M.B.'s account can be found on page 202.

9. C.H. is an eighty-one-year-old widowed father who is a retired electrician. His hobby is photography, and he volunteers to assist other seniors who are depressed and lonely. Raised as a Protestant, he worships as a Catholic today. He is certain that divine beings are watching over him and guiding him.

10. K.C. is a fifty-six-year-old married mother of one; she works as a secretary and enjoys reading, art, music, and working with stained glass. She is a lifelong Catholic, prays daily, and has had encounters with Jesus and angels, as well as with Mary. She says that miracles often happen when her faith is strong.

7. The Way of Surrender

1. C. S. Lewis, *Mere Christianity* (New York: Macmillan, 1952), p. 167.

2. E. Underhill, *Mysticism* (Cleveland: Meridian, 1955), p. 386.

3. B.F. is a forty-two-year-old married man who is a social worker. Raised as a Catholic, he turned to Eastern philosophy and practices as a reaction to his upbringing, which he believed had failed him.

4. A. C. Emmerich, *The Life of the Blessed Virgin Mary: From the Visions of Anne Catherine Emmerich* (Rockford, Illinois: Tan Books, 1970), p. 352.

5. K.F. is a thirty-five-year-old married mother of two; she works as a dance instructor. She is currently pursuing further training in floristry, aromatherapy, and gardening as a result of having received guidance from higher beings. Raised as a Lutheran, she remains active in the same church that her parents attended before her birth. She attended an all-women's Catholic college, which she believes was an important part of her spiritual development. She has had many mystical experiences, meditates regularly, and works with her dreams as a part of her spiritual path.

6. T.A. is a fifty-two-year-old married mother of three; she works as an auditor. Her hobbies are gardening, walking, and travel. Raised as a Protestant, she worshiped as a Catholic in her early adulthood; currently, she considers herself a nondenominational Christian.

8. Imitating Mary

1. C. S. Lewis, *Mere Christianity* (New York: Macmillan, 1952), p. 161.

2. M.B. is a fifty-eight-year-old divorced mother of six; she manages a New Age conference center. She was raised a Catholic but is unaffiliated with a particular denomination today. Her mystical relationship with Mary arose within her Catholic upbringing, then flowered in the context of a less structured spiritual journey. She has meditated daily for twenty-five years, and she has had an encounter with Christ, on one occasion.

3. Actually, this is not entirely possible from the standpoint of the Catholic dogma of the Immaculate Conception (1854), which declared that Mary was conceived without the stain of original sin. This dogma, by implication, prevents the rest of us from serving in quite the way that she did. But for Protestants, who may not subscribe to this dogma, it remains within the realm of possibility for any of us to serve as fully as Mary did.

4. A. C. Emmerich, *The Life of the Blessed Virgin Mary: From the Visions of Anne Catherine Emmerich* (Rockford, Illinois: Tan Books, 1970), pp. 4–20.

5. R. H. Drummond, *A Broader Vision—Perspectives on the Buddha and the Christ* (Virginia Beach, Virginia: A.R.E. Press, 1995), p. 25.

6. J. Elson, "The New Testament's Unsolved Mysteries," *Time*, December 18, 1995, p. 79.

7. C.R. is a forty-eight-year-old married mother of three and a housewife. Raised as a Catholic, she meditates and prays daily. She feels drawn to serve as a trance channeler, even though her religious upbringing conflicts with this direction.

8. H. O. J. Brown, *Heresies: The Image of Christ in the Mirror of Heresy and Orthodoxy from the Apostles to the Present* (Garden City, New York: Doubleday, 1984), p. 201.

9. A. Govinda, *Foundations of Tibetan Mysticism* (New York: Weiser, 1971).

10. M. Warner, *Alone of All Her Sex* (New York: Alfred A. Knopf, 1976), p. 254.

11. Maria Esperanza is the principal visionary of a series of Marian apparitions in Betania, Venezuela. For more information, see J. T. Connell's *Meetings with Mary: Visions of the Blessed Mother* (New York: Ballantine, 1995).

12. Dorothy Cox is a fifty-nine-year-old married mother of two. She is involved in artistic hobbies, such as poetry writing and weaving. Raised in the Anglican church, she has studied the yogic traditions and often worships in the Catholic church. She has published a booklet of Mary's messages entitled *From My Immaculate Heart*, available by writing to her at 584 Hopkins Avenue, Peterborough, Ontario, Canada K9H 2S1.

13. L.N. is a forty-six-year-old divorced mother of one; she works as a counselor and artist. Raised in her early childhood as a Catholic, she had no religious preference in her teens. As an adult, she refers to herself as an agnostic Christian Buddhist with an eclectic approach to her spiritual path. She exhibits a remarkably permanent sense of Mary's abiding

presence with her, and she regards her mission as one of assisting others to welcome the same joyfulness and communion into their lives.

14. C. S. Lewis, *That Hideous Strength* (New York: Macmillan, 1946), p. 316.

15. S.E. is a married mother of two. Raised as a Catholic, she is a third-order Carmelite. She has studied meditation extensively under the Maharishi, and she worships in a Southern Baptist church. She is guided by Mary to work toward the unity of all faiths. She has had innumerable experiences of the eternal light and various higher beings.

16. See G. S. Sparrow, *I Am with You Always: True Stories of Encounters with Jesus* (New York: Bantam, 1995), p. 92.

17. C.L. is a fifty-seven-year-old divorced mother of four; she works as a federal disability examiner. Trained also as an X-ray technician, she enjoys writing, camping, and gardening. Raised in the Catholic church, she is currently a member of the Methodist church. She prays twice daily and has done so since she entered Catholic school when she was six years old. She often receives psychic impressions concerning individuals who need her help; she has found the work of Edgar Cayce to be helpful in understanding her gift.

9. Responding to Mary's Request

1. J. M. Haffert, *The Meaning of Akita* (Asbury, New Jersey: 101 Foundation, 1989), p. 23.

2. W. Y. Evans-Wentz, *Tibet's Great Yogi Milarepa* (London: Oxford University Press, 1951), p. 158.

3. R. Roth, *The Rosary: Praying with Mary for Healing* (LaSalle, Illinois: Roth Publications, 1985), p. 4.

4. J. A. Pelletier, *God Speaks at Garabandal: The Message of Garabandal with a Summary and Picture Story of the Apparitions* (Worcester, Massachusetts: Assumption, 1970), p. 561.

5. A. Govinda, *Foundations of Tibetan Mysticism* (New York: Weiser, 1971), p. 19.

6. D.S. is a twenty-eight-year-old married man who works in banking and enjoys various artistic activities such as harp playing, singing, acting,

and ice-skating. He was raised a Methodist and remains an active member of the church today. He also practices meditation and prayer work on a regular basis.

7. See W. Y. Evans-Wentz, *Tibet's Great Yogi Milarepa* (London: Oxford University Press, 1951).

8. A.G. is a sixty-two-year-old married mother of three; she has been mystically inclined all her life. Raised in the Greek Orthodox church, she worships today in the Catholic church. She has had numerous encounters with Mary and Jesus and other spiritual beings, and is well-known in the Northeast for her research into UFOs and paranormal healing.

9. A. Govinda, *The Way of the White Clouds: A Buddhist Pilgrim in Tibet* (London: Hutchinson and Co., 1966), p. 5.

10. See J. Arguelles and M. Arguelles, *Mandala* (Berkeley: Shambala, 1970), p. 65.

Appendix A: How to Recite the Rosary

1. M. O'Carroll, *Theotokos: A Theological Encyclopedia of the Blessed Virgin Mary* (Wilmington, Delaware: Michael Glazier, Inc., 1982), p. 165.

2. St. Louis Mary de Montfort, *The Secret of the Rosary*, trans. Mar Barbour (Bay Shore, New York: Montfort Publications, 1995).

3. See R. Roth, *The Rosary: Praying with Mary for Healing* (LaSalle, Illinois: Roth Publications, 1985), p. 4.

About the Author

G. Scott Sparrow, Ed.D., is a psychotherapist in private practice who specializes in transpersonal approaches to therapy. He has lectured and taught courses across the United States and Canada on topics such as meditation, mystical experiences, and methods of dream work. He is the author of the well-received *Lucid Dreaming—Dawning of the Clear Light* as well as of several articles in the general field of dream theory and dream analysis. He has also written *I Am with You Always: True Stories of Encounters with Jesus*, which investigates the phenomenon of encountering Jesus in dreams and visions.